Officers and Soldiers in the Service of the Province of Pennsylvania

1744 to 1764

Craig R. Scott, CG, FUGA

HERITAGE BOOKS
2015

HERITAGE BOOKS
AN IMPRINT OF HERITAGE BOOKS, INC.

Books, CDs, and more—Worldwide

For our listing of thousands of titles see our website
at
www.HeritageBooks.com

Published 2015 by
HERITAGE BOOKS, INC.
Publishing Division
5810 Ruatan Street
Berwyn Heights, Md. 20740

Copyright © 2015 Craig R. Scott, CG, FUGA

Heritage Books by the author:

Index to the Fairfax County, Virginia Register of Marriages, 1853–1933
Constance K. Ring and Craig R. Scott

The "Lost" Pensions: Settled Accounts of the Act of 6 April 1838, Revised Edition

New Jerusalem Lutheran Church Cemetery
Marty Hiatt and Craig R. Scott

Officers and Soldiers in the Service of the Province of Pennsylvania, 1744 to 1764

Scott Family Finding Aids, Volume #1: Marriages, 1700–1900

*Understanding Revolutionary War and Invalid Pension Ledgers, 1818–1872
and the Pension Payment Vouchers They Represent*

All rights reserved. No part of this book may be reproduced or transmitted in any form or by any means, electronic or mechanical, including photocopying, recording or by any information storage and retrieval system without written permission from the author, except for the inclusion of brief quotations in a review.

International Standard Book Numbers
Paperbound: 978-0-7884-5653-4
Clothbound: 978-0-7884-6190-3

Table of Contents

Preface v
A 1
B 12
C 36
D 59
E 72
F 76
G 86
H 100
I 122
J 124
K 131
L 139
M 149
N 186
O 192
P 194
Q 207
R 207
S 220
T 246
U 253
V 253
W 256
Y 273
Z 274
Appendix A 277
Appendix B 281
Appendix C 283

Preface

For as long as I can remember, I have had an interest in the French and Indian War. A decade ago I purchased a set of the appropriate volumes of the *Pennsylvania Archives* and began a journey. It was an intermittent journey. I saw the need to create a finding aid to the information for my personal use and in this volume I am sharing it with others. I have combined individual entries together where I felt there was sufficient information to do so. They are my evaluations; I rely on the reader since this is my finding aid to find their own way.

I am an avid user and fan of Fold3.com and the *Pennsylvania Archives* are available there for free. The data entry for this work was completed long before there was a Footnote.com or a Fold3.com. I found using my finding aid to be quicker and it made it easier for me to find things and did not rely on annotations and indexing. However, since the information was available online I decided not to publish this work. Basically, I have changed my mind since others told me I was being selfish.

Craig R. Scott, CG, FUGA

Abbott, James, enlisted 20 May 1758 in Captain French Battell's company of Lower County Provincials.

Abel, Peter, age 30, laborer, born Germany, enlisted 01 May 1758. On a return of Captain John Bull's company dated 01 July 1758.

Abivon, George, Surgeon of the provincial ship *Pennsylvania* on 17 August 1757.

Ableren, John, a private in Captain Edward Jones's Independent Company of Horse, Philadelphia in 1756.

Ache, John Lewis, a private in Captain Adam Heylman's Company, of the St. Vincent and Puke's Land Association on 10 May 1756.

Achenbach, John, private who enlisted 19 April 1756 in Captain Joseph Shippen's company in Colonel William Clapham's Regiment in 1756, the regiment in garrison at Fort Augusta, Shamokin, and listed in Shippen's Account Book.

Ackin, Michael, *see* Eakin, Michael.

Ackland, Andrew, age 25, mariner, born Sweedland, enlisted 30 April 1758. On a weekly return of Captain Samuel Jones's company in 1758.

Ackley, Joseph, age 17, wheelwright, born Pennsylvania, enlisted 01 May 1758. On a return of Captain John Bull's company dated 01 July 1758.

Acre, Henry, age 23, born Pennsylvania, enlisted 01 September 1757, Corporal in Captain John Nicholas Weatherholt's company which enlisted for a term of three years and was stationed in Heydelberg Township, Northampton County, in March and April 1758April 1758.

Adams, Emanuel, age 28, wool-comber, born Ireland, enlisted 01 August 1746 in Captain William Trent's company.

Adams, James, ensign in the Associated Regiment of Bucks County in 1748.

Adams, John, age 28, laborer, born Scotland, enlisted 18 August 1746 in Captain William Trent's company.

Adams, John, ensign in one of the Associated Companies of Bucks County in 1756.

Addam, John, age 21, born Holland, private in Captain John Wright's company of the Lower County. On a muster dated 11 May 1759.

Age, Michael, a private in Captain Edward Jones's Independent Company of Horse, Philadelphia in 1756.

Agnew, James, captain in one of the Associated Companies of York County in 1756.

Aidley, John, age 23, born Dublin, Ireland, private in Captain John Haslett's company enlisted on 08 May 1758 and last paid on 21 May 1758.

Aiken, Hugh, landsman on the provincial ship *Pennsylvania* on 17 August 1757.

Aiken, John, age 16, weaver, born Pennsylvania, enlisted 03 May 1759, private in Captain John Haslet's company in the Pennsylvania Regiment. On a list of recruits dated 20 May 1759.

Aiken, William, age 24, laborer, born Antrim, Ireland, enlisted 10 May 1759, private in Captain John Haslet's company in the Pennsylvania Regiment. On a list of recruits dated 20 May 1759.

Akin, Alexander, age 20, laborer, enlisted 14 May 1759, private in Captain James Armstrong's company in Colonel William Clapham's Pennsylvania Regiment. On a return dated 01 June 1759.

Albright, George, private who enlisted 27 April 1756 in Captain Joseph Shippen's company in Colonel William Clapham's Regiment in 1756, the regiment in garrison at Fort Augusta, Shamokin, and listed in Shippen's Account Book. At Hunter's Fort.

Aldevey, Jacob, age 19, carpenter, born Pennsylvania, enlisted 18 May 1749 in Captain Richard Gardiner's company in Colonel William Denney's Pennsylvania Regiment.

Alexander, Alexander, a private in Captain Edward Jones's Independent Company of Horse, Philadelphia in 1756.

Alexander, Jedediah, captain in the Associated Regiment of the West End of Lancaster County in 1747–8.

Alexander, John, lieutenant in the Associated Regiment of the West End of Lancaster County in 1747–8.

Alfree, Paul, lieutenant in one of two regiments of New Castle County in 1747–8.

All, William, age 34, laborer, born Ireland, enlisted 01 May 1758 by Captain Benjamin Noxon.

Allan, William, a private in Captain John Kidd's Independent Company of Foot, Philadelphia in 1756.

Allee, Jacob, lieutenant in one of the Associated Companies of Kent County in 1747–8.

Allen, David, enlisted 05 May 1759, private in Captain Henry Van Bibber's company of the Lower County. On a return dated 04 June 1759.

Allen, George, master of the Battoe, 1757–8

Allen, John, age 28, born Derry, Ireland, weaver, private in Captain John Haslett's company enlisted on 14 May 1758 and last paid on 21 May 1758.

Allen, Peter, age 22, born Chester, Pennsylvania, saddler, private in Captain John Haslett's company enlisted on 07 May 1758 and last paid on 21 May 1758.

Allen, Samuel, lieutenant in Captain John Van Etten's company of the First Battalion from 19 May 1756. Commissioned from 02 December 1757, stationed eastward of Susquehanna. Captain Lieutenant of what appears to be the headquarters company of Colonel William Denny's Regiment, 09 January 1758. This company was originally Smith's Company stationed east of the Susquehanna. On a List of Officers in the Province Pay, 1756 in the First Battalion of the Pennsylvania Regiment with a commission date of 19 May 1756. {PA5, I, 88}

Allen, Thomas, hired 30 May 1757 as a battoe man, Master George Allen.

Allen, Ulrich, age 25, laborer, enlisted 28 June 1746 in Captain John Deimer's company.

Allen, William, captain in one of the companies of Colonel Jacob Duché's Philadelphia Regiment in 1756.

Allison, Hector, Chaplain from March 1759 of the Second Battalion. Chaplain of the First Battalion in 1760.

Allison, John, captain in one of the Associated Companies of Lancaster County in 1756. Captain of one of the new levies in May 1758.

Allison, Patrick, ensign of Captain John Hambright's Company, Third Battalion (known as the Augusta Regiment) from 20 August 1756. Lieutenant from 16 December 1757 in the same company, now in the Second Battalion, while stationed at Fort Augusta. First lieutenant from 02 May 1758 in Captain John Hambright's troop of Light Horse. Promoted to lieutenant after serving in the Pennsylvania Regiment of Three Battalions in 1758 and 1759.

Allison, Robert, lieutenant in the Associated Regiment of Chester County in 1747.

Allison, Samuel, on a list of men recruited by Captain Andrew McDowell's company in the Second Battalion, Pennsylvania Regiment dated 04 June 1759.

Allison, Thomas, age 20, miller, born Ireland, enlisted 03 May 1759 in Captain Robert Boyd's company [probably in the Third Battalion]. On a return dated May and June 1759.

Allison, William, lieutenant in the Associated Regiment of the West End of Lancaster County in 1747–8.

Allwinkle, Joseph, age 22, laborer, born Maryland, enlisted 21 April 1758 by Captain Benjamin Noxon, enlisted 01 May 1759, private in Captain Henry Van Bibber's company of the Lower County. On a return dated 04 June 1759.

Almond, John, captain in one of two regiments of New Castle County in 1747–8.

Almond, Thomas, age 20, laborer, born Ireland, enlisted 15 July 1746 in Captain Samuel Perry's company.

Alricks, Samuel, ensign in one of two regiments of New Castle County in 1747–8. Lieutenant in the New Castle Hundred company of Colonel William Armstrong's Upper Regiment of New Castle County in 1756.

Althain, Nicholas, age 24, born Germany, enlisted 01 January 1758, private in Captain John Nicholas Weatherholt's company which enlisted for a term of three years and was stationed in

Heydelberg Township, Northampton County, in March and April 1758April 1758.

Altum, James, enlisted 28 May 1758 in Captain French Battell's company of Lower County Provincials.

Anderson, Andrew, age 30, cordwainer, born Jersey, enlisted 30 April 1759, private in Captain Robert Curry's company in Colonel William Clapham's Pennsylvania Regiment. On a return dated June 1759.

Anderson, David, age 23, laborer, born Ireland, enlisted 01 May 1758. On a return of Captain John Blackwood's company in the Third Battalion dated 22 May 1758.

Anderson, Edward, age 24, born Richmond, private in Captain John Wright's company of the Lower County. On a muster dated 11 May 1759.

Anderson, Edward, private, laborer, born Ireland, enlisted May 1758 for the campaign in the lower counties. On a return of Captain McClughan's company dated 17 May 1758.

Anderson, James, a private in Captain George Armstrong's Company, Second Battalion in 1756; killed at Kittanning.

Anderson, James, age 21, laborer, born Ireland, enlisted 02 May 1758. On a weekly return of Captain Samuel Jones's company in 1758.

Anderson, James, age 30, born Germany, enlisted 14 May 1759, private in Captain Robert Curry's company in Colonel William Clapham's Pennsylvania Regiment. On a return dated June 1759.

Anderson, James, lieutenant in the Associated Regiment of the West End of Lancaster County in 1747–8. Captain in one of the Associated Companies of Lancaster County in 1756.

Anderson, John, private in Captain Samuel Mifflin's Association Battery Company of Philadelphia in 1756.

Anderson, John, ensign in the Associated Regiment of Lancaster County over the Susquehanna in 1747–8. Ensign in the St. George's Hundred company of Colonel Jacob Van Bibber's Lower Regiment of New Castle County in 1756.

Anderson, Joshua, lieutenant in one of the Associated Companies of Lancaster County in 1756.

Anderson, Robert, adjutant of the First Battalion (John Armstrong's) of Colonel William Denny's Regiment, 05 December 1757; promoted to first lieutenant, 30 April 1758. Reported as an Ensign in Captain Hugh Mercer's Company of the First Battalion on 05 December 1757 and promoted to lieutenant on 17 March 1759. Captain of a company of the Second Battalion of the Pennsylvania Regiment from 25 April 1760.

Anderson, Robert, lieutenant in the Associated Regiment of Chester County in 1747.

Anderson, Robert, ensign in Captain Hugh Mercer's Company from 05 December 1757, stationed westward of the Susquehanna. Promoted to first lieutenant from 30 April 1758 in Captain William Thompson's troop of Light Horse in the First Battalion. Lieutenant in Captain John Nicholas Wetterholt's company in the First Battalion on 18 March 1759.

Anderson, Robert, promoted to captain after serving in the Pennsylvania Regiment of Three Battalions in 1758 and 1759. Reported "Regular Service".

Anderson, Samuel, age 19, laborer, born Kent, Delaware, enlisted 16 July 1746 in Captain John Shannon's company of foot.

Anderson, Samuel, captain in the Associated Regiment of the West End of Lancaster County in 1747–8. Captain in one of the Associated Companies of Lancaster County in 1756.

Anderson, William, lieutenant of Captain James Burd's Company, Third Battalion (known as the Augusta Regiment) from 10 May 1756.

Andover, Joseph, Quartermaster of the provincial ship *Pennsylvania* on 17 August 1757.

Anslow, Richard, age 34, born Ireland, private in Captain John Wright's company of the Lower County. On a muster dated 11 May 1759.

Anstill, Isaac, age 21, laborer, born Virginia, enlisted 21 April 1758 by Captain Benjamin Noxon.

Anthony, Thomas, age 25, mariner, born England, enlisted 08 May 1758. On a weekly return of Captain Samuel Jones's company in 1758.

Anthony, William, age 20, laborer, born Sussex, Delaware, private in Captain John Wright's company of the Lower County. On a muster dated 11 May 1759.

Antonio, Manuel, age 22, mariner, born East Indies, enlisted 01 May 1758. On a weekly return of Captain Samuel Jones's company in 1758.

Appleby, George, a private in Captain George Armstrong's Company, Second Battalion in 1756; missing at the capture of Kittanning.

Ardis, Joshua, landsman on the provincial ship *Pennsylvania* on 17 August 1757.

Armgost, George, age 28, laborer, born Germany, enlisted 09 May 1758. On a return of Captain John Bull's company dated 01 July 1758.

Armitage, Samuel, age 27, born Chester, Pennsylvania, private in Captain John Singleton's company in service between 01 May and 08 May 1758.

Armour, Thomas, captain one of the new levies in May 1758 from York County.

Armsbie, Luke, age 27, laborer, born Ireland, enlisted 08 July 1746 in Captain Samuel Perry's company.

Armstrong, Abel, lieutenant in one of two regiments of New Castle County in 1747–8.

Armstrong, Alexander, lieutenant in one of two regiments of New Castle County in 1747–8.

Armstrong, Alexander, lieutenant in the Associated Regiment of the West End of Lancaster County in 1747–8.

Armstrong, Archibald, age 32, laborer, born Tyrone, Ireland, enlisted 26 April 1759, private in Captain James Armstrong's company in Colonel William Clapham's Pennsylvania Regiment. On a return dated 01 June 1759.

Armstrong, Archibald, captain in one of two regiments of New Castle County in 1747–8.

Armstrong, Edward, lieutenant in Captain Edward Ward's Company, Second Battalion from 22 May 1756; killed at the capture and burning of Ft. Granville, 30 July 1756.

Armstrong, George, captain of a company in the Second Battalion from 22 May 1756. Captain of a company in the First Battalion (John Armstrong's) of Colonel William Denny's Regiment from 12 December 1757 stationed westward of the Susquehanna. Major from of the Third Battalion. Lieutenant Colonel of the Second Battalion of the Pennsylvania Regiment from 13 April 1760.

Armstrong, James, captain in the Associated Regiment of the West End of Lancaster County in 1747-8.

Armstrong, James, ensign from 15 May 1758 in Captain Archibald McGrew's company in the Third Battalion. Promoted to captain after serving in the Pennsylvania Regiment of Three Battalions in 1758 and 1759. Captain from 13 May 1759 of a company of Colonel William Clapham's Regiment of New Levies. Reported as "dead".

Armstrong, James, sergeant, age 25, shoemaker, born Fermanagh, Ireland, enlisted 20 April 1758 for the campaign in the lower counties. On a return of Captain McClughan's company dated 17 May 1758.

Armstrong, John, a member of Captain Joseph Armstrong's Company on 07 August 1755, raised in Cumberland County.

Armstrong, John, age 22, laborer, born Ireland, enlisted 08 May 1758. On a return of Captain John Bull's company dated 01 July 1758.

Armstrong, John, captain of a company in the Second Battalion from January 1756; Lt. Col., of the Second Battalion from 11 May 1756; wounded at Kittanning, 07 September 1756. Captain of a company in the First Battalion of Colonel William Denny's Regiment, 02 December 1757. Stationed westward of Susquehanna.

Armstrong, John, Colonel Commandant of the First Battalion of Colonel William Denny's Regiment, 27 May 1758. Colonel of the First Battalion of the Pennsylvania Regiment in 1759, promoted to the rank of Colonel after having served in the Pennsylvania Regiment of Three Battalions, 1758 and 1759.

Armstrong, John, lieutenant in the Christiana Hundred Company of Colonel William Armstrong's Upper Regiment of New Castle County in 1756.

Armstrong, Joseph, age 23, laborer, born Ireland, enlisted 27 June 1746 in Captain William Trent's company.

Armstrong, Joseph, captain of a company from Cumberland County on 07 August 1755.

Armstrong, Joseph, ensign in Captain John Nicholas Wetterholt's company of the First Battalion, 22 February 1758. Also reported as an ensign in Captain Edward Ward's company from 22 February 1758 stationed westward of the Susquehanna.

Armstrong, Joseph, Captain of a company in Lieutenant Colonel Commandant Asher Clayton's Second Battalion of the Pennsylvania Regiment commanded by the Hon. J. Penn from 17 July 1763.

Armstrong, Joseph, Junr., ensign from 22 February 1758 in Captain Jacob Morgan's company stationed eastward of the Susquehanna.

Armstrong, Joseph, lieutenant in Captain John Lytle's company of the Second Battalion of the Pennsylvania Regiment from 01 May 1760.

Armstrong, Nehemiah, on a return of Captain David Hunter's Company [probably from York County] in Colonel William Clapham's Regiment of New Levies dated 26 May 1759.

Armstrong, Thomas, ensign in the Associated Regiment of Bucks County in 1748.

Armstrong, Thomas, a member of Captain Joseph Armstrong's Company on 07 August 1755, raised in Cumberland County.

Armstrong, William, captain in one of two regiments of New Castle County in 1747–8.

Armstrong, William, colonel of the Upper Regiment of New Castle County in 1756.

Armstrong, William, corporal, age 28, laborer, born Fermanagh, Ireland, enlisted 20 April 1758 for the campaign in the lower counties. On a return of Captain McClughan's company dated 17 May 1758.

Armstrong, William, lieutenant in Captain John Potter's Company, Second Battalion from 10 May 1756. Promoted to captain after serving in the Pennsylvania Regiment of Three Battalions in 1758 and 1759. Promoted to major of the Second Battalion of the Regiment Commanded by the Hon. J. Penn, Esquire, from 02 July 1764.

Armstrong, William, captain in a company in the First Battalion from 24 December 1757 stationed westward of the Susquehanna.

Arnett, James, age 22, laborer, born Dorset, Maryland, enlisted 18 May 1759, private in Captain John Mathers's company in the Pennsylvania Regiment. On a return dated 15 June 1759.

Arnold, Joseph, age 40, laborer, born England, enlisted 16 July 1746 in Captain William Trent's company.

Arnold, Martin, age 21, wheelwright, enlisted Captain John Deimer's company, 22 July 1746.

Arsell, James, age 26, tailor, born Ireland, enlisted 01 May 1758. On a weekly return of Captain Samuel Jones's company in 1758.

Arthurs, William, a private in Captain Joseph Inslee's Company of Foot, Newtown, Bucks County, in 1756.

Ashburn, Jacob, a private in Captain Joseph Inslee's Company of Foot, Newtown, Bucks County, in 1756.

Ashton, George, Captain from 08 May 1758 in a company in the Third Battalion.

Ashton, George, captain in the Associated Regiment of Chester County in 1747.

Ashton, George, Jun., ensign from 18 May 1758 in Captain John Clark's company in the Third Battalion. Lieutenant in Captain Edward Biddle's company of the Second Battalion of the Pennsylvania Regiment from 24 April 1760.

Ashton, Isaac, ensign in one of the companies of Colonel Jacob Duché's Philadelphia Regiment in 1756. Lieutenant in the Associated Regiment in the County of Philadelphia in 1748.

Ashton, William, age 28, laborer, born Pennsylvania, enlisted 05 May 1758. On a weekly return of Captain Samuel Jones's company in 1758.

Askey, Thomas, ensign in Captain James Piper's company in Lieutenant Colonel Commandant Asher Clayton's Second Battalion of the Pennsylvania Regiment commanded by the Hon. J. Penn from 15 July 1763.

Atchinson, James, age 22, butcher, born Delaware, enlisted 26 May 1749 in Captain Richard Gardiner's company in Colonel William Denney's Pennsylvania Regiment.

Atkins, William, enlisted 11 July 1746 in Captain William Trent's company—deserted 07 August 1746.

Atkinson, Cornelius, private who enlisted 20 April 1756 in Captain Joseph Shippen's company in Colonel William Clapham's Regiment, the regiment in garrison at Fort Augusta, Shamokin, and listed in Shippen's Account Book.

Atkinson, George, quartermaster of the provincial ship *Pennsylvania* on 17 August 1757.

Atkinson, John, private in Captain Joseph Inslee's Company of Foot, Newtown, Bucks County, in 1756.

Atlee, Samuel J., ensign of Captain Thomas Lloyd's Company, Third Battalion (known as the Augusta Regiment) from 23 April 1756. Lieutenant from 07 December 1757 in Captain Patrick Work's company in the Second Battalion, stationed at Fort Augusta. Captain from March 1759 in a company in the Second Battalion, vice Weiser. Captain from 15 May 1759 of a company in the Old Levies. Captain in of a company of the First Battalion of the Pennsylvania Regiment from 14 April 1760.

Atlee, Samuel J., promoted to Captain after serving in the Pennsylvania Regiment of Three Battalions in 1758 and 1759.

Avery, Charles, landsman on the provincial ship *Pennsylvania* on 17 August 1757.

Awl, Robert, ensign in the Associated Regiment of Chester County in 1747.

Awl, William, *see* William All.

Ayres, John, hired 07 May 1757 as a battoe man, Master George Allen.

Ayres, John, private in Captain Patterson's company from 26 December 1757 stationed eastward of the Susquehanna. On a muster roll dated 08 March 1758.

Ayres, William, age 20, mariner, born England, enlisted 27 April 1758. On a return of Captain John Blackwood's company in the Third Battalion dated 22 May 1758.

Babe, Innocent, seaman on the provincial ship *Pennsylvania* on 17 August 1757.

Baecker, Vangul, landsman on the provincial ship *Pennsylvania* on 17 August 1757.

Baem, David, age 32, weaver, born Ireland, enlisted 17 July 1746 in Captain William Trent's company.

Bailey, Edward, age 21, born Kent, Delaware, private in Captain John Wright's company of the Lower County. On a muster dated 11 May 1759.

Bailey, Thomas, enlisted 19 May 1758 in Captain French Battell's company of Lower County Provincials.

Bailey, William, age 21, weaver, born Ireland, enlisted 28 April 1759 in Captain Charles Stewart's company [probably one of the Associated Companies of Bucks County] on a return dated June 1759.

Bailitz, Nicholas, private who enlisted 10 May 1756 in Captain Joseph Shippen's company in Colonel William Clapham's Regiment in 1756, the regiment in garrison at Fort Augusta, Shamokin, and listed in Shippen's Account Book. Transferred to the Colonel's Company and promoted to Corporal 14 November 1756.

Baird, John, ensign from 13 March 1758 in Captain Patrick Work's company in the Second Battalion.

Baird, John, lieutenant in Captain John Prentice's company of the Second Battalion of the Pennsylvania Regiment from 18 April 1760.

Baird, John, promoted to lieutenant after serving in the Pennsylvania Regiment of Three Battalions in 1758 and 1759. Reported as "dead".

Baker, Jacob, age 18, laborer, born Philadelphia, Pennsylvania, enlisted 30 April 1759, private in Captain Joseph Richardson's company of the Third Battalion in the Pennsylvania Regiment. On a return of recruits dated 1759.

Baker, John, a private in Captain Hugh Mercer's Company, Second Battalion in 1756; killed at Kittanning.

Baker, Robert, captain in the Associated Regiment of the West End of Lancaster County in 1747–8. Major, in the Associated Regiment of the West End of Lancaster County in 1747–8.

Baker, William, a private in Captain George Armstrong's Company, Second Battalion in 1756; missing at the capture of Kittanning.

Balance, John, a private in Captain Joseph Inslee's Company of Foot, Newtown, Bucks County, in 1756.

Ball, Michael, age 27, laborer, born Ireland, enlisted 16 May 1758 by Lieutenant William McClay for Captain John Montgomery's company.

Ball, William, ensign in the Miln Creek Hundred company of Colonel William Armstrong's Upper Regiment of New Castle County in 1756.

Balls, Richard, enlisted 07 July 1746 in Captain William Trent's company—died 27 July 1746.

Bally, William, on a list of men recruited by Captain Andrew McDowell's company in the Second Battalion, Pennsylvania Regiment dated 04 June 1759.

Bambridge, James, lieutenant from 09 May 1759 in Captain Andrew McDowell's company of Colonel William Clapham's Regiment of New Levies.

Bambridge, James, promoted to lieutenant after serving in the Pennsylvania Regiment of Three Battalions in 1758 and 1759. Reported as "discontinued".

Bambridge, James, sergeant in Captain Joseph Shippen's company in Colonel William Clapham's Regiment in 1756, the regiment in garrison at Fort Augusta, Shamokin, and listed in Shippen's Account Book. Enlisted 03 May 1756 and discharged 10 May 1757.

Bambury, John, age 21, laborer, born Kent, Delaware, enlisted 14 July 1746 in Captain John Shannon's company of foot.

Bane, Reuben, age 20, tanner, born Pennsylvania, enlisted 20 May 1759 in Captain Robert Boyd's company [probably in the Third Battalion]. On a return dated May and June 1759.

Bane, Samuel, age 24, shoemaker, born Pennsylvania, enlisted 08 July 1746 in Captain Samuel Perry's company.

Barber, James, ensign in the Associated Regiment of Bucks County in 1748.

Barclay, Alexander, private in Captain Edward Jones's Independent Company of Horse, Philadelphia in 1756.

Barclay, Gilbert, private in Captain John Kidd's Independent Company of Foot, Philadelphia in 1756.

Barclay, Robert, a private in Captain Charles Batho's Independent Company of Foot, Philadelphia in 1756.

Bard, Peter, Commissary of Provisions, of the Third Battalion (known as the Augusta Regiment) in 1756. Commissary from 1758 of the Second Battalion. Commissary General of Stores to the Pennsylvania Regiment commanded by the Hon. J. Penn, Esqr., from 08 June 1764.

Bard, Samuel, age 25, born Ireland, private in Captain John Wright's company of the Lower County. On a muster dated 11 May 1759.

Barge, John, ensign, then lieutenant on 04 August 1748, in the Associated Regiment in the County of Philadelphia in 1748. Elected in the room of Jacob Leech. [CR,V, 325]

Barker, Herman, age 40, born Hungary, enlisted 27 April 1758. On a return of Captain John Blackwood's company in the Third Battalion dated 22 May 1758. Sergeant of Light Horse.

Barkley, John, ensign in one of the Associated Companies of Lancaster County in 1756.

Barkley, John, ensign in the Associated Regiment of the West End of Lancaster County in 1747–8.

Barloon, John, age 25, mariner, born Ireland, enlisted 01 May 1758. On a weekly return of Captain Samuel Jones's company in 1758.

Barlow, Samuel, private, age 33, dyer, born Lancaster, England, enlisted 12 May 1758 for the campaign in the lower counties.

On a return of Captain McClughan's company dated 17 May 1758.

Barnes, Barnabas, landsman on the provincial ship *Pennsylvania* on 17 August 1757.

Barnes, John, captain in the Upper Part of Little Creek Hundred company of Colonel John Vining's Regiment of Kent County Militia, Upon Delaware in 1756.

Barnes, John, ensign in one of the Associated Companies of York County in 1756.

Barnes, William, landsman on the provincial ship *Pennsylvania* on 17 August 1757.

Barnet, James, a member of Captain Joseph Armstrong's Company on 07 August 1755, raised in Cumberland County.

Barnet, John, a member of Captain Joseph Armstrong's Company on 07 August 1755, raised in Cumberland County.

Barnet, Joshua, a member of Captain Joseph Armstrong's Company on 07 August 1755, raised in Cumberland County

Barnet, Thomas, Jun., a member of Captain Joseph Armstrong's Company on 07 August 1755, raised in Cumberland County

Barnet, Thomas, Sr., a member of Captain Joseph Armstrong's Company on 07 August 1755, raised in Cumberland County

Barnett, James, age 22, laborer, born Ireland, enlisted 21 July 1746 in Captain Samuel Perry's company.

Barnett, John, a member of Captain David Jameson's Company at McCord's Fort on 02 April 1756 when he was wounded.

Barnt, Bernhard, a private in Captain Charles Batho's Independent Company of Foot, Philadelphia in 1756.

Baron, John, a private in Captain John Kidd's Independent Company of Foot, Philadelphia in 1756.

Baronnight, Charles, age 43, laborer, born England, enlisted 27 April 1758. On a return of Captain John Blackwood's company in the Third Battalion dated 22 May 1758.

Barr, David, lieutenant in the Pencader Hundred company of Colonel Jacob Van Bibber's Lower Regiment of New Castle County in 1756.

Barr, Thomas, age 30, weaver, born Ireland, enlisted 30 July 1746 in Captain Samuel Perry's company.

Barr, William, private in Captain Patterson's company from 29 December 1757 stationed eastward of the Susquehanna. On a muster roll dated 08 March 1758.

Barrett, James, age 23, laborer, born Ireland, enlisted 24 April 1758 by Captain Benjamin Noxon. Formerly with the Royal Americans.

Barrett, James, age 30, laborer, born Antrim, Ireland, enlisted 02 May 1759, private in Captain John Haslet's company in the Pennsylvania Regiment. On a list of recruits dated 20 May 1759.

Barrett, John, on a list of men recruited by Captain Andrew McDowell's company in the Second Battalion, Pennsylvania Regiment dated 04 June 1759.

Bartholomew, George, captain in one of the companies of Colonel Jacob Duché's Philadelphia Regiment in 1756.

Bartiel, Rudy, in Captain Robert Eastburn's company in the Second Battalion.

Bartley, George, private in Captain Patterson's company from 20 December 1757 stationed eastward of the Susquehanna. On a muster roll dated 08 March 1758.

Bartley, James, on a list of men recruited by Captain Andrew McDowell's company in the Second Battalion, Pennsylvania Regiment dated 04 June 1759.

Bartolimus, Peter, age 23, smith, age 25, laborer, enlisted 28 June 1746 in Captain John Deimer's company.

Barton, Rev. Thomas, captain in the provincial service in 1755. Chaplain of Colonel William Denny's Regiment, 11 June 1758

Bartram, Andrew, age 28, cooper, born Switzerland, enlisted 05 August 1746 in Captain John Deimer's company.

Baskell, William, *see* Baskins, William.

Baskins, Thomas, hired 27 May 1757 as a battoe man, Master George Allen.

Baskins, William, ensign in the Associated Regiment of the West End of Lancaster County in 1747–8.

Basset, John, age 26, laborer, born Wales, enlisted 29 April 1758 by Captain Benjamin Noxon.

Bassett, John, landsman on the provincial ship *Pennsylvania* on 17 August 1757.

Baston, John, age 28, laborer, born America, enlisted 07 May 1758 by Captain Benjamin Noxon.

Bates, Edward, age 58, laborer, born Norfolk, England, enlisted 20 May 1759, private in Captain John Mathers's company in the Pennsylvania Regiment. On a return dated 15 June 1759.

Batho, Charles, captain in Independent Company of Foot, Philadelphia on 12 March 1756.

Battell, French, ensign in one of two regiments of New Castle County in 1747–8. Captain of a company of Lower County Provincials. Lieutenant in the Town of Dover company of Colonel John Vining's Regiment of Kent County Militia, Upon Delaware in 1756. First lieutenant from 20 April 1758 in Captain Richard Wells company raised for the campaign in the lower counties. Quartermaster from 07 June 1758. On a list of officers of the lower government on Delaware, 1758/9. Captain from 22 May 1759 of a company from the Lower County.

Batten, Daniel, private who enlisted 16 April 1756 in Captain Joseph Shippen's company in Colonel William Clapham's Regiment in 1756, the regiment in garrison at Fort Augusta, Shamokin, and listed in Shippen's Account Book.

Baxter, Hope, age 34, laborer, born Leicester, England, enlisted 10 May 1759, private in Captain John Mathers's company in the Pennsylvania Regiment. On a return dated 15 June 1759.

Bay, Andrew, Chaplain from July 1758 of the Third Battalion. Chaplain from 01 May 1759 of Colonel William Clapham's Regiment of New Levies.

Bayer, Jacob, *see* Byer, Jacob.

Bayer, Thomas, seaman on the provincial ship *Pennsylvania* on 17 August 1757.

Bayman, Nathaniel, age 30, baker, born Ireland, enlisted 01 July 1746 in Captain William Trent's company.

Bayne, Andrew, private who enlisted 29 April 1756 in Captain Joseph Shippen's company in Colonel William Clapham's Regiment in 1756, the regiment in garrison at Fort Augusta,

Shamokin, and listed in Shippen's Account Book. Described as being of Colonel's company.

Bayst, Sebastian, age 30, tailor, born Germany, enlisted 17 July 1746 in Captain John Deimer's company.

Beain, William, Corporal in Captain Patterson's company from 26 January 1758 stationed eastward of the Susquehanna. On a muster roll dated 08 March 1758.

Beales, John, musician of the provincial ship *Pennsylvania* on 17 August 1757.

Beane, William, age 25, cordwainer, born Maryland, enlisted 29 April 1758 by Captain Benjamin Noxon.

Beard, John, age 21, laborer, born Germany, enlisted 20 July 1746 in Captain Samuel Perry's company.

Beard, John, lieutenant in the Associated Regiment of Bucks County in 1748.

Beatty, Charles, Chaplain of the First Battalion (John Armstrong's) of Colonel William Denny's Regiment, 09 June 1758.

Beatty, John, age 24, weaver, born Ireland, enlisted 01 May 1758 by Captain Benjamin Noxon.

Beatty, Patrick, age 25, laborer, born Ireland, enlisted 17 May 1758 by Lieutenant William McClay for Captain John Montgomery's company.

Beatty, Samuel, age 16, laborer, born Tyrone, Ireland, enlisted 01 May 1759, private in Captain John Haslet's company in the Pennsylvania Regiment. On a list of recruits dated 20 May 1759.

Beaulguard, John, age 24, combmaker, born Germany, enlisted 11 May 1758. On a weekly return of Captain Samuel Jones's company in 1758.

Beckley, William, age 30, cooper, born Pennsylvania, enlisted 15 May 1749 in Captain Richard Gardiner's company in Colonel William Denney's Pennsylvania Regiment.

Bedford, Gunning, promoted to lieutenant after serving in the Pennsylvania Regiment of Three Battalions in 1758 and 1759. Lieutenant in Major Thomas Smallman's company of the

Second Battalion of the Pennsylvania Regiment from 03 May 1760.

Begs, Robert, on a list of men recruited by Captain Andrew McDowell's company in the Second Battalion, Pennsylvania Regiment dated 04 June 1759.

Beker, John, a private in Captain Adam Heylman's Company, of the St. Vincent and Puke's Land Association on 10 May 1756.

Bell, John, a private in Captain Joseph Inslee's Company of Foot, Newtown, Bucks County, in 1756.

Bell, Pearson, promoted to lieutenant after serving in the Pennsylvania Regiment of Three Battalions in 1758 and 1759. Reported as "left the Province".

Bell, Reason, lieutenant from 10 May 1759 in Captain Evan Shelley's company of Colonel William Clapham's Regiment of New Levies.

Bell, William, a private in Captain Joseph Inslee's Company of Foot, Newtown, Bucks County, in 1756.

Bell, William, age 18, tanner, born Maryland, enlisted 05 May 1758 by Captain Benjamin Noxon.

Bell, William, captain in the Associated Regiment of Chester County in 1747.

Bellville, John, age 16, tailor, born Delaware, enlisted 26 April 1758 by Captain Benjamin Noxon.

Bellville, Nicholas, age 35, weaver, born New York, enlisted 29 April 1758 by Captain Benjamin Noxon.

Bellville, Philip, age 19, tailor, born Delaware, enlisted 25 April 1758 by Captain Benjamin Noxon.

Beltz, Michael, lieutenant in Captain Charles Foulk's company of the First Battalion in 1755/6.

Bembrook, William, age 45, laborer, born Ireland, enlisted 09 May 1749 in Captain Richard Gardiner's company in Colonel William Denney's Pennsylvania Regiment.

Bender, Jacob, a private in Captain Edward Jones's Independent Company of Horse, Philadelphia in 1756.

Bender, Jacob, a private in Captain John Kidd's Independent Company of Foot, Philadelphia in 1756.

Bender, John, private in Captain Charles Batho's Independent Company of Foot, Philadelphia in 1756.

Benezet, Daniel, a private in Captain John Kidd's Independent Company of Foot, Philadelphia in 1756.

Benezet, Philio, ensign in the Associated Regiment of Foot of Philadelphia on 29 Dec 1747.

Benn, Benjamin, age 27, laborer, born England, enlisted 01 July 1746 in Captain William Trent's company.

Benn, David, age 34, laborer, enlisted 23 July 1746 in Captain John Deimer's company.

Benner, Michael, age 45, blacksmith, born Platz, Germany, enlisted 24 May 1759, private in Captain John Mathers's company in the Pennsylvania Regiment. On a return dated 15 June 1759.

Bennett, George, captain in the Associated Regiment of Bucks County in 1748.

Bennett, Isaac, age 30, laborer, born East Jersey, enlisted 13 July 1746 in Captain John Shannon's company of foot.

Bennett, Stephen, private, age 30, laborer, born Ipswich, Massachusetts, enlisted 12 May 1758 for the campaign in the lower counties. On a return of Captain McClughan's company dated 17 May 1758.

Bennett, Thomas, ensign in one of two regiments of New Castle County in 1747–8. Ensign in the Apoquinimink Hundred company of Colonel Jacob Van Bibber's Lower Regiment of New Castle County in 1756.

Bentley, George, lieutenant in the Associated Regiment of Chester County in 1747.

Berret, John, *see* John Barrett.

Berry, Thomas, age 20, laborer, born Philadelphia, Pennsylvania, enlisted 28 April 1759, private in Captain Joseph Richardson's company of the Third Battalion in the Pennsylvania Regiment. On a return of recruits dated 1759.

Best, Joseph, landsman on the provincial ship *Pennsylvania* on 17 August 1757.

Bevard, Charles, age 28, born Chester, Pennsylvania, weaver, private in Captain John Singleton's company in service between 01 May and 08 May 1758.

Bey, William, captain in one of the companies of Colonel Jacob Duché's Philadelphia Regiment in 1756.

Beyers, John, promoted to captain after serving in the Pennsylvania Regiment of Three Battalions in 1758 and 1759.

Bezoom, Frederick, ensign in Captain Robert Anderson's company of the Second Battalion of the Pennsylvania Regiment from 01 May 1760.

Bickley, Joseph, age 21, laborer, born England, enlisted 09 May 1758 by Captain Benjamin Noxon.

Biddle, Edward, ensign, provincial officer in 1754, ensign from 03 December 1757 in Captain Samuel Weiser's company in the Second Battalion, stationed eastward of Susquehanna. Promoted to lieutenant in Captain William Thompson's company of the First Battalion 01 February 1759. Promoted to captain after serving in the Pennsylvania Regiment of Three Battalions in 1758 and 1759.Captain of a company of the Second Battalion of the Pennsylvania Regiment from 24 April 1760.

Bierlyh, Casper, private in Captain Patterson's company from 07 February 1758 stationed eastward of the Susquehanna. On a muster roll dated 08 March 1758.

Bigger, John, age 22, weaver, born Ireland, enlisted 17 May 1759 in Captain Robert Boyd's company [probably in the Third Battalion]. On a return dated May and June 1759.

Bigger, Peacock, captain in the Associated Regiment of Foot of Philadelphia on 29 Dec 1747.

Biles, William, captain from 14 May 1758 of a company in the Third Battalion. Captain in one of the new levies in May 1758 from Bucks County.

Billik, Frederick, age 19, born Pennsylvania, enlisted 01 September 1757, private in Captain John Nicholas Weatherholt's company which enlisted for a term of three years and was stationed in Heydelberg Township, Northampton County, in March and April 1758April 1758.

Bines, Robert, ensign from 28 April 1758 in Captain John Haslett's company in the Second Battalion and last paid on 21 May 1758. Surgeon from 09 May 1758 in the Third Battalion.

Bingham, William, a private in Captain Charles Batho's Independent Company of Foot, Philadelphia in 1756.

Bingham, William, ensign in the Associated Regiment of Foot of Philadelphia on 29 Dec 1747.

Bird, Empsena, lieutenant in the Christiana Hundred company of Colonel William Armstrong's Upper Regiment of New Castle County in 1756.

Bird, Jacob, age 18, height 7 ft., 7 ½ inches, laborer, born Jersey, enlisted 30 April 1759, private in Captain Joseph Richardson's company of the Third Battalion in the Pennsylvania Regiment. On a return of recruits dated 1759.

Bishop, George, age 20, weaver, born Germany, enlisted 15 May 1758. On a return of Captain John Bull's company dated 01 July 1758.

Blacbly, William, age 25, mason, born England, enlisted 01 July 1746 in Captain John Deimer's company.

Black, George, private, age 24, weaver, born Armagh, Ireland, enlisted 20 April 1758 for the campaign in the lower counties. On a return of Captain McClughan's company dated 17 May 1758.

Black, Hugh, age 25, born Ireland, enlisted 28 May 1759, sergeant in Captain Robert Curry's company in Colonel William Clapham's Pennsylvania Regiment. On a return dated June 1759.

Black, James, landsman on the provincial ship *Pennsylvania* on 17 August 1757.

Black, Thomas, age 20, cooper, born Ireland, enlisted 09 July 1746 in Captain John Shannon's company of foot.

Black, William, age 28, weaver, born Scotland, enlisted 21 July 1746 in Captain William Trent's company.

Blackshire, Robert, captain in one of the Associated Companies of Kent County in 1747–8.

Blackwood, John, Captain from 02 May 1758 in a company in the Third Battalion. On a return dated 22 May 1758. Promoted to captain after serving in the Pennsylvania Regiment of Three Battalions in 1758 and 1759. Reported as "dead". Captain of a company of the Second Battalion of the Pennsylvania Regiment from 01 May 1760.

Blackwood, John, ensign in Captain William Vanderspeigle's Philadelphia Company in 1760.

Blades, Edmond, age 26, carpenter, born Maryland, enlisted 02 May 1758 by Captain Benjamin Noxon.

Blair, James, John, a member of Captain David Jameson's Company at McCord's Fort on 02 April 1756 when he was killed.

Blair, John (Thomas), Surgeon of the First Battalion (John Armstrong's) of Colonel William Denny's Regiment, 02 December 1757.

Blair, John, *see* John Blear.

Blair, Thomas, age 26, laborer, born Antrim, Ireland, enlisted 01 May 1759, private in Captain John Haslet's company in the Pennsylvania Regiment. On a list of recruits dated 20 May 1759.

Blair, Thomas, lieutenant in the Associated Regiment of Bucks County in 1748.

Blake, Adam, a private in Captain Samuel Mifflin's Association Battery Company of Philadelphia in 1756.

Blankenstone, Frederick, a private in Captain John Kidd's Independent Company of Foot, Philadelphia in 1756.

Blear, John, age 30, laborer, born Ireland, enlisted May 1758. On a return of Captain John Bull's company dated 01 July 1758.

Blyth(e), William, lieutenant from 24 December 1757 in Captain William Armstrong's company stationed westward of the Susquehanna. Promoted to lieutenant after serving in the Pennsylvania Regiment of Three Battalions in 1758 and 1759. Lieutenant in Captain Caleb Grayden's company in the First Battalion of the Pennsylvania Regiment from 21 August 1763.

Boadman, Matthew, age 28, laborer, born Germany, enlisted 07 August 1746 in Captain William Trent's company.

Boark, Thomas, age 25, miller, born Ireland, enlisted 13 July 1746 in Captain John Shannon's company of foot.

Bogart, James, lieutenant in the Associated Regiment of Bucks County in 1748.

Boggs, Andrew, ensign in the Associated Regiment of the West End of Lancaster County in 1747–8.

Boggs, James, age 17, tailor, born Pennsylvania, enlisted 15 May 1758 by Lieutenant William McClay for Captain John Montgomery's company.

Boggs, William, age 30, born Cecil, Maryland, private in Captain John Singleton's company in service between 01 May and 08 May 1758.

Boggs, William, age 40, born Chester, Pennsylvania, private in Captain John Haslett's company enlisted on 06 May 1758 and last paid on 21 May 1758.

Bogonar, Tobias, age 27, laborer, born Germany, enlisted 09 May 1758. On a return of Captain John Bull's company dated 01 July 1758.

Boham, John, private who enlisted 15 April 1756 in Captain Joseph Shippen's company in Colonel William Clapham's Regiment in 1756, the regiment in garrison at Fort Augusta, Shamokin, and listed in Shippen's Account Book.

Bond, John, enlisted 17 May 1758 in Captain French Battell's company of Lower County Provincials.

Bond, John, Surgeon of Colonel William Denny's Regiment at Fort Augusta, 11 May 1758. Lieutenant and surgeon in Captain Samuel West's company of the First Battalion of the Pennsylvania Regiment from 30 April 1760.

Bond, Thomas, captain in the Associated Regiment of Foot of Philadelphia on 29 Dec 1747.

Bonner, Dennis, age 36, mariner, born Ireland, enlisted 29 April 1758. On a weekly return of Captain Samuel Jones's company in 1758.

Boom, Jacob, age 23, laborer, born England, enlisted 23 July 1746 in Captain John Deimer's company.

Boon, Anthony, landsman on the provincial ship *Pennsylvania* on 17 August 1757.

Boon, Evan, *see* Evan Bown.

Boon, William, Midshipman of the provincial ship *Pennsylvania* on 17 August 1757.

Booth, Joseph, enlisted 10 May 1758 in Captain French Battell's company of Lower County Provincials.

Booth, Richard, age 31, born Derby, England, private in Captain John Haslett's company enlisted on 10 May 1758 and last paid on 21 May 1758.

Bordner, Jacob, age 26, laborer, enlisted 14 July 1746 in Captain John Deimer's company.

Bossing, Dewalt, sergeant, in Captain Charles Foulk's company of the First Battalion in 1755/6.

Bouden, James, enlisted 13 May 1758 in Captain French Battell's company of Lower County Provincials.

Bound, John, a private in Captain Adam Heylman's Company, of the St. Vincent and Puke's Land Association on 10 May 1756.

Bourgeois, Benjamin, age 28, laborer, born Switzerland, enlisted 31 May 1758 by Lieutenant William McClay for Captain John Montgomery's company.

Bourne, Thomas, captain in the Associated Regiment of Foot of Philadelphia on 29 Dec 1747.

Bowbeck, Michael, age 35, laborer, born Alson, Germany, enlisted 11 May 1759, private in Captain John Mathers's company in the Pennsylvania Regiment. On a return dated 15 June 1759.

Bowen, George, enlisted 17 May 1759, private in Captain Henry Van Bibber's company of the Lower County. On a return dated 04 June 1759.

Bower, Henry, age 22, cooper, enlisted 11 July 1746 in Captain John Deimer's company.

Bowern, Valentine, private who enlisted 23 April 1756 in Captain Patrick Work's company in Colonel William Clapham's Regiment in 1756, the regiment in garrison at Fort Augusta, Shamokin, and listed in Shippen's Account Book.

Bowler, Samuel John, age 27, shoemaker, born Barbados, enlisted 15 May 1758. On a return of Captain John Blackwood's company in the Third Battalion dated 22 May 1758.

Bowler, Thomas, age 33, shoemaker, born Barbados, enlisted 15 May 1758. On a return of Captain John Blackwood's company in the Third Battalion dated 22 May 1758.

Bowman, Christian, age 22, born Germany, enlisted 01 September 1757, private in Captain John Nicholas Weatherholt's company which enlisted for a term of three years and stationed in Heydelberg Township, Northampton County, in March and April 1758April 1758.

Bowman, Samuel, age 18, cordwainer, born Pennsylvania, enlisted 12 May 1749 in Captain Richard Gardiner's company in Colonel William Denney's Pennsylvania Regiment.

Bown, Evan, age 31, laborer, born Pennsylvania, enlisted 03 May 1758. On a return of Captain John Bull's company dated 01 July 1758.

Bown, Samuel, a member of Captain Joseph Armstrong's Company on 07 August 1755, raised in Cumberland County

Bownrife, John, private who enlisted 16 April 1756 in Captain Joseph Shippen's company in Colonel William Clapham's Regiment in 1756, the regiment in garrison at Fort Augusta, Shamokin, and listed in Shippen's Account Book.

Boyd, Adam, promoted to lieutenant after serving in the Pennsylvania Regiment of Three Battalions in 1758 and 1759.

Boyd, Alex, an ensign stationed on the frontier in Northampton County with Captain John Nebb, one sergeant, and twenty-five men at Fort Penn on 01 June 1764 as part of a unit under the command of Major Asher Clayton.

Boyd, Alexander, ensign in Captain John Webb's company in the First Battalion of the Pennsylvania Regiment from 29 November 1763.

Boyd, Daniel, lieutenant from 01 May 1758 in Captain Robert Boyd's company in the Third Battalion. Captain from 26 April 1759 in Colonel William Clapham's Regiment of New Levies.

Boyd, John, a member of Captain Joseph Armstrong's Company on 07 August 1755, raised in Cumberland County

Boyd, John, age 19, weaver, born Ireland, enlisted 16 July 1746 in Captain Samuel Perry's company.

Boyd, John, enlisted 14 May 1759, private in Captain Henry Van Bibber's company of the Lower County. On a return dated 04 June 1759.

Boyd, John, lieutenant in the Associated Regiment of Chester County in 1747.

Boyd, Robert, Promoted to captain after serving in the Pennsylvania Regiment of Three Battalions in 1758 and 1759. Captain from 01 May 1758 of a company in the Third Battalion. Reported as "discontinued".

Boyd, William, captain in the Associated Regiment of Chester County in 1747.

Boyd, William, enlisted 15 July 1746 in Captain Samuel Perry's company.

Boyd, William, lieutenant from 23 April 1759 in Captain Robert Boyd's company of Colonel William Clapham's Regiment of New Levies.

Boyle, James, age 27, laborer, born Ireland, enlisted 04 August 1746 in Captain William Trent's company.

Boyle, Philip, private who enlisted 04 May 1756 in Captain Joseph Shippen's company in Colonel William Clapham's Regiment in 1756, the regiment in garrison at Fort Augusta, Shamokin, and listed in Shippen's Account Book.

Boyssen, Bay, age 25, mariner, born Sweedland, enlisted 01 May 1758. On a weekly return of Captain Samuel Jones's company in 1758.

Braden, James, hired 27 May 1757 as a battoe man, Master George Allen.

Bradford, William, lieutenant in the Associated Regiment of Foot of Philadelphia on 29 Dec 1747.

Brady, John, ensign in Captain (Brigade Major) David Jamison's Company of the First Battalion of the Pennsylvania Regiment from 18 April 1760. Captain of a company in Lieutenant Colonel Commandant Asher Clayton's Second Battalion of the Pennsylvania Regiment commanded by the Hon. J. Penn from 19 July 1763.

Bragg, Henry, carpenter of the provincial ship *Pennsylvania* on 17 August 1757.

Brandon, Timothy, private who enlisted 20 April 1756 in Captain Joseph Shippen's company in Colonel William Clapham's Regiment in 1756, the regiment in garrison at Fort Augusta, Shamokin, and listed in Shippen's Account Book.
Braning, Edward, *see* Brennan, Edward.
Brannan, James, *see* Brennan, James.
Bratt, Samuel, a private in Captain Joseph Inslee's Company of Foot, Newtown, Bucks County, in 1756.
Bratton, Ephraim, a private in Captain Edward Ward's Company, Second Battalion in 1756; wounded at Kittanning.
Braun, Jacob, a private in Captain Adam Heylman's Company, of the St. Vincent and Puke's Land Association on 10 May 1756.
Breasland, James, private in Captain John Singleton's company in service between 01 May and 08 May 1758.
Breckill, George, age 24, laborer, born Ireland, enlisted 07 May 1759 in Captain Robert Boyd's company [probably in the Third Battalion]. On a return dated May and June 1759.
Bredan, William, age 25, laborer, born Derry, Ireland, enlisted 06 May 1759, private in Captain John Haslet's company in the Pennsylvania Regiment. On a list of recruits dated 20 May 1759.
Brennan, Edward, age 21, laborer, born Ireland, enlisted 21 July 1746 in Captain Samuel Perry's company.
Brennan, George, ensign in the Associated Regiment of Lancaster County over the Susquehanna in 1747–8.
Brennan, James, age 23, laborer, born Ireland, enlisted 19 July 1746 in Captain Samuel Perry's company.
Bresland, James, age 50, mason, born Templemore, Ireland, enlisted 22 May 1759, private in Captain John Mathers's company in the Pennsylvania Regiment. On a return dated 15 June 1759.
Brich, Jacob, private in Captain Edward Jones's Independent Company of Horse, Philadelphia in 1756.
Brickle, Benjamin, captain in the Lower Part of Mispillim Hundred company of Colonel John Vining's Regiment of Kent County Militia, Upon Delaware in 1756.

Brieslin, James, age 17, born Chester, Pennsylvania, private in Captain John Haslett's company enlisted on 12 May 1758 and last paid on 21 May 1758.

Brinckle, John, captain in the Lower Part of Little Creek Hundred company of Colonel John Vining's Regiment of Kent County Militia, Upon Delaware in 1756. Lt. Col. in Colonel John Vining's Regiment of Militia for Kent County, upon the Delaware in 1756.

Brinckle, Joseph, enlisted 24 May 1758 in Captain French Battell's company of Lower County Provincials.

Brind, Isaac, enlisted 07 May 1759, private in Captain Henry Van Bibber's company of the Lower County. On a return dated 04 June 1759.

Brind, Isaac, private, age 34, shoemaker, born Wiltshire, England, enlisted 01 May 1758 for the campaign in the lower counties. On a return of Captain McClughan's company dated 17 May 1758.

Brining, Philip, age 27, born Germany, enlisted 01 September 1757, private in Captain John Nicholas Weatherholt's company which enlisted for a term of three years and stationed in Heydelberg Township, Northampton County, in March and April 1758April 1758.

Brinley, Robert, age 19, laborer, born Ireland, enlisted 25 May 1758 by Lieutenant William McClay for Captain John Montgomery's company.

Brisbane, John, ensign from 26 April 1759 in Captain Samuel Nelson's company of Colonel William Clapham's Regiment of New Levies.

Brischert, Richard, a private in Captain Adam Heylman's Company, of the St. Vincent and Puke's Land Association on 10 May 1756.

Broadass, Arthur, a private in Captain Joseph Inslee's Company of Foot, Newtown, Bucks County, in 1756.

Brochson, Joseph, private, age 17, planter, born Three Runs, Delaware, enlisted 19 April 1758 for the campaign in the lower counties. On a return of Captain McClughan's company dated 17 May 1758.

Brodhead, Charles, ensign of Captain Thomas Lloyd's Company, Third Battalion (known as the Augusta Regiment) from 29 April 1756. Lieutenant in Captain Levi Trump's company (also reported Captain Patrick Davis company of the First Battalion) from 08 December 1757 stationed at Fort Augusta. Promoted to captain in March 1759 of a company in the Second Battalion, vice Bussè. Captain from 16 May 1759 of a company in the Old Levies.

Brodhead, Charles, promoted to Captain after serving in the Pennsylvania Regiment of Three Battalions in 1758 and 1759. Reported as "left the Province".

Brodie, William, age 25, born Scotland, 30 July 1746 in Captain John Deimer's company.

Brooks, Robert, age 22, laborer, born England, enlisted 22 July 1746 in Captain William Trent's company.

Broomfield, Francis, age 16, tailor, born Charlestown, Maryland, enlisted 29 April 1759, private in Captain James Armstrong's company in Colonel William Clapham's Pennsylvania Regiment. On a return dated 01 June 1759.

Brown, George, age 23, born Germany, butcher, enlisted 01 September 1757, private in Captain John Nicholas Weatherholt's company which enlisted for a term of three years and stationed in Heydelberg Township, Northampton County, in March and April 1758April 1758.

Brown, George, captain in the Associated Regiment of Lancaster County over the Susquehanna in 1747–8.

Brown, George, Corporal, age 26, tanner, born Derry, Ireland, enlisted 25 April 1758 for the campaign in the lower counties. On a return of Captain McClughan's company dated 17 May 1758.

Brown, George, landsman on the provincial ship *Pennsylvania* on 17 August 1757.

Brown, Jacob, age 23, baker, born Germany, enlisted 09 May 1758. On a return of Captain John Bull's company dated 01 July 1758.

Brown, James, private in Captain Patterson's company from 04 November 1757 stationed eastward of the Susquehanna. On a muster roll dated 08 March 1758.

Brown, James, private in Lieutenant Miller's detachment of Captain Frederick Smith's Company killed by Indians on 06 August 1756 at Manity [Manada] Fort.

Brown, John, age 33, barber, born Ireland, enlisted 04 May 1759, private in Captain William Johnston's company in the Pennsylvania Regiment. On a return dated 12 May 1759.

Brown, John, private who enlisted 28 April 1756 in Captain Joseph Shippen's company in Colonel William Clapham's Regiment in 1756, the regiment in garrison at Fort Augusta, Shamokin, and listed in Shippen's Account Book.

Brown, Joseph, a private in Captain Samuel Mifflin's Association Battery Company of Philadelphia in 1756.

Brown, Peter, age 45, laborer, born Ireland, enlisted 08 May 1759 in Captain Charles Stewart's company [probably one of the Associated Companies of Bucks County]. On a return dated June 1759.

Brown, Samuel, a member of Captain Joseph Armstrong's Company on 07 August 1755, raised in Cumberland County.

Brown, Thomas, age 24, laborer, born Ireland, enlisted 03 May 1759, private in Captain James Armstrong's company in Colonel William Clapham's Pennsylvania Regiment. On a return dated 01 June 1759.

Brown, Thomas, age 25, laborer, born England, enlisted 01 May 1758. On a weekly return of Captain Samuel Jones's company in 1758.

Brown, Thomas, ensign in the Associated Regiment of Chester County in 1747.

Brownholtz, Frederick, age 18, laborer, born Germany, enlisted 30 April 1759, private in Captain Joseph Richardson's company of the Third Battalion in the Pennsylvania Regiment. On a return of recruits dated 1759.

Brubaker, Nicholas, enlisted 13 July 1746 in Captain Samuel Perry's company.

Bryan, _____, lieutenant of Captain Nathan Miles's Company, Third Battalion (known as the Augusta Regiment) in 1756.

Bryan, Arthur, age 30, born Philadelphia, bricklayer, "much pitted with the Smallpox", private in Captain John Singleton's company in service between 01 May and 08 May 1758.

Bryan, Charles, Sen., ensign in one of two regiments of New Castle County in 1747–8.

Bryan, Francis, private who enlisted 20 April 1756 in Captain David Jameson's company in Colonel William Clapham's Regiment in 1756, the regiment in garrison at Fort Augusta, Shamokin, and listed in Shippen's Account Book.

Bryan, John, Captain of a company of the First Battalion of the Pennsylvania Regiment from 02 May 1760.

Bryan, John, ensign in the New Castle Hundred company of Colonel William Armstrong's Upper Regiment of New Castle County in 1756.

Bryan, John, ensign in the St. George's Hundred company of Colonel Jacob Van Bibber's Lower Regiment of New Castle County in 1756. Second lieutenant from 22 April 1758 in Captain John McClughan's company raised for the campaign in the lower counties.

Bryan, William, private, age 34, planter, born St. Martin's, Maryland, enlisted 03 May 1758 for the campaign in the lower counties. On a return of Captain McClughan's company dated 17 May 1758.

Buchanan, John, age 29, laborer, born Lancaster, Pennsylvania, enlisted 08 May 1759, private in Captain John Haslet's company in the Pennsylvania Regiment. On a list of recruits dated 20 May 1759.

Buchanan, William, age 18, laborer, born Lancaster, Pennsylvania, enlisted 08 May 1759, private in Captain John Haslet's company in the Pennsylvania Regiment. On a list of recruits dated 20 May 1759.

Buchanan, William, age 25, laborer, born Donegal, Ireland, enlisted 08 May 1759, private in Captain John Haslet's company in the Pennsylvania Regiment. On a list of recruits dated 20 May 1759.

Buchanan, William, ensign in Captain James Hyndshaw's company of the Second Battalion of the Pennsylvania Regiment from 21 April 1760.

Buchanan, William, ensign in William Armstrong's company in Lieutenant Colonel Commandant Asher Clayton's Second Battalion of the Pennsylvania Regiment commanded by the Hon. J. Penn from 14 July 1763.

Buchanan, William, lieutenant in the Associated Regiment of Chester County in 1747.

Bucher, Conrad, Adjutant in Lieutenant Colonel Commandant Asher Clayton's Second Battalion of the Pennsylvania Regiment commanded by the Hon. J. Penn from 07 September 1764.

Bucher, Conrad, ensign from 01 April 1758 in Captain William Armstrong's company stationed westward of the Susquehanna.

Bucher, Conrad, lieutenant in Captain James Piper's company in Lieutenant Colonel Commandant Asher Clayton's Second Battalion of the Pennsylvania Regiment commanded by the Hon. J. Penn from 16 July 1763.

Bucher, Conrad, lieutenant in Lieutenant Colonel George Armstrong's company of the Second Battalion of the Pennsylvania Regiment from 19 April 1760.

Bucher, Conrad, promoted to lieutenant after serving in the Pennsylvania Regiment of Three Battalions in 1758 and 1759. Reported as "joined Colonel Francis".

Buckhammer, John, age 25, born Germany, enlisted 01 September 1757, private in Captain John Nicholas Weatherholt's company which enlisted for a term of three years and stationed in Heydelberg Township, Northampton County, in March and April 1758April 1758.

Buckmaster, Wilson, lieutenant in the Lower Part of Little Creek Hundred company of Colonel John Vining's Regiment of Kent County Militia, Upon Delaware in 1756.

Budd, John, enlisted 13 May 1759, private in Captain Henry Van Bibber's company of the Lower County. On a return dated 04 June 1759.

Budden, Richard, a private in Captain Samuel Mifflin's Association Battery Company of Philadelphia in 1756.

Bulger, Thomas, a private in Captain Joseph Inslee's Company of Foot, Newtown, Bucks County, in 1756.

Bulkeley, John, Master's Mate of the provincial ship *Pennsylvania* on 17 August 1757.

Bull, John, Captain from 12 May 1758 of a company in the Third Battalion and listed on a return dated 01 July 1758. Captain from 29 April 1759 of a company of Colonel William Clapham's Regiment of New Levies.

Bull, John, promoted to Captain after serving in the Pennsylvania Regiment of Three Battalions in 1758 and 1759.

Bullet, Bedy, age 21, born Maryland, private in Captain John Wright's company of the Lower County. On a muster dated 11 May 1759.

Bullock, George, age 26, weaver, born Ireland, enlisted 15 May 1758 by Captain Benjamin Noxon.

Bummer, Peter, age 20, laborer, born Pennsylvania, enlisted 10 May 1758. On a return of Captain John Blackwood's company in the Third Battalion dated 22 May 1758.

Bunn, Serejah, age 20, stonemason, born Jersey, enlisted 10 May 1758. On a return of Captain John Bull's company dated 01 July 1758.

Burch, Thomas, age 22, laborer, born England, enlisted 30 July 1746 in Captain William Trent's company.

Burd, James was promoted to the rank of Colonel after having served in the Pennsylvania Regiment of Three Battalions, 1758 and 1759.

Burd, James, Colonel, First Battalion, Pennsylvania Regiment from 12 April 1760.

Burd, James, Lt. Col., in the provincial service in 1755. Stationed at Fort Augusta. Captain of a company of the Third Battalion (known as the Augusta Regiment) promoted Major from 24 April 1756. Captain of a company in the Second Battalion from 03 December 1757. Colonel from 28 May 1758 of the Second Battalion of Col. William Denny's Regiment. Colonel of the Second Battalion of the Pennsylvania Regiment in 1759.

Burk, Edward, age 17, joiner, born Maryland, enlisted 15 May 1758. On a return of Captain John Blackwood's company in the Third Battalion dated 22 May 1758.

Burk, Edward, age 17, joiner, born Queen's, Maryland, enlisted 04 May 1759, private in Captain William Johnston's company in the Pennsylvania Regiment. On a return dated 12 May 1759.

Burk, John, age 26, laborer, born Ireland, enlisted 08 May 1759 in Captain Robert Boyd's company [probably in the Third Battalion]. On a return dated May and June 1759.

Burke, Thomas, private in Captain Hugh Mercer's Company, Second Battalion in 1756; missing at the capture of Kittanning.

Burke, Thomas, *see* Boark, Thomas.

Burn, Edward, age 24, laborer, born Ireland, enlisted 26 June 1746 in Captain William Trent's company.

Burnes, Nathaniel, private in Captain John Singleton's company in service between 01 May and 08 May 1758.

Burneston, Joseph, age 24, shoemaker, born Ireland, enlisted 11 July 1746 in Captain John Deimer's company.

Burnett, James, age 28, laborer, born Scotland, enlisted 11 July 1746 in Captain Samuel Perry's company.

Burnett, John, age 21, laborer, born England, enlisted 22 July 1746 in Captain Samuel Perry's company.

Burns, Edward, age 26, laborer, born Ireland, enlisted 22 July 1746 in Captain Samuel Perry's company.

Burns, John, age 24, blacksmith, born Ireland, enlisted 24 July 1746 in Captain Samuel Perry's company.

Burns, Nathaniel, on a list of men recruited by Captain Andrew McDowell's company in the Second Battalion, Pennsylvania Regiment dated 04 June 1759.

Burton, John, lieutenant in the Southern District of Indian River Hundred in Captain Burton Waples's company of Colonel Jacob Kollock's Regiment of Sussex County in 1756/8.

Busby, John, age 20, laborer, born Ireland, enlisted 01 May 1759 in Captain Charles Stewart's company [probably one of the Associated Companies of Bucks County]. On a return dated June 1759.

Bush, Charles, ensign in one of two regiments of New Castle County in 1747–8.

Bush, David, captain in one of two regiments of New Castle County in 1747–8.

Bussé, Christian, captain provincial officer in 1754 at Fort Henry, in the provincial service in 1755. Captain in a company of the First Battalion from 05 January 1756. On a List of Officers in the Province Pay, 1756 in the First Battalion of the Pennsylvania Regiment with a commission date of 5 January, 1756. {PA5, I, 88} Captain from 05 December 1757 of a company in the Second Battalion, stationed eastward of the Susquehanna. {See A Journal in 1754, A(1) 2: 159}

Butler, Benjamin, ensign in the Associated Regiment of Bucks County in 1748.

Butler, John, a private in Captain Edward Jones's Independent Company of Horse, Philadelphia in 1756.

Butler, Simon, captain in the Associated Regiment of Bucks County in 1748.

Byer, Jacob, age 21, carpenter, born Germany, enlisted 10 July 1746 in Captain Samuel Perry's company.

Byer, John, age 24, tailor, born Germany, enlisted 01 May 1758. On a return of Captain John Blackwood's company in the Third Battalion dated 22 May 1758.

Byers, John, Captain from 27 April 1758 of a company in the Second Battalion.

Byles, Daniel, lieutenant, Captain William Trent's company, in winter quarters in Albany, N.Y., 1746–7, being discharged 31 October 1747.

Byles, Daniel, Major, in one of the companies of the Philadelphia Regiment on 09 April 1756.

Byles, Langhorne, captain in the Associated Regiment of Bucks County in 1748.

Byrn, Charles, age 27, joiner, born Ireland, enlisted 21 July 1746 in Captain William Trent's company.

C____, Joseph, ensign in the Associated Regiment of the West End of Lancaster County in 1747–8.

Cadwallader, Thomas, a private in Captain Charles Batho's Independent Company of Foot, Philadelphia in 1756.

Caffey, Thomas, a private in Captain Joseph Inslee's Company of Foot, Newtown, Bucks County, in 1756.

Cahoon, John, ensign in the Upper Part of Duck Creek Hundred company of Colonel John Vining's Regiment of Kent County Militia, Upon Delaware in 1756.

Cain, Miles, *see* Kain, Miles.

Caldwell, Alexander, a member of Captain Joseph Armstrong's Company on 07 August 1755, raised in Cumberland County

Caldwell, James, ensign in the Tidberry company of Colonel John Vining's Regiment of Kent County Militia, Upon Delaware in 1756. Ensign in Captain John Caton's company from Upper District of Mother-Kill Hundred prior to March 1758. Promoted to lieutenant of that company 29 March 1758 vice Joseph Caldwell.

Caldwell, Joseph, ensign from 23 May 1759 of a company from the Lower County.

Caldwell, Joseph, lieutenant in the Tidberry company of Colonel John Vining's Regiment of Kent County Militia, Upon Delaware in 1756. Lieutenant in Captain John Caton's company from Upper District of Mother-Kill Hundred in March 1758. Resigned before 29 March 1758.

Caldwell, Robert, a member of Captain Joseph Armstrong's Company on 07 August 1755, raised in Cumberland County

Caldwell, Robert, age 25, laborer, born Ireland, enlisted 21 July 1746 in Captain Samuel Perry's company.

Calladine, Abraham, age 19, locksmith, born Germany, enlisted 07 July 1746 in Captain Samuel Perry's company.

Callahann, Edward, enlisted 22 May 1758 in Captain French Battell's company of Lower County Provincials.

Callender, Robert, lieutenant in Captain John Armstrong's company of the Second Battalion; Captain Lieutenant from 16 January 1756. Captain of a company in the First Battalion from 15 December 1757 stationed westward of the Susquehanna.

Callender, Robert, promoted to Captain after serving in the Pennsylvania Regiment of Three Battalions in 1758 and 1759.

Callican, Thomas, age 20, born Chester, Pennsylvania, private in Captain John Singleton's company in service between 01 May and 08 May 1758.

Cally, James, age 30, gardener, born England, enlisted 07 July 1746 in Captain William Trent's company.

Calvin, Luther, lieutenant in one of the Associated Companies of Bucks County in 1756.

Cameron, Daniel, age 23, clerk, born Inverness, Scotland, enlisted 02 May 1759, private in Captain James Armstrong's company in Colonel William Clapham's Pennsylvania Regiment. On a return dated 01 June 1759.

Camock, John, carpenter's mate of the provincial ship *Pennsylvania* on 17 August 1757.

Campbell, Cleary, ensign from 21 April 1759 in Captain John Mather's company in Colonel William Clapham's Regiment of New Levies. Ensign in Captain Patrick Work's Company of the First Battalion of the Pennsylvania Regiment from 12 April 1760.

Campbell, Edward, on a list of men recruited by Captain Andrew McDowell's company in the Second Battalion, Pennsylvania Regiment dated 04 June 1759.

Campbell, George, age 22, born Cumberland, Pennsylvania, "a cut on his cheek, Irish man", private in Captain John Singleton's company in service between 01 May and 08 May 1758.

Campbell, George, age 24, laborer, born Antrim, Ireland, enlisted 13 June 1759, private in Captain John Mathers's company in the Pennsylvania Regiment. On a return dated 15 June 1759.

Campbell, James, a member of Captain David Jameson's Company at McCord's Fort on 02 April 1756 when he was wounded.

Campbell, James, a private in Captain John Kidd's Independent Company of Foot, Philadelphia in 1756.

Campbell, James, age 22, born Antrim, Ireland, weaver, private in Captain John Haslett's company enlisted on 13 May 1758 and last paid on 21 May 1758.

Campbell, John, age 22, laborer, born Chester, Pennsylvania, enlisted 13 June 1759 in Captain Robert Boyd's company [probably in the Third Battalion]. On a return dated May and June 1759.

Campbell, John, age 31, collier, born Scotland, enlisted 27 June 1746 in Captain William Trent's company.

Campbell, John, armourer of the provincial ship *Pennsylvania* on 17 August 1757.

Campbell, Robert, age 21, born Maryland, cooper, private in Captain John Singleton's company in service between 01 May and 08 May 1758.

Campbell, Robert, age 22, born Antrim, Ireland, laborer, private in Captain John Haslett's company enlisted on 11 May 1758 and last paid on 21 May 1758.

Campbell, Samuel, on a list of men recruited by Captain Andrew McDowell's company in the Second Battalion, Pennsylvania Regiment dated 04 June 1759.

Campbell, William, age 27, born Cecil, Maryland, miller, private in Captain John Singleton's company in service between 01 May and 08 May 1758.

Camphlin, Thomas, private in Captain Patterson's company from 23 December 1757 stationed eastward of the Susquehanna. On a muster roll dated 08 March 1758.

Campleton, Thomas, an ensign stationed on the frontier in Lancaster County with fifteen men at Godfried Young's, Hanover Township, on 01 June 1764 as part of a unit under the command of Major Asher Clayton.

Campleton, Thomas, ensign in Captain Timothy Green's company in Lieutenant Colonel Commandant Asher Clayton's Second Battalion of the Pennsylvania Regiment commanded by the Hon. J. Penn from 11 November 1763.

Camplin, Thomas, a private in Captain George Armstrong's Company, Second Battalion in 1756; wounded at Kittanning.

Cannaberry, Terence, a private in Captain John Steel's Company, Second Battalion in 1756, missing at the capture of Kittanning.

Canton, John, captain in one of the Associated Companies of Kent County in 1747–8.

Captain Morgan, Reece, lieutenant from 01 December 1744, Earl Town, Lancaster County.

Carber, Henry, age 19, laborer, born Germany, enlisted 07 July 1746 in Captain Samuel Perry's company.

Carlin, John, age 21, laborer, born Maryland, enlisted 03 May 1758 by Captain Benjamin Noxon.

Carmichael, Daniel, on a return of Captain David Hunter's Company [probably from York County] in Colonel William Clapham's Regiment of New Levies dated 26 May 1759.

Carnahan, James, captain in the Associated Regiment of Lancaster County over the Susquehanna in 1747–8.

Carnes, John, age 16, laborer, born Maryland, enlisted 03 May 1758 by Captain Benjamin Noxon.

Carney, Daniel, age 34, laborer, born Ireland, enlisted 20 July 1746 in Captain Samuel Perry's company.

Carney, Michael, private in Captain Patterson's company from 26 December 1757 stationed eastward of the Susquehanna. On a muster roll dated 08 March 1758.

Carpenter, Ulrick, hired 17 June 1757 as a battoe man, Master George Allen.

Carpenter, William, age 25, cordwainer, born Maryland, enlisted 04 July 1746 in Captain William Trent's company.

Carr, George, age 21, laborer, born Ireland, enlisted 30 July 1746 in Captain Samuel Perry's company.

Carr, Lawrence, captain in one of the companies of Colonel Jacob Duché's Philadelphia Regiment in 1756.

Carr, William, age 31, laborer, born Ireland, enlisted 21 July 1746 in Captain John Shannon's company of foot.

Carr, William, enlisted 07 May 1759, private in Captain Henry Van Bibber's company of the Lower County. On a return dated 04 June 1759.

Carr, William, ensign in the Associated Regiment of Chester County in 1747.

Carrigan, Bryan, a private in Captain Hugh Mercer's Company, Second Battalion in 1756; killed at Kittanning.

Carroll, Dennis, age 26, laborer, enlisted 04 August 1746 in Captain John Deimer's company.

Carroll, John, age 19, laborer, born Ireland, enlisted 22 July 1746 in Captain Samuel Perry's company.

Carroll, John, on a list of men recruited by Captain Andrew McDowell's company in the Second Battalion, Pennsylvania Regiment dated 04 June 1759.

Carson, Andrew, a private in Captain Samuel Mifflin's Association Battery Company of Philadelphia in 1756.

Carson, Charles, age 36, tailor, born Scotland, enlisted 30 June 1746 in Captain William Trent's company.

Carson, Charles, lieutenant in the Apoquinimink Hundred company of Colonel Jacob Van Bibber's Lower Regiment of New Castle County in 1756.

Carson, Robert, age 24, glover, born Ireland, enlisted 23 July 1746 in Captain Samuel Perry's company.

Carson, Samuel, a private in Captain Samuel Mifflin's Association Battery Company of Philadelphia in 1756.

Carson, William, private who enlisted 16 April 1756 in Captain Joseph Shippen's company in Colonel William Clapham's Regiment in 1756, the regiment in garrison at Fort Augusta, Shamokin, and listed in Shippen's Account Book.

Carter, Ashe, private in Captain Joseph Inslee's Company of Foot, Newtown, Bucks County, in 1756.

Carter, Henry, private in Captain Joseph Inslee's Company of Foot, Newtown, Bucks County, in 1756.

Carter, James, landsman on the provincial ship *Pennsylvania* on 17 August 1757.

Carter, John, private who enlisted 19 April 1756 in Captain Joseph Shippen's company in Colonel William Clapham's Regiment in 1756, the regiment in garrison at Fort Augusta, Shamokin, and listed in Shippen's Account Book. Discharged 10 May 1757.

Carter, Joseph, age 24, born Maryland, private in Captain John Wright's company of the Lower County. On a muster dated 11 May 1759.

Cartland, Nathaniel, ensign in Captain George Armstrong's Company, Second Battalion from 22 May 1756; left out in the reorganization of December 1757.

Cartwright, Jacob, enlisted 19 May 1759, private in Captain Henry Van Bibber's company of the Lower County. On a return dated 04 June 1759.

Carty, Henry, quartermaster of the provincial ship *Pennsylvania* on 17 August 1757.

Carty, Thomas, age 30, tailor, born Ireland, enlisted 05 July 1746 in Captain John Shannon's company of foot.

Caruthers, James, private in Captain Lieutenant Robert Callender's Company, Second Battalion in 1756; wounded at Kittanning.

Carver, Jacob, age 22, laborer, born Germany, enlisted 05 May 1758. On a return of Captain John Blackwood's company in the Third Battalion dated 22 May 1758.

Casedy, Thomas, private who enlisted 16 April 1756 in Captain Joseph Shippen's company in Colonel William Clapham's Regiment in 1756, the regiment in garrison at Fort Augusta, Shamokin, and listed in Shippen's Account Book.

Cass, Peter, age 26, born Germany, shipper, enlisted 01 September 1757, sergeant in Captain John Nicholas Weatherholt's company which enlisted for a term of three years and stationed in Heydelberg Township, Northampton County, in March and April 1758April 1758.

Cassiday, Thomas, age 23, laborer, born Germany, enlisted 02 May 1758. On a return of Captain John Bull's company dated 01 July 1758.

Cassiday, William, age 21, carpenter, born Chester, Pennsylvania, enlisted 20 April 1759, private in Captain Joseph Richardson's company of the Third Battalion in the Pennsylvania Regiment. On a return of recruits dated 1759.

Casson, Charles, *see* Carson, Charles.

Castner, Samuel, age 21, shoemaker, born Pennsylvania, enlisted 09 May 1758. On a return of Captain John Bull's company dated 01 July 1758.

Catchmore, Thomas, enlisted 13 May 1759, private in Captain Henry Van Bibber's company of the Lower County. On a return dated 04 June 1759.

Catin, Benjamin, ensign from 26 April 1758 in Captain Richard Well's company raised for the campaign in the lower counties. Lieutenant from 21 May 1759 of a company from the Lower County.

Catlin, Robert, lieutenant in one of the Associated Companies of Kent County in 1747–8.

Caton, John, captain in the Tidberry company of Colonel John Vining's Regiment of Kent County Militia, Upon Delaware in 1756. Captain in a company from Upper District of Mother-Kill Hundred in March 1758.

Cayton, Edward, age 21, laborer, born Ireland, enlisted 22 July 1746 in Captain Samuel Perry's company.

Cesna, John, ensign in the Associated Regiment of Lancaster County over the Susquehanna in 1747–8.

Chaband, John, gunner of the provincial ship *Pennsylvania* on 17 August 1757.

Chalfin, John, age 28, laborer, born Pennsylvania, enlisted 05 May 1758. On a weekly return of Captain Samuel Jones's company in 1758.

Chambers, Benjamin, captain in the Associated Regiment of Lancaster County over the Susquehanna in 1747–8.

Chambers, Benjamin, colonel in the Associated Regiment of Lancaster County over the Susquehanna in 1747–8.

Chambers, Benjamin, lieutenant colonel in the provincial service in 1755.

Chambers, James, lieutenant in Captain Samuel Lindsay's company in Lieutenant Colonel Commandant Asher Clayton's Second Battalion of the Pennsylvania Regiment commanded by the Hon. J. Penn from 19 July 1763.

Chambers, John, captain in the Associated Regiment of Lancaster County over the Susquehanna in 1747–8.

Chambers, Joseph, age 20, laborer, born Maryland, enlisted 29 April 1758 by Captain Benjamin Noxon.

Chambers, Robert, captain in the Associated Regiment of Lancaster County over the Susquehanna in 1747–8.

Chambers, Samuel, a private in Captain Edward Ward's Company, Second Battalion in 1756; missing at the capture of Kittanning.

Chambers, William, a member of Captain David Jameson's Company at McCord's Fort on 02 April 1756 when he was killed.

Chanadler, David, private, age 21, weaver, born Greenwick, New Jersey, enlisted 24 April 1758 for the campaign in the lower counties. On a return of Captain McClughan's company dated 17 May 1758.

Chance, Alexander, captain in the Apoquinimink Hundred company of Colonel Jacob Van Bibber's Lower Regiment of New Castle County in 1756.

Chance, Alexander, lieutenant in one of two regiments of New Castle County in 1747–8.

Chanullor, Samuel, a private in Captain Samuel Mifflin's Association Battery Company of Philadelphia in 1756.

Chapham, William, *see* Clapham, William.

Chapman, Michael, age 23, shoemaker, born Pennsylvania, enlisted 04 May 1758. On a return of Captain John Blackwood's company in the Third Battalion dated 22 May 1758.

Charles, Esaias, a private in Captain Adam Heylman's Company, of the St. Vincent and Puke's Land Association on 10 May 1756.

Cheese, Richard, house carpenter, born Jersey, enlisted 26 June 1746 in Captain William Trent's company.

Cherrington, Clem'ce, age 48, currier, born Cheltenham, England, enlisted 22 May 1759, private in Captain John Mathers's company in the Pennsylvania Regiment. On a return dated 15 June 1759.

Chipman, James, lieutenant in the Northern District of Broad Kiln Hundred in Captain John Haverloe's company of Colonel Jacob Kollock's Regiment of Sussex County in 1756. Reported as dead in 1758.

Chisholm, Charles, quartermaster of the provincial ship *Pennsylvania* on 17 August 1757.

Christ, Michael, age 27, miller, born Germany, enlisted 15 July 1746 in Captain John Deimer's company.

Christie, William, ensign in Captain Samuel West's company of the First Battalion of the Pennsylvania Regiment from 26 April 1760.

Cladwell, Andrew, Major in Colonel John Vining's Regiment of Militia for Kent County, upon the Delaware in 1756.

Clapham, William, Jr., lieutenant of Captain David Jameson's Company, Third Battalion (known as the Augusta Regiment) from 20 August 1756. Lieutenant from 09 January 1758 in Captain Samuel Weiser's company in the Second Battalion.

Clapham, William, captain of a company of the Third Battalion (known as the Augusta Regiment) before his promotion to Lt. Col. of the Third Battalion from 29 March 1756. Captain from 21 April 1759 of a company of the New Levies. Colonel of the New Levies in 1759.

Clapham, William, Jr., Captain of a company of the First Battalion of the Pennsylvania Regiment from 23 April 1760.

Clapham, William, Second lieutenant from 02 May 1758 in Captain John Hambright's troop of Light Horse.

Clare, John, Mathematician of the provincial ship *Pennsylvania* on 17 August 1757.

Clark, Daniel, lieutenant of Captain Patrick Work's Company, Third Battalion (known as the Augusta Regiment) from 01 May 1756.

Clark, David, captain in the Upper Part of Duck Creek Hundred company of Colonel John Vining's Regiment of Kent County Militia, Upon Delaware in 1756.

Clark, David, lieutenant in one of the Associated Companies of Kent County in June 1748.

Clark, Hector, age 28, laborer, born Scotland, enlisted 03 May 1758. On a return of Captain John Blackwood's company in the Third Battalion dated 22 May 1758.

Clark, James, age 20, born Pennsylvania, private in Captain John Haslett's company enlisted on 15 May 1758 and last paid on 21 May 1758.

Clark, John, age 29, laborer, born Ireland, enlisted May 24 April 1758 by Captain Benjamin Noxon.

Clark, John, age 30, husbandman, born England, enlisted 19 July 1746 in Captain William Trent's company.

Clark, John, Captain from 18 May 1758 in a company in the Third Battalion. Captain from 02 May 1759 of a company of Colonel William Clapham's Regiment of New Levies.

Clark, John, on a list of men recruited by Captain Andrew McDowell's company in the Second Battalion, Pennsylvania Regiment dated 04 June 1759.

Clark, John, private who enlisted 19 May 1756 in Captain Joseph Shippen's company in Colonel William Clapham's Regiment in 1756, the regiment in garrison at Fort Augusta, Shamokin, and listed in Shippen's Account Book.

Clark, John, promoted to Captain after serving in the Pennsylvania Regiment of Three Battalions in 1758 and 1759.

Clark, Nathaniel, age 25, weaver, born England, enlisted 08 May 1759 in Captain Robert Boyd's company [probably in the Third Battalion]. On a return dated May and June 1759.

Clark, Robert Quarter-Master in Lieutenant Colonel Commandant Asher Clayton's Second Battalion of the Pennsylvania Regiment commanded by the Hon. J. Penn from 07 June 1764.

Clark, Robert, private in Captain John Kidd's Independent Company of Foot, Philadelphia in 1756.

Clarke, Thomas, captain in the Upper Part of Mispillim Hundred company of Colonel John Vining's Regiment of Kent County Militia, Upon Delaware in 1756.

Clarke, Thomas, ensign in the Associated Regiment of Chester County in 1747.

Clawson, John, age 32, cordwainer, born Pennsylvania, enlisted 27 June 1746 in Captain William Trent's company.

Claypoole, George, ensign in the Northern District of Broad Kiln Hundred in Captain John Haverloe's company of Colonel Jacob Kollock's Regiment of Sussex County in 1756/8.

Claypoole, James, ensign in the Associated Regiment of Foot of Philadelphia on 29 Dec 1747.

Clayton, _____, ensign from 17 March 1759 in Captain Samuel Weiser's company in the Second Battalion.

Clayton, Asher, lieutenant in Captain Joseph Shippen's company in Colonel William Clapham's Regiment in 1756, the regiment in garrison at Fort Augusta, Shamokin, and listed in Shippen's Account Book. Major in the First Battalion of the Pennsylvania Regiment from 12 April 1760. Promoted to the rank of Lieutenant Colonel after having served in the Pennsylvania Regiment of Three Battalions, 1758 and 1759 and joined Colonel Francis. Lieutenant Colonel Commandant of the Second Battalion of the Regiment commanded by the Hon. J. Penn, Esquire, from 02 July 1764.

Clayton, Asher, lieutenant of Captain Elisha Salter's Company, Third Battalion (known as the Augusta Regiment) from 10 May 1756. Adjutant, of the Third Battalion (known as the Augusta Regiment) from 24 May 1756. Commissioned 01 December 1757 Late Clapham's Company stationed at Fort Augusta. Captain from 09 January 1758 in a company in the Second Battalion. Quartermaster from 08 June 1758 of the Second Battalion. Wounded at Grant's defeat near Fort Duquesne on 14 September 1758.

Clayton, John, captain in the Town of Dover company of Colonel John Vining's Regiment of Kent County Militia, Upon Delaware in 1756.

Clegg, John, landsman on the provincial ship *Pennsylvania* on 17 August 1757.

Clifford, John, age 18, born Maryland, enlisted 30 April 1759, private in Captain Robert Curry's company in Colonel William Clapham's Pennsylvania Regiment. On a return dated June 1759.

Clifft, Ezekiel, age 20, laborer, born Pennsylvania, enlisted 16 May 1758. On a return of Captain John Bull's company dated 01 July 1758.

Clift, George, a private in Captain Joseph Inslee's Company of Foot, Newtown, Bucks County, in 1756.

Clinepup, Jacob in Captain Robert Eastburn's company in the Second Battalion.

Clingan, George, lieutenant in one of the Associated Companies of Lancaster County in 1756.

Clinton, William, captain in the Associated Regiment of Chester County in 1747.

Clinton, William, lieutenant from 28 April 1758 in Captain John Haslett's company in the Second Battalion and last paid on 21 May 1758. Lieutenant from 22 April 1759 in Captain Thomas Hamilton's company of Colonel William Clapham's Regiment of New Levies.

Clinton, William, promoted to lieutenant after serving in the Pennsylvania Regiment of Three Battalions in 1758 and 1759. Reported as "doubtful".

Clos, John, seaman on the provincial ship *Pennsylvania* on 17 August 1757.

Clow, Cheany, age 24, laborer, born Maryland, enlisted 02 May 1758 by Captain Benjamin Noxon.

Clow, Cheny, landsman on the provincial ship *Pennsylvania* on 17 August 1757.

Clower, Thomas, age 45, laborer, born Philadelphia, Pennsylvania, enlisted 11 May 1759, private in Captain John Mathers's company in the Pennsylvania Regiment. On a return dated 15 June 1759.

Cloyd, Thomas, age 33, tailor, born Ireland, enlisted 18 May 1759, private in Captain Robert Curry's company in Colonel William Clapham's Pennsylvania Regiment. On a return dated June 1759.

Cluse, James, age 18, cooper, born Pennsylvania, enlisted 24 April 1758. On a weekly return of Captain Samuel Jones's company in 1758.

Clyne, Abraham, age 16, drummer, born Germany, enlisted 28 April 1758. On a return of Captain John Blackwood's company in the Third Battalion dated 22 May 1758.

Coates, William, 2nd lieutenant in the Associated Regiment in the County of Philadelphia in 1748.

Cochran, Alexander, on a list of men recruited by Captain Andrew McDowell's company in the Second Battalion, Pennsylvania Regiment dated 04 June 1759.

Cochran, James, lieutenant in the Associated Regiment of Chester County in 1747.

Cochran, Stephen, lieutenant in one of the new levies in May 1758.

Cogleton, Benjamin, enlisted 21 May 1759, private in Captain Henry Van Bibber's company of the Lower County. On a return dated 04 June 1759.

Cole, Richard, private in Captain Charles Batho's Independent Company of Foot, Philadelphia in 1756.

Colegate, John, age 23, cordwainer, born America, enlisted 01 May 1758 by Captain Benjamin Noxon.

Coleman, Conrad, age 33, laborer, born Germany, enlisted 07 May 1749 in Captain Richard Gardiner's company in Colonel William Denney's Pennsylvania Regiment.

Colesbury, Henry, lieutenant in one of two regiments of New Castle County in 1747–8.

Coletrap, Matthew, hired 17 June 1757 as a battoe man, Master George Allen.

Coll, Isaac, age 42, born London, private in Captain John Wright's company of the Lower County. On a muster dated 11 May 1759.

Collins, Thomas, age 22, born Donegal, Ireland, private in Captain John Haslett's company enlisted on 13 May 1758 and last paid on 21 May 1758.

Collins, Timothy, age 24, laborer, born Ireland, enlisted 10 May 1758. On a weekly return of Captain Samuel Jones's company in 1758.

Collis, Thomas, age 22, mariner, born England, enlisted 03 May 1758. On a return of Captain John Blackwood's company in the Third Battalion dated 22 May 1758.

Coltas, George, *see* Coultas, George.

Colter, Thomas, age 22, born Sussex, Delaware, private in Captain John Wright's company of the Lower County. On a muster dated 11 May 1759.

Colter, William, age 20, born Sussex, Delaware, private in Captain John Wright's company of the Lower County. On a muster dated 11 May 1759.

Combs, William, age 24, mariner, born England, enlisted 13 May 1758 by Captain Benjamin Noxon.

Coney, John, age 27, laborer, born Ireland, enlisted 02 June 1759 in Captain Robert Boyd's company [probably in the Third Battalion]. On a return dated May and June 1759.

Connell, William, lieutenant in Captain John Wright's company of the Lower County. On a muster dated 11 May 1759.

Connelly, Bernard, age 20, born Lowthe, Ireland, private in Captain John Haslett's company enlisted on 17 May 1758 and last paid on 21 May 1758.

Connelly, Bryan, private, age 20, laborer, born Monaghan, Ireland, enlisted 20 April 1758 for the campaign in the lower counties. On a return of Captain McClughan's company dated 17 May 1758.

Conner, John, enlisted 21 May 1759, private in Captain Henry Van Bibber's company of the Lower County. On a return dated 04 June 1759.

Conner, Thomas, age 21, born Donegal, enlisted 27 May 1759, private in Captain Robert Curry's company in Colonel William Clapham's Pennsylvania Regiment. On a return dated June 1759.

Conner, Thomas, age 45, shoemaker, born Cork, Ireland, enlisted 23 May 1759, private in Captain John Mathers's company in the Pennsylvania Regiment. On a return dated 15 June 1759.

Connolly, Thomas, age 17, born Chester, Pennsylvania, private in Captain John Singleton's company in service between 01 May and 08 May 1758.

Connolly, Thomas, on a return of Captain David Hunter's Company [probably from York County] in Colonel William Clapham's Regiment of New Levies dated 26 May 1759.

Conolly, James, private who enlisted 29 April 1756 in Captain Joseph Shippen's company in Colonel William Clapham's Regiment in 1756, the regiment in garrison at Fort Augusta, Shamokin, and listed in Shippen's Account Book.

Conrad, Duras, private who enlisted 23 April 1756 in Captain Joseph Shippen's company in Colonel William Clapham's Regiment in 1756, the regiment in garrison at Fort Augusta,

Shamokin, and listed in Shippen's Account Book. Stationed at Hunter's Fort. May have been in Captain Elisha Saltar's company instead of Captain Shippen's.

Conrad, Leonard, age 35, smith, born Germany, enlisted 14 July 1746 in Captain John Deimer's company.

Conrad, Michael, private in Captain Adam Heylman's Company, of the St. Vincent and Puke's Land Association on 10 May 1756.

Conrad, Nicholas, ensign in Captain Frederick Smith's company of the First Battalion from 29 December 1755. Lieutenant in Captain James Patterson's company of the First Battalion from 22 December 1757 stationed eastward of the Susquehanna. On a muster roll dated 08 March 1758.

Conrad, Nicholas, promoted to lieutenant after serving in the Pennsylvania Regiment of Three Battalions in 1758 and 1759.

Conrad, Peter, age 21, born Germany, enlisted 19 May 1759, private in Captain Robert Curry's company in Colonel William Clapham's Pennsylvania Regiment. On a return dated June 1759.

Conwell, Elias, age 20, born Sussex, Delaware, Corporal in Captain John Wright's company of the Lower County. On a muster dated 11 May 1759.

Conwell, William Lieutenant from 23 May 1759 of a company from the Lower County.

Conyngham, Hugh, lieutenant from 25 May 1758 in Captain Ludowick Stone's company in the Third Battalion.

Cooch, Thomas, captain in the Pencader Hundred company of Colonel Jacob Van Bibber's Lower Regiment of New Castle County in 1756.

Cook, Edward, landsman on the provincial ship *Pennsylvania* on 17 August 1757.

Cook, George, private who enlisted 16 April 1756 in Captain Joseph Shippen's company in Colonel William Clapham's Regiment in 1756, the regiment in garrison at Fort Augusta, Shamokin, and listed in Shippen's Account Book. Deserted 14 October 1756.

Cook, John, age 30, born Ireland, enlisted 19 May 1759, private in Captain Robert Curry's company in Colonel William Clapham's Pennsylvania Regiment. On a return dated June 1759.

Cook, John, age 30, laborer, born Tyrone, Ireland, enlisted 28 April 1759, private in Captain James Armstrong's company in Colonel William Clapham's Pennsylvania Regiment. On a return dated 01 June 1759.

Cook, John, private in Captain John Singleton's company in service between 01 May and 08 May 1758.

Cook, John, private who enlisted 08 May 1756 in Captain Nathaniel Miles's company in Colonel William Clapham's Regiment in 1756, the regiment in garrison at Fort Augusta, Shamokin, and listed in Shippen's Account Book.

Cooke, Daniel, age 21, laborer, born Newcastle, Delaware, enlisted 08 July 1746 in Captain John Shannon's company of foot.

Cooke, Nathaniel, private, age 19, farmer, born Whitly Creek, Delaware, enlisted 05 May 1758 for the campaign in the lower counties. On a return of Captain McClughan's company dated 17 May 1758.

Cookson, Thomas, Colonel, in the Associated Regiment of the West End of Lancaster County in 1747–8.

Cooley, William, age 27, laborer, born Ireland, enlisted 10 July 1746 in Captain Samuel Perry's company.

Cooper, James, age 30, laborer, born Ireland, enlisted 02 May 1759, private in Captain James Armstrong's company in Colonel William Clapham's Pennsylvania Regiment. On a return dated 01 June 1759.

Cooper, James, enlisted 12 May 1758 in Captain French Battell's company of Lower County Provincials.

Cooper, John, seaman on the provincial ship *Pennsylvania* on 17 August 1757.

Cooper, Richard, enlisted 14 May 1758 in Captain French Battell's company of Lower County Provincials.

Coove, William, age 36, carpenter, born Germany, enlisted 25 May 1759 in Captain Charles Stewart's company [probably one of the Associated Companies of Bucks County]. On a return dated June 1759.

Cope, Robert, enlisted 15 May 1758 in Captain French Battell's company of Lower County Provincials.

Corbet, John, age 34, laborer, born Ireland, enlisted 09 July 1746 in Captain William Trent's company.

Cord, Joseph, captain in the Southern District of Broad Kiln Hundred company of Colonel Jacob Kollock's Regiment of Sussex County in 1756/8.

Cordbird, Garret, age 26, laborer, born England, enlisted 16 July 1746 in Captain John Shannon's company of foot.

Corkem, James, a private in Captain John Potter's Company, Second Battalion, captured by Indians in November 1756.

Corkerlin, James, enlisted 20 May 1758 in Captain French Battell's company of Lower County Provincials.

Corneallie, Cornelius, age 22, laborer, born Ireland, enlisted 17 July 1746 in Captain Samuel Perry's company.

Corner, Jacob, a private in Captain Adam Heylman's Company, of the St. Vincent and Puke's Land Association on 10 May 1756.

Cornman, Conrad, age 21, laborer, 13 July 1746 in Captain John Deimer's company.

Cornwall, William, a private in Captain John Potter's Company, Second Battalion, captured by Indians in November 1756

Cornwell, Samuel, age 22, born Virginia, private in Captain John Wright's company of the Lower County. On a muster dated 11 May 1759.

Correy, John, lieutenant in one of the Associated Companies of York County in 1756.

Corson, Henry, captain in the Associated Regiment of Bucks County in 1748.

Cosby, David, age 30, born Ireland, laborer, private in Captain John Shannon's Company, enlisted 21 July 1746. On a roll of deserters dated 22 July 1746. [B3:422:18]

Cosgrift, John, age 28, laborer, born Ireland, enlisted 25 April 1758 by Captain Benjamin Noxon.

Coulson, William, age 21, shoemaker, born Pennsylvania, enlisted 05 May 1758. On a weekly return of Captain Samuel Jones's company in 1758.

Coultas, George, age 24, shoemaker, 07 August 1746 in Captain John Deimer's company.

Coultas, James, captain in the Associated Regiment of Foot of Philadelphia on 29 Dec 1747.

Coultas, James, Lt. Col., in one of the companies of the Philadelphia Regiment on 09 April 1756.

Countz, Henry, *see* Kountz, Henry.

Courchod, Daniel, lieutenant not assigned in the First Battalion of the Pennsylvania Regiment from 04 May 1760.

Courchod, Daniel, promoted to lieutenant after serving in the Pennsylvania Regiment of Three Battalions in 1758 and 1759. Reported as "dead".

Cowpland, David, private in Captain John Singleton's company in service between 01 May and 08 May 1758.

Cox, Edward, age 27, watchmaker, born Ireland, enlisted 27 April 1758. On a return of Captain John Blackwood's company in the Third Battalion dated 22 May 1758.

Cox, Jacob, age 38, laborer, born Pennsylvania, enlisted 18 May 1749 in Captain Richard Gardiner's company in Colonel William Denney's Pennsylvania Regiment.

Cox, William, a private in Captain Charles Batho's Independent Company of Foot, Philadelphia in 1756.

Coyle, Charles, age 32, cordwainer, born Ireland, enlisted 14 July 1746 in Captain John Shannon's company of foot.

Craig, _____, captain in the provincial service in 1755 in Lehigh Township, Northampton County

Craig, James, a private in Captain Samuel Mifflin's Association Battery Company of Philadelphia in 1756.

Craig, John, lieutenant from 24 April 1758 in Captain Richard Walker's company in the First Battalion.

Craig, Robert, a private in Captain Charles Batho's Independent Company of Foot, Philadelphia in 1756.

Craig, Thomas, ensign in the Lower Part of Murder Kiln [or Mother-Kill] Hundred company of Colonel John Vining's Regiment of Kent County Militia, Upon Delaware in 1756.

Craig, William, captain in the Associated Regiment of Bucks County in 1748.

Craig, William, lieutenant in the Southern District of Broad Kiln Hundred company of Colonel Jacob Kollock's Regiment of Sussex County in 1756.

Craige, William, lieutenant in Captain Joseph Cord's Company from the Southern District of Broad-Kill Hundred, Sussex County, Delaware, in Colonel Jacob Killock's Regiment in 1758.

Craighead, George, Captain of a company of the First Battalion of the Pennsylvania Regiment from 26 April 1760.

Craighead, George, ensign from 08 December 1757 in Captain Christian Bussè's company in the Second Battalion, stationed eastward of the Susquehanna.

Craighead, George, promoted to captain after serving in the Pennsylvania Regiment of Three Battalions in 1758 and 1759.

Craighead, Patrick, lieutenant from 09 May 1758 in Captain Charles McClung's company in the Third Battalion.

Cramp, Charles, a private in Captain Adam Heylman's Company, of the St. Vincent and Puke's Land Association on 10 May 1756.

Crampton, James, hired 30 May 1757 as a battoe man, Master George Allen.

Crane, Thomas, age 23, laborer, born Kent, Delaware, enlisted 16 July 1746 in Captain John Shannon's company of foot.

Cranne, John, *see* John Cranne.

Cranney, John, on a list of men recruited by Captain Andrew McDowell's company in the Second Battalion, Pennsylvania Regiment dated 04 June 1759.

Crantlemeyer, Philip, age 21, born Germany, enlisted 01 September 1757, private in Captain John Nicholas Weatherholt's company which enlisted for a term of three years and stationed in Heydelberg Township, Northampton County, in March and April 1758April 1758.

Crassert, John, a private in Captain Adam Heylman's Company, of the St. Vincent and Puke's Land Association on 10 May 1756.

Crawford, Alexander, on a list of men recruited by Captain Andrew McDowell's company in the Second Battalion, Pennsylvania Regiment dated 04 June 1759.

Crawford, Hugh, ensign in Captain Hance Hamilton's company of the First Battalion of Colonel William Denny's Regiment from 11 March 1758 stationed westward of the Susquehanna. At Fort Bedford, 12 April 1759.

Crawford, Hugh, lieutenant in Captain James Patterson's company of the First Battalion in 1755/6.

Crawford, James, ensign in Captain (Major) Asher Clayton's Company of the First Battalion of the Pennsylvania Regiment from 15 April 1760.

Crawford, James, on a list of men recruited by Captain Andrew McDowell's company in the Second Battalion, Pennsylvania Regiment dated 04 June 1759.

Crawford, John, lieutenant in the Associated Regiment of the West End of Lancaster County in 1747–8.

Crawford, John, private, age 25, laborer, born Donegal, Ireland, enlisted 29 April 1758 for the campaign in the lower counties. On a return of Captain McClughan's company dated 17 May 1758.

Crawford, Robert, ensign from 24 April 1758 in Captain Richard Walker's company in the First Battalion.

Crawford, Robert, seaman on the provincial ship *Pennsylvania* on 17 August 1757.

Crawford, William, lieutenant in the Associated Regiment of the West End of Lancaster County in 1747–8.

Crawford, Samuel, captain in the Associated Regiment of the West End of Lancaster County in 1747–8.

Creader, George, *see* George Creider.

Creamer, George, age 22, bottlemaker, born Germany, enlisted 14 July 1746 in Captain Samuel Perry's company.

Creekery [Gregory], George, age 16, born Pennsylvania, enlisted 01 September 1757, private in Captain John Nicholas Weatherholt's company which enlisted for a term of three years and stationed in Heydelberg Township, Northampton County, in March and April 1758April 1758.

Creely, Daniel, age 38, laborer, born Ireland, enlisted 02 May 1758. On a weekly return of Captain Samuel Jones's company in 1758.

Creider, George, age 35, born Ireland, enlisted 17 May 1759, private in Captain Robert Curry's company in Colonel William Clapham's Pennsylvania Regiment. On a return dated June 1759.

Cremer, Jacob, private, age 19, laborer, born Thorlowitz, Germany, enlisted 11 May 1758 for the campaign in the lower counties. On a return of Captain McClughan's company dated 17 May 1758.

Crochford, Thomas, age 18, barber, born Ireland, enlisted 02 May 1758. On a weekly return of Captain Samuel Jones's company in 1758.

Croll, Theodorus, age 26, shoemaker, born Germany, enlisted 21 July 1746 in Captain Samuel Perry's company.

Crook, John, age 23, laborer, born England, enlisted 22 July 1746 in Captain William Trent's company.

Cropper, Levin ensign in the Northern District of Cedar Creek Hundred in Captain Benjamin Wynkoop's company of Colonel Jacob Kollock's Regiment of Sussex County in 1756.

Cross, John, age 25, born Chester, Pennsylvania, cordwainer, "pock pitted", private in Captain John Singleton's company in service between 01 May and 08 May 1758.

Crouter, Melchoir, age 40, shoemaker, born Neise, Germany, enlisted 14 June 1759, private in Captain John Mathers's company in the Pennsylvania Regiment. On a return dated 15 June 1759.

Crowley, Bartholomew, age 21, tinner, born Ireland, enlisted 02 July 1746 in Captain John Shannon's company of foot.

Crowley, James, age 28, laborer, born Ireland, enlisted 04 August 1746 in Captain John Shannon's company of foot.

Crowley, Owen, age 28, laborer, enlisted 19 May 1759, private in Captain James Armstrong's company in Colonel William

Clapham's Pennsylvania Regiment. On a return dated 01 June 1759.

Crozier, Matthew, ensign in the Upper Part of Little Creek Hundred company of Colonel John Vining's Regiment of Kent County Militia, Upon Delaware in 1756.

Cruiss, Christopher, private who enlisted 18 April 1756 in Captain Joseph Shippen's company in Colonel William Clapham's Regiment in 1756, the regiment in garrison at Fort Augusta, Shamokin, and listed in Shippen's Account Book.

Crull, Theodorus, *see* Croll, Theodorus.

Crum, William, lieutenant in the Associated Regiment of the West End of Lancaster County in 1747–8.

Crumbach, Peter, *see* Krumbach, Peter.

Cruthers, John, age 16, born Chester, Pennsylvania, "stout made", private in Captain John Singleton's company in service between 01 May and 08 May 1758.

Cuck, John, *see* John Cook.

Cuff, (a Negro), seaman on the provincial ship *Pennsylvania* on 17 August 1757.

Culbertson, Alexander, captain in the provincial service in 1755 of Lurgan Township, Cumberland County.

Culbertson, Alexander, captain of a company in the Second Battalion; killed by Indians near McCord's Fort in April 1756.

Culbertson, James, ensign from 01 May 1758 in Captain Robert Boyd's company in the Third Battalion.

Culbertson, John, lieutenant in the Associated Regiment of Chester County in 1747.

Culbertson, John, lieutenant in the Associated Regiment of Chester County in 1747.

Culbertson, Samuel, sergeant major in 1758 of the Third Battalion.

Cumming, William, ensign in the Associated Regiment of Chester County in 1747.

Cummings, James, ensign in one of the Associated Companies of Bucks County in 1756.

Cummings, Robert, lieutenant in one of the Associated Companies of Bucks County in 1756.

Cummings, Robert, lieutenant in the Associated Regiment of Bucks County in 1748.

Cunningham, John, lieutenant in the Associated Regiment of Chester County in 1747.

Cunningham, Matthew, ensign in one of the Associated Companies of Lancaster County in 1756.

Cunningham, Thomas, quartermaster of the provincial ship *Pennsylvania* on 17 August 1757.

Cunrad, Nicholas, ensign on a List of Officers in the Province Pay, 1756 in the First Battalion of the Pennsylvania Regiment with a commission date of 29 December 1755. {PA5, I, 88}

Currie, Robert, captain of a company of the Second Battalion of the Pennsylvania Regiment from 17 April 1760.

Curry, Marks, hired 30 May 1757 as a battoe man, Master George Allen.

Curry, Niel, age 35, cooper, born Scotland, enlisted 22 April 1758 by Captain Benjamin Noxon.

Curry, Robert, Captain from 23 April 1759 of a company in Colonel William Clapham's Regiment of New Levies. On a return dated June 1759.

Curry, Robert, promoted to Captain after serving in the Pennsylvania Regiment of Three Battalions in 1758 and 1759. Reported as "doubtful".

Cuthbert, John, lieutenant in the Associated Regiment of Chester County in 1747.

D'Armond, Edward, age 23, laborer, born Ireland, enlisted 23 July 1746 in Captain Samuel Perry's company.

D'Normandie, Anthony, lieutenant in the Associated Regiment of Bucks County in 1748.

D'Normandie, John, Major, in the Associated Regiment of Bucks County in 1748.

Dadson, Richard, age 24, born Pennsylvania, enlisted 28 November 1757, private in Captain John Nicholas Weatherholt's company which enlisted for a term of three years and stationed in Heydelberg Township, Northampton County, in March and April 1758April 1758.

Dagley, Elias, age 46, spectacle maker, born St. Ann's, England, enlisted 09 June 1759, private in Captain John Mathers's company in the Pennsylvania Regiment. On a return dated 15 June 1759.

Dainty, John, private, age 25, miller, born Grapner, England, enlisted 01 May 1758 for the campaign in the lower counties. On a return of Captain McClughan's company dated 17 May 1758.

Daley, Edward, *see* Dealy, Edward.

Dalmaster, Lorenzo, *see* Dalmater, Lorenzo.

Dalmater, Lorenzo, seaman on the provincial ship *Pennsylvania* on 17 August 1757.

Danefels, Jacob, a private in Captain Adam Heylman's Company, of the St. Vincent and Puke's Land Association on 10 May 1756.

Danford, William, captain in one of two regiments of New Castle County in 1747–8.

Daniel, Isaac, age 30, wheelwright, born England, enlisted 31 July 1746 in Captain John Deimer's company.

Danily, Abner, age 20, born Maryland, private in Captain John Wright's company of the Lower County. On a muster dated 11 May 1759.

Darbeyshire, John, a private in Captain Joseph Inslee's Company of Foot, Newtown, Bucks County, in 1756.

Darling, Jeremiah, age 42, sawyer, born Pennsylvania, enlisted 14 July 1746 in Captain William Trent's company.

Darlington, William, lieutenant in the Associated Regiment of Chester County in 1747.

Darrach, William, promoted to lieutenant after serving in the Pennsylvania Regiment of Three Battalions in 1758 and 1759.

Darragh, James, ensign in Captain Robert Currie's company of the Second Battalion of the Pennsylvania Regiment from 25 April 1760.

Darragh, William, lieutenant from 29 April 1759 in Captain Robert Curry's company in Colonel William Clapham's Regiment of New Levies.

Darwen, Andrew, landsman on the provincial ship *Pennsylvania* on 17 August 1757.

Davenport, Eleazer, ensign from 11 May 1758 in Captain Paul Jackson's company in the Third Battalion.

Davenport, Josiah, lieutenant from 30 April 1758 in Captain Robert Eastburn's company in the Second Battalion.

Davenport, Josiah, promoted to lieutenant after serving in the Pennsylvania Regiment of Three Battalions in 1758 and 1759.

David, Joshua, landsman on the provincial ship *Pennsylvania* on 17 August 1757.

Davies, Patrick, *see* Davis, Patrick.

Davis, _____, lieutenant in the provincial service in 1755.

Davis, Benjamin, ensign in the Associated Regiment in the County of Philadelphia in 1748.

Davis, David, age 22, laborer, born Pennsylvania, enlisted 25 April 1759 in Captain Charles Stewart's company [probably one of the Associated Companies of Bucks County]. On a return dated June 1759.

Davis, David, age 25, laborer, born Pennsylvania, enlisted 09 May 1758. On a return of Captain John Bull's company dated 01 July 1758.

Davis, Edward, Jun., ensign in the Associated Regiment of the West End of Lancaster County in 1747–8.

Davis, Edward, age 23, laborer, born Ireland, enlisted 06 August 1746 in Captain Samuel Perry's company.

Davis, Gabriel, captain in the Associated Regiment of the West End of Lancaster County in 1747–8.

Davis, James, age 21, perukemaker, born Philadelphia, enlisted 28 June 1746 in Captain John Shannon's company of foot.

Davis, James, lieutenant in the Associated Regiment of Bucks County in 1748.

Davis, James, private, age 19, farmer, born Down, Ireland, enlisted 22 April 1758 for the campaign in the lower counties. On a return of Captain McClughan's company dated 17 May 1758.

Davis, John, age 27, flatsman, born England, enlisted 23 July 1746 in Captain William Trent's company.

Davis, Nehemiah, age 23, laborer, born Wales, enlisted 06 May 1759, private in Captain Joseph Richardson's company of the Third Battalion in the Pennsylvania Regiment. On a return of recruits dated 1759.

Davis, Nehemiah, ensign in the Southern District of Cedar Creek Hundred Captain Thomas Till's company of Colonel Jacob Kollock's Regiment of Sussex County in 1756. Described as Slaughter Neck District company in 1758.

Davis, Patrick, lieutenant of Captain Thomas Lloyd's Company, Third Battalion (known as the Augusta Regiment) from 04 April 1756. Captain of a company in the First Battalion from 22 December 1757 stationed eastward of the Susquehanna.

Davis, Patrick, promoted to captain after serving in the Pennsylvania Regiment of Three Battalions in 1758 and 1759. Reported "dead."

Davis, Thomas, age 22, laborer, born Maryland, enlisted 14 July 1746 in Captain John Shannon's company of foot.

Davis, Thomas, age 23, laborer, born New England, enlisted 15 May 1749 in Captain Richard Gardiner's company in Colonel William Denney's Pennsylvania Regiment.

Davis, Thomas, age 40, cooper, born England, enlisted 01 May 1759, private in Captain Robert Curry's company in Colonel William Clapham's Pennsylvania Regiment. On a return dated June 1759.

Davis, Valentine, age 30, cordwainer, born Ireland, enlisted 20 July 1746 in Captain John Shannon's company of foot.

Davis, Walter, ensign in the Associated Regiment of Lancaster County over the Susquehanna in 1747–8.

Davis, William, age 25, laborer, born England, enlisted 14 July 1746 in Captain John Shannon's company of foot.

Davis, William, ensign in the Associated Regiment of Bucks County in 1748.

Davise, Hugh, age 20, born Chester, Pennsylvania, smith, private in Captain John Singleton's company in service between 01 May and 08 May 1758.

Davon, John, *see* Dawson, John.

Davyer, William, age 21, laborer, born Maryland, enlisted 06 May 1758. On a return of Captain John Bull's company dated 01 July 1758.

Dawson, John, age 21, laborer, born Pennsylvania, enlisted 05 August 1746 in Captain William Trent's company.

De Haas, John Philip, captain stationed on the frontier in Berks County with one sergeant and eighteen men at Fort Henry, Bethel Township, on 01 June 1764 as part of a unit under the command of Major Asher Clayton.

de Haas, John Philip, ensign, Captain Robert Callender's company of the First Battalion, 03 January 1758. Adjutant of the First Battalion (John Armstrong's) of Colonel William Denny's Regiment, 30 April 1758. Major in 1759. Reported to have joined Colonel Francis. Captain of a company of the First Battalion of the Pennsylvania Regiment from 28 April 1760.

De Haas, John Phillip, Major in the Pennsylvania Regiment commanded by the Hon. J. Penn, Esqr., from 09 June 1764.

Dealy, Edward, landsman on the provincial ship *Pennsylvania* on 17 August 1757.

Dealy, Thomas, landsman on the provincial ship *Pennsylvania* on 17 August 1757.

Deatenberger, Henry, age 36, born Germany, enlisted 01 September 1757, private in Captain John Nicholas Weatherholt's company which enlisted for a term of three years and stationed in Heydelberg Township, Northampton County, in March and April 1758.

Deatry, Nicholas, age 18, born Germany, enlisted 01 September 1757, private in Captain John Nicholas Weatherholt's company which enlisted for a term of three years and stationed in Heydelberg Township, Northampton County, in March and April 1758.

DeFrau, Jacob, a private in Captain Adam Heylman's Company, of the St. Vincent and Puke's Land Association on 10 May 1756.

Dehaas, John Philip, ensign in Captain Robert Callender's company in December 1757 stationed westward of the Susquehanna.

Dehaven, Abraham, captain, in the Associated Regiment in the County of Philadelphia in 1748.

Deimer, John, captain of Pennsylvania troops in Albany, N.Y. on 21 October 1746 and at least through 12 November 1746.

Demler, Peter, a private in Captain Adam Heylman's Company, of the St. Vincent and Puke's Land Association on 10 May 1756.

Dennahew, Florence, age 40, laborer, born Ireland, enlisted 07 July 1746 in Captain William Trent's company.

Denny, David, hired 27 May 1757 as a battoe man, Master George Allen.

Denny, William, Lieutenant Governor of the Province and Colonel-in-Chief of a Pennsylvania Regiment consisting of three battalions. Colonel and Governor in December 1757.

Dermott, Matthew, age 28, carpenter, born Ireland, enlisted 19 July 1746 in Captain William Trent's company.

Derr, Leonard, sergeant, in Captain John Van Etten's company of the First Battalion in 1756.

Derry, William, age 23, cooper, born Delaware, enlisted 24 April 1758 by Captain Benjamin Noxon.

Described as being of Captain company.

Described as being of the Major's Company.

Described as being of the Major's Company.

Desert, Benjamin, age 17, cordwainer, born Cumberland, Pennsylvania, enlisted 05 May 1759, private in Captain James Armstrong's company in Colonel William Clapham's Pennsylvania Regiment. On a return dated 01 June 1759.

Deveney, Samuel, private in Captain Patterson's company from 01 December 1757 stationed eastward of the Susquehanna. On a muster roll dated 08 March 1758.

Dick, Alexander, age 18, born Lancaster, Pennsylvania, blacksmith, private in Captain John Haslett's company enlisted on 10 May 1758 and last paid on 21 May 1758.

Dick, John, age 29, shoemaker, born Ireland, enlisted 26 July 1746 in Captain Samuel Perry's company.

Dickey, James, private, age 29, smith, born Octoraro, Pennsylvania, enlisted 24 April 1758 for the campaign in the lower counties. On a return of Captain McClughan's company dated 17 May 1758.

Dickey, Moses, captain, in the Associated Regiment of Chester County in 1747.

Diemer, John, captain, company in winter quarters in Albany, N.Y., 1746–7, being discharged 31 October 1747.

Diermont, George, hired 21 June 1757 as a battoe man, Master George Allen.

Dieus, William, enlisted 15 May 1759, private in Captain Henry Van Bibber's company of the Lower County. On a return dated 04 June 1759.

Dill, Matthew, captain, in the Associated Regiment of Lancaster County over the Susquehanna in 1747–8.

Dinney, James, a member of Captain Joseph Armstrong's Company on 07 August 1755, raised in Cumberland County

Dinney, William, a member of Captain Joseph Armstrong's Company on 07 August 1755, raised in Cumberland County Discharged 10 May 1757.

Dishler, Hans Joseph, age 40, mason, born Germany, enlisted 02 June 1759, private in Captain John Mathers's company in the Pennsylvania Regiment. On a return dated 15 June 1759.

Divine, James, age 25, laborer, born Donaghadee, Ireland, enlisted 23 May 1759, private in Captain John Mathers's company in the Pennsylvania Regiment. On a return dated 15 June 1759.

Dix, John, *see* Dick, John.

Dixon, George, lieutenant in Colonel Hugh Mercer's company of the Second Battalion of the Pennsylvania Regiment from 23 April 1760.

Dixon, George, promoted to lieutenant after serving in the Pennsylvania Regiment of Three Battalions in 1758 and 1759.

Dixon, John, landsman on the provincial ship *Pennsylvania* on 17 August 1757.

Dixson, Robert, a member of Captain Joseph Armstrong's Company on 07 August 1755, raised in Cumberland County

Dixson, William, a member of Captain Joseph Armstrong's Company on 07 August 1755, raised in Cumberland County

Dixson, William, private, age 25, farmer, born New Castle, Delaware, enlisted 22 April 1758 for the campaign in the lower counties. On a return of Captain McClughan's company dated 17 May 1758.

Donald, John, ensign in the Associated Regiment of Chester County in 1747.

Donally, Felix, age 21, laborer, born Ireland, enlisted 17 July 1746 in Captain Samuel Perry's company.

Donelly, Bernard, age 19, born Ireland, private in Captain John Haslett's company enlisted on 09 May 1758 and last paid on 21 May 1758.

Donnahow, Lawrence, a private in Captain Edward Ward's Company, Second Battalion in 1756; missing at the capture of Kittanning.

Donnelly, Abner, *see* Abner Danily.

Donnelly, John, age 30, laborer, born Ireland, enlisted 22 July 1746 in Captain John Shannon's company of foot.

Donner, Thomas, a private in Captain Edward Jones's Independent Company of Horse, Philadelphia in 1756.

Donohue, Timothy, laborer, born Ireland, enlisted July 1746 in Captain Samuel Perry's company.

Dormeyer, Jacob, age 23, born Germany, enlisted 01 September 1757, private in Captain John Nicholas Weatherholt's company, which enlisted for a term of three years, and stationed in Heydelberg Township, Northampton County, in March and April 1758.

Dorraugh, James, age 20, laborer, born Chester, Pennsylvania, enlisted 11 May 1759 in Captain Robert Boyd's company [probably in the Third Battalion]. On a return dated May and June 1759.

Dorsey, Basil, a private in Captain John Kidd's Independent Company of Foot, Philadelphia in 1756.

Dorsey, Patrick, age 26, laborer, born Ireland, enlisted 27 April 1759 in Captain Charles Stewart's company [probably one of the Associated Companies of Bucks County]. On a return dated June 1759.

Douché, Jacob, colonel in one of the companies of the Philadelphia Regiment on 09 April 1756.

Doudle, James, age 20, weaver, born Ireland, 09 August 1746 in Captain John Deimer's company.

Dougherty, Charles, sergeant, age 29, farmer, born Donegal, Ireland, enlisted 22 April 1758 for the campaign in the lower counties. On a return of Captain McClughan's company dated 17 May 1758.

Dougherty, Cornelius, age 20, laborer, born Donegal, Ireland, enlisted 05 May 1759, private in Captain John Haslet's company in the Pennsylvania Regiment. On a list of recruits dated 20 May 1759.

Dougherty, John, ensign in the Associated Regiment of the West End of Lancaster County in 1747–8.

Dougherty, John, landsman on the provincial ship *Pennsylvania* on 17 August 1757.

Dougherty, John, private, age 17, farmer, born Donegal, Ireland, enlisted 05 May 1758 for the campaign in the lower counties. On a return of Captain McClughan's company dated 17 May 1758.

Dougherty, Neal, landsman on the provincial ship *Pennsylvania* on 17 August 1757.

Dougherty, Owen, private, age 33, laborer, born Donegal, Ireland, enlisted 26 April 1758 for the campaign in the lower counties. On a return of Captain McClughan's company dated 17 May 1758.

Dougherty, Patrick, private, age 24, laborer, born Donegal, Ireland, enlisted 23 April 1758 for the campaign in the lower counties. On a return of Captain McClughan's company dated 17 May 1758.

Dougherty, Peter, hired 27 May 1757 as a battoe man, Master George Allen.

Doughty, Jacob, a private in Captain Joseph Inslee's Company of Foot, Newtown, Bucks County, in 1756.

Doughty, Thomas, a private in Captain Joseph Inslee's Company of Foot, Newtown, Bucks County, in 1756.

Douglass, Andrew, a private in Captain John Potter's Company, Second Battalion in 1756.

Douglass, Duncan, age 21, laborer, born Scotland, enlisted 01 July 1746 in Captain John Shannon's company of foot.

Douglass, Thomas, landsman on the provincial ship *Pennsylvania* on 17 August 1757.

Dowell, William, a private in Captain Samuel Mifflin's Association Battery Company of Philadelphia in 1756.

Down, John, age 34, born Germany, enlisted 08 August 1746 in Captain John Deimer's company.

Downs, Joseph, age 30, laborer, born London, enlisted 01 May 1759, private in Captain James Armstrong's company in Colonel William Clapham's Pennsylvania Regiment. On a return dated 01 June 1759.

Downs, Thomas, age 20, glassblower, born England, enlisted 29 April 1758 by Captain Benjamin Noxon.

Downs, Thomas, age 46, baker, born Dublin, Ireland, enlisted 26 April 1759, private in Captain William Johnston's company in the Pennsylvania Regiment. On a return dated 12 May 1759.

Downs, Thomas, laborer, born Maryland, enlisted 29 April 1758 by Captain Benjamin Noxon.

Downs, Thomas, landsman on the provincial ship *Pennsylvania* on 17 August 1757.

Doyle, James, age 38, laborer, born Ireland, enlisted 07 May 1759 in Captain Robert Boyd's company [probably in the Third Battalion]. On a return dated May and June 1759.

Doyle, John, private in Captain Patterson's company from 01 January 1758 stationed eastward of the Susquehanna. On a muster roll dated 08 March 1758.

Doyle, Peter, age 26, sailor, born Dublin, Ireland, enlisted 03 May 1759, private in Captain William Johnston's company in the Pennsylvania Regiment. On a return dated 12 May 1759.

Drum, James Heroit, age 19, laborer, born New Castle, Delaware, enlisted 03 May 1759, private in Captain James Armstrong's company in Colonel William Clapham's Pennsylvania Regiment. On a return dated 01 June 1759.

Drummer, Sampson, seaman on the provincial ship *Pennsylvania* on 17 August 1757.

Drumming, John, age 21, laborer, born England, enlisted 30 June 1746 in Captain William Trent's company.

Drummond, Daniel, on a return of Captain David Hunter's Company [probably from York County] in Colonel William Clapham's Regiment of New Levies dated 26 May 1759.

Drysdale, William, landsman on the provincial ship *Pennsylvania* on 17 August 1757.

Dudleston, Henry, age 22, shoemaker, born Ireland, enlisted 07 May 1758. On a weekly return of Captain Samuel Jones's company in 1758.

Duell, Dennis, age 25, laborer, born Ireland, enlisted 11 May 1758. On a return of Captain John Blackwood's company in the Third Battalion dated 22 May 1758.

Duff, Thomas, ensign in the Christiana Hundred company of Colonel William Armstrong's Upper Regiment of New Castle County in 1756.

Duffell, William, ensign in one of the Associated Companies of York County in 1756.

Duffield, Jacob, captain in one of the companies of Colonel Jacob Duché's Philadelphia Regiment in 1756.

Duffield, Ratchford, ensign from 05 May 1759 in Captain Andrew McDowell's company of Colonel William Clapham's Regiment of New Levies.

Duffield, Richard, age 24, born Philadelphia, Pennsylvania, private in Captain John Singleton's company in service between 01 May and 08 May 1758.

Duffy, Michael, private who enlisted 15 April 1756 in Captain Joseph Shippen's company in Colonel William Clapham's Regiment in 1756, the regiment in garrison at Fort Augusta, Shamokin, and listed in Shippen's Account Book.

Duffy, Philip, age 28, tanner, born Ireland, enlisted 06 May 1758. On a return of Captain John Blackwood's company in the Third Battalion dated 22 May 1758.

Dugan, James, seaman on the provincial ship *Pennsylvania* on 17 August 1757.

Dugan, John, age 23, laborer, born Scotland, enlisted 09 July 1746 in Captain William Trent's company.

Dummes, Ezekiel, lieutenant from 21 April 1759 in Captain John Mather's company in Colonel William Clapham's Regiment of New Levies.

Dunbar, John, age 21, laborer, born Ireland, enlisted 15 July 1746 in Captain Samuel Perry's company.

Dunbar, John, age 26, laborer, born Ireland, enlisted 08 May 1759, private in Captain James Armstrong's company in Colonel William Clapham's Pennsylvania Regiment. On a return dated 01 June 1759.

Dunbar, John, private, age 24, weaver, born Tyrone, Ireland, enlisted 25 April 1758 for the campaign in the lower counties. On a return of Captain McClughan's company dated 17 May 1758.

Dunfee, Michael, private, age 22, laborer, born Wexford, Ireland, enlisted 02 May 1758 for the campaign in the lower counties. On a return of Captain McClughan's company dated 17 May 1758.

Dunlap, John, landsman on the provincial ship *Pennsylvania* on 17 August 1757.

Dunlap, John, private, age 28, laborer, born Ireland, enlisted 06 May 1758 for the campaign in the lower counties. On a return of Captain McClughan's company dated 17 May 1758.

Dunlap, Mathew, age 19, carpenter, born Scotland, enlisted 11 May 1758. On a return of Captain John Blackwood's company in the Third Battalion dated 22 May 1758.

Dunlap, Mathew, age 24, born Ireland, cordwainer, private in Captain John Shannon's Company, enlisted 20 July 1746. On a roll of deserters dated 22 July 1746. [B3:422:18]

Dunn, Ralph, a private in Captain Joseph Inslee's Company of Foot, Newtown, Bucks County, in 1756.

Dunn, Ralph, ensign in the Associated Regiment of Bucks County in 1748.

Dunn, Ralph, ensign in the Associated Regiment of Bucks County in 1748.

Dunn, Robert, lieutenant in the Associated Regiment in the County of Philadelphia in 1748.

Dunn, Thomas, lieutenant in the White Clay Creek Hundred company of Colonel William Armstrong's Upper Regiment of New Castle County in 1756.

Dunning, Ezekiel, lieutenant from 27 April 1758 in Captain John Byers's company in the Second Battalion.

Dunning, Robert, captain, in the Associated Regiment of Lancaster County over the Susquehanna in 1747–8.

Dunning, Robert, lt. colonel, in the Associated Regiment of Lancaster County over the Susquehanna in 1747–8.

Dunwoody, Hugh, captain, in one of the Associated Companies of York County in 1756.

Durborrow, Isaac, enlisted 28 May 1758 in Captain French Battell's company of Lower County Provincials.

Durmot, Matthew, *see* Dermott, Matthew.

Dushane, Jerome, lieutenant in the St. George's Hundred company of Colonel Jacob Van Bibber's Lower Regiment of New Castle County in 1756.

Dusheene, Isaac, ensign in one of two regiments of New Castle County in 1747–8.

Dusheene, Jerome, lieutenant in one of two regiments of New Castle County in 1747–8.

Dusier, William, age 23, laborer, born Pennsylvania, enlisted 04 May 1758. On a weekly return of Captain Samuel Jones's company in 1758.

Dwine, John, private who enlisted 10 April 1756 in Captain Joseph Shippen's company in Colonel William Clapham's Regiment in 1756, the regiment in garrison at Fort Augusta, Shamokin, and listed in Shippen's Account Book.

Dyartt, James, *see* James Dysart.

Dyer, Henry, captain, in one of two regiments of New Castle County in 1747–8.

Dysart, James, ensign in the Associated Regiment of Chester County in 1747. Lieutenant in the Associated Regiment of Lancaster County over the Susquehanna in 1747–8.

Eagert, Robert, hired 29 May 1757 as a battoe man, Master George Allen.

Eagle, Jacob, lieutenant in one of the companies of Colonel Jacob Duché's Philadelphia Regiment in 1756.

Eakin, Michael, age 21, wheelwright, born Ireland, enlisted 26 July 1746 in Captain Samuel Perry's company.

Eastburn, Robert, captain from 30 April 1758 of a company in the Second Battalion. Reported as a prisoner at Canada.

Eastburn, Robert, promoted to captain after serving in the Pennsylvania Regiment of Three Battalions in 1758 and 1759.

Eaton, James, a member of Captain Joseph Armstrong's Company on 07 August 1755, raised in Cumberland County

Eaton, John, a member of Captain Joseph Armstrong's Company on 07 August 1755, raised in Cumberland County

Eaton, Joshua, a member of Captain Joseph Armstrong's Company on 07 August 1755, raised in Cumberland County

Eckard, George William, age 23, bricklayer, enlisted 07 August 1746 in Captain John Deimer's company.

Eckart, Abraham, age 20, laborer, born Germany, enlisted 10 May 1758. On a return of Captain John Blackwood's company in the Third Battalion dated 22 May 1758.

Eckbret, Daniel, age 31, laborer, born Germany, enlisted 09 May 1758. On a return of Captain John Bull's company dated 01 July 1758.

Edgin, Benjamin, age 24, born Maryland, private in Captain John Wright's company of the Lower County. On a muster dated 11 May 1759.

Edinfields, William, age 25, born Kent on Delaware, laborer, private in Captain John Shannon's Company, enlisted 14 July 1746. On a roll of deserters dated 22 July 1746. [B3:422:18]

Edwards, James, captain, in one of the Associated Companies of Kent County in August 1748.

Edwards, John, age 19, laborer, born Bucks, Pennsylvania, enlisted 25 April 1759, private in Captain Joseph Richardson's company of the Third Battalion in the Pennsylvania Regiment. On a return of recruits dated 1759.

Edwards, John, captain, in one of two regiments of New Castle County in August 1748.

Edwards, Josiah, age 21, tailor, born Wales, enlisted 22 April 1758 by Captain Benjamin Noxon.

Edwards, Thomas, captain from 01 December 1744

Egbertson, James, lieutenant in one of two regiments of New Castle County in 1747–8.

Elder, James, a member of Captain Joseph Armstrong's Company on 07 August 1755, raised in Cumberland County

Elliott, Andrew, a private in Captain John Kidd's Independent Company of Foot, Philadelphia in 1756.

Elliott, John, ensign in the Brandy Wine Hundred company of Colonel William Armstrong's Upper Regiment of New Castle County in 1756.

Elliott, William, ensign in Captain Samuel West's company of the First Battalion of the Pennsylvania Regiment from 09 May 1760.

Ellis, David, private who enlisted 15 April 1756 in Captain Joseph Shippen's company in Colonel William Clapham's Regiment in 1756, the regiment in garrison at Fort Augusta, Shamokin, and listed in Shippen's Account Book.

Ellis, Francis, hired 23 June 1757 as a battoe man, Master George Allen.

Ellis, Jacob, private in Lieutenant Miller's detachment of Captain Frederick Smith's Company, killed by Indians on 06 August 1756 at Manity [Manada] Fort.

Ellis, John, age 15, sailor, born Ireland, enlisted 13 June 1759 in Captain Charles Stewart's company [probably one of the Associated Companies of Bucks County]. On a return dated June 1759.

Ellis, Robert, lieutenant in the Associated Regiment of the West End of Lancaster County in 1747–8.

Elms, Christopher, drummer, age 15, laborer, born Conococheague, Pennsylvania, enlisted 06 May 1758 for the campaign in the lower counties. On a return of Captain McClughan's company dated 17 May 1758.

Elson, William, age 49, brass founder, born London, enlisted 02 May 1758. On a return of Captain John Bull's company dated 01 July 1758.

Elwell, Elias, landsman on the provincial ship *Pennsylvania* on 17 August 1757.

Emmery, William, age 25, laborer, born Talbot, Maryland, enlisted 26 May 1759, private in Captain John Mathers's company in the Pennsylvania Regiment. On a return dated 15 June 1759.

Emmitt, John, ensign in the Associated Regiment of Chester County in 1747. Lieutenant from 29 April 1758 in Captain John Singleton's company in the Second Battalion in service between 01 May and 08 May 1758.

Empsom, William, captain, in the Brandy Wine Hundred company of Colonel William Armstrong's Upper Regiment of New Castle County in 1756.

Endless, John, private, age 34, laborer, born Gregory Stroke, England, enlisted 21 April 1758 for the campaign in the lower counties. On a return of Captain McClughan's company dated 17 May 1758.

Endsworth, Benjamin, private in Captain Patterson's company from 26 December 1757 stationed eastward of the Susquehanna. On a muster roll dated 08 March 1758.

Engel, Andrew, lieutenant on a List of Officers in the Province Pay, 1756 in the First Battalion of the Pennsylvania Regiment with a commission date of 5 January 1756. {PA5, I, 88}

Engle, Andrew, lieutenant in Captain Jacob Morgan's company of the First Battalion from 05 January 1756. Lieutenant in Captain Andrew Engle's company from 09 December 1757 stationed eastward of the Susquehanna.

English, James, hired 30 May 1757 as a battoe man, Master George Allen.

Ennis, John, on a list of men recruited by Captain Andrew McDowell's company in the Second Battalion, Pennsylvania Regiment dated 04 June 1759.

Ennis, Robert, age 22, weaver, born Scotland, enlisted 03May 1758 by Captain Benjamin Noxon.

Ensley, John, age 21, cooper, born Ireland, enlisted 10 July 1746 in Captain John Shannon's company of foot.

Enslow, Isaac, ensign in Colonel Hugh Mercer's company of the Second Battalion of the Pennsylvania Regiment from 23 April 1760.

Ernst, John Valentine, a private in Captain Adam Heylman's Company, of the St. Vincent and Puke's Land Association on 10 May 1756.

Erwin, Joseph, ensign in Captain John Proctor's company in the First Battalion of the Pennsylvania Regiment during or after 1763.

Erwine, John, *see* Irvine, John.

Esdam, James, age 19, born England, enlisted 26 July 1746 in Captain John Deimer's company.

Essary, James, age 31, laborer, born England, enlisted 02 August 1746 in Captain John Shannon's company of foot.

Etter, Peter, ensign in the Associated Regiment of Foot of Philadelphia on 29 Dec 1747.

Eules, James, age 22, born Tyrone, Ireland, private in Captain John Haslett's company enlisted on 12 May 1758 and last paid on 21 May 1758.

Evans, Daniel, enlisted 20 May 1758 in Captain French Battell's company of Lower County Provincials.

Evans, David, age 25, laborer, born Pennsylvania, enlisted 03 May 1749 in Captain Richard Gardiner's company in Colonel William Denney's Pennsylvania Regiment.

Evans, John, age 19, born Maryland, private in Captain John Wright's company of the Lower County. On a muster dated 11 May 1759.

Evans, John, age 25, laborer, born Pennsylvania, enlisted 03 July 1746 in Captain William Trent's company.

Evans, John, age 50, farmer, born England, enlisted 21 May 1759 in Captain Charles Stewart's company [probably one of the Associated Companies of Bucks County]. On a return dated June 1759.

Evans, John, lieutenant in one of the Associated Companies of Lancaster County in 1756.

Evans, Solomon, age 36, whitesmith, born Newcastle, Delaware, enlisted 02 July 1746 in Captain John Shannon's company of foot.

Eve, Oswald, lieutenant in Captain Samuel Mifflin's Association Battery Company of Philadelphia in 1756.

Everhard, Conrad, age 23, born Germany, weaver, enlisted 13 October 1757, private in Captain John Nicholas Weatherholt's company which enlisted for a term of three years and was stationed in Heydelberg Township, Northampton County, in March and April 1758.

Everhard, Yost, a private in Captain Adam Heylman's Company, of the St. Vincent and Puke's Land Association on 10 May 1756.

Everhart, Martin, ensign in Captain William Parson's Company in the First Battalion from 20 December 1755. Left out in the reorganization of December 1757.

Everhart, Martin, ensign on a List of Officers in the Province Pay, 1756 in the First Battalion of the Pennsylvania Regiment with a commission date of 20 December 1755. {PA5, I, 88}

Ewald, John, age 36, laborer, born Germany, enlisted 16 May 1758. On a return of Captain John Blackwood's company in the Third Battalion dated 22 May 1758. Formerly in Clapham's Provincials.

Ewing, James, lieutenant from 10 May 1758 in Captain Robert McPherson's company in the Third Battalion. Adjutant from 07 June 1758 of the Third Battalion.

Ewing, William, lieutenant from 01 May 1759 in Captain John Bull's company of Colonel William Clapham's Regiment of New Levies. Adjutant from 30 May 1759 in Colonel William Clapham's Regiment of New Levies.

Ewing, William, promoted to lieutenant after serving in the Pennsylvania Regiment of Three Battalions in 1758 and 1759.

Eyres, William, *see* William Ayres.

Faire, Jacob, private who enlisted 29 April 1756 in Captain Patrick Work's company in Colonel William Clapham's Regiment in 1756, the regiment in garrison at Fort Augusta, Shamokin, and listed in Shippen's Account Book.

Faires, Daniel, age 24, laborer, born Ireland, enlisted 08 May 1749 in Captain Richard Gardiner's company in Colonel William Denney's Pennsylvania Regiment.

Falconer, _____, Sergt., present at the battle of Sideling Hill in August 1756. {PA1, III, 315} {B8:1691:625}

Falconer, Joseph, ensign, commissioned 07 December 1757 in Late Clapham's Company stationed at Fort Augusta. Also reported as an ensign from 07 December 1757 in Captain Asher Clayton's company in the Second Battalion. Lieutenant in Captain (Major) Asher Clayton's Company of the First Battalion of the Pennsylvania Regiment from 15 April 1760.

Falconer, Joseph, promoted to lieutenant after serving in the Pennsylvania Regiment of Three Battalions in 1758 and 1759.

Falstead, Adam, landsman on the provincial ship *Pennsylvania* on 17 August 1757.

Fanstiel, Ernst, a private in Captain Adam Heylman's Company, of the St. Vincent and Puke's Land Association on 10 May 1756.

Farb, Casper, age 23, laborer, born Germany, enlisted 13 May 1749 in Captain Richard Gardiner's company in Colonel William Denney's Pennsylvania Regiment.

Farmer, Richard, lieutenant in the Associated Regiment of Foot of Philadelphia on 29 Dec 1747.

Farquer, Hugh, age 26, born Down, Ireland, private in Captain John Haslett's company enlisted on 09 May 1758 and last paid on 21 May 1758.

Farrell, James, age 31, laborer, born Maryland, enlisted 15 April 1758 by Captain Benjamin Noxon.

Farrell, James, private, age 31, laborer, born Maryland, enlisted 15 April 1758 for the campaign in the lower counties and is believed to be in Captain McClughan's company, but not on a return dated 17 May 1758.

Fay, see Foy.

Feran, Matthew, on a list of men recruited by Captain Andrew McDowell's company in the Second Battalion, Pennsylvania Regiment dated 04 June 1759.

Ferguson, James, sergeant in Captain Patterson's company from 03 March 1758 stationed eastward of the Susquehanna. On a muster roll dated 08 March 1758.

Ferguson, John, sergeant in Captain Patterson's company from 03 March 1758 stationed eastward of the Susquehanna. On a muster roll dated 08 March 1758.

Ferral, John, a private in Captain George Armstrong's Company, Second Battalion in 1756; wounded at Kittanning.

Ferrill, John, private in Captain Patterson's company from 10 February 1758 stationed eastward of the Susquehanna. On a muster roll dated 08 March 1758.

Ferris, William, lieutenant in one of two regiments of New Castle County in 1747–8.

Fifer, Martin, private who enlisted 20 April 1756 in Captain Patrick Work's company in Colonel William Clapham's Regiment in 1756, the regiment in garrison at Fort Augusta, Shamokin, and listed in Shippen's Account Book.

Fillson, Samuel, age 18, tailor, born Chester, Pennsylvania, enlisted 06 June 1759 in Captain Robert Boyd's company [probably in the Third Battalion]. On a return dated May and June 1759.

Fimill, Nicholas, landsman on the provincial ship *Pennsylvania* on 17 August 1757.

Findley, Andrew, captain in one of the Associated Companies of York County in 1756.

Findley, William, a private in Captain George Armstrong's Company, Second Battalion in 1756; wounded at Kittanning.

Fink, Conrad, age 25, tailor, enlisted 07 July 1746 in Captain John Deimer's company.

Fink, George, age 25, laborer, enlisted 28 June 1746 in Captain John Deimer's company.

Finley, Andrew, lieutenant in the Associated Regiment of Lancaster County over the Susquehanna in 1747–8. Lieutenant from 25 April 1758 in Captain David Hunter's company in the First Battalion. Lieutenant from 02 May 1759 in Captain David Hunter's company of Colonel William Clapham's Regiment of New Levies.

Finley, Andrew, promoted to lieutenant after serving in the Pennsylvania Regiment of Three Battalions in 1758 and 1759.

Finley, Archibald, age 21, laborer, born Bucks, Pennsylvania, enlisted 04 May 1759, private in Captain Joseph Richardson's company of the Third Battalion in the Pennsylvania Regiment. On a return of recruits dated 1759.

Finley, Archibald, lieutenant in Captain Robert Currie's company of the Second Battalion of the Pennsylvania Regiment from 09 May 1760.

Finley, Archibald, lieutenant in the Associated Regiment of Bucks County in 1748.

Finley, John, age 22, laborer, born Scotland, enlisted 06 May 1749 in Captain Richard Gardiner's company in Colonel William Denney's Pennsylvania Regiment.

Finley, Samuel, lieutenant in Captain William Piper's company in Lieutenant Colonel Commandant Asher Clayton's Second Battalion of the Pennsylvania Regiment commanded by the Hon. J. Penn from 16 July 1763. Promoted to captain.

Finney, Archibald, ensign from 24 April 1758 in Captain Benjamin Noxon's company; promoted to second lieutenant 16 June 1758. On a list of officers of the lower government on Delaware, 1758/9.

Finney, David, captain in one of two regiments of New Castle County in 1747–8.

Finney, James, ensign in the Associated Regiment of the West End of Lancaster County in 1747–8.

Finney, John, Lt. Col. of the Upper Regiment of New Castle County in 1756.

Finney, William, ensign in the Associated Regiment in the County of Philadelphia in 1748.

Fisher, Alexander, private in Captain Patterson's company from 01 December 1757 stationed eastward of the Susquehanna. On a muster roll dated 08 March 1758.

Fisher, John, age 22, laborer, born Germany, enlisted 08 July 1746 in Captain Samuel Perry's company.

Fisher, Matthias, age 20, born Germany, enlisted 01 September 1757, private in Captain John Nicholas Weatherholt's company which enlisted for a term of three years and stationed in Heydelberg Township, Northampton County, in March and April 1758.

Fisher, Samuel, ensign in the Associated Regiment of Lancaster County over the Susquehanna in 1747–8.

Fitz Randolph, Edward, captain in one of two regiments of New Castle County in 1747–8.

Fitzgerald, John, Drummer, age 15, smith, born Queen Anne's, Maryland, enlisted 02 May 1758 for the campaign in the lower counties. On a return of Captain McClughan's company dated 17 May 1758.

Fitzgibbins, Richard, a private in Captain Hugh Mercer's Company, Second Battalion in 1756; wounded at Kittanning.

Fitzpatrick, Dennis, age 26, laborer, born Ireland, enlisted 23 July 1746 in Captain William Trent's company.

Fitzsimmons, John, private, age 27, laborer, born Dublin, Ireland, enlisted 11 May 1758 for the campaign in the lower counties. On a return of Captain McClughan's company dated 17 May 1758.

Fitzsimons, John, a private in Captain Charles Batho's Independent Company of Foot, Philadelphia in 1756.

Flack, John, age 25, born Germany, enlisted 01 September 1757, private in Captain John Nicholas Weatherholt's company which enlisted for a term of three years and stationed in Heydelberg Township, Northampton County, in March and April 1758.

Flackhardie, Daniel, landsman on the provincial ship *Pennsylvania* on 17 August 1757.

Flannigan, George, age 40, cordwainer, born Ireland, enlisted 16 July 1746 in Captain William Trent's company.

Flannigan, Patrick, age 19, laborer, born Ireland, enlisted 15 July 1746 in Captain John Deimer's company.

Fleeson, Plunkett, ensign in the Associated Regiment of Foot of Philadelphia on 29 Dec 1747.

Fleming, George, age 17, mariner, born Ireland, enlisted 10 May 1758. On a return of Captain John Blackwood's company in the Third Battalion dated 22 May 1758.

Fleming, George, age 17, mariner, born Ireland, enlisted 10 May 1758. On a return of Captain John Blackwood's company in the Third Battalion dated 22 May 1758.

Fleming, John, age 21, laborer, born Germany, enlisted 16 May 1758. On a return of Captain John Blackwood's company in the Third Battalion dated 22 May 1758. Formerly in Clapham's Provincials.

Fleming, John, age 21, shoemaker, born Germany, enlisted 07 May 1758. On a return of Captain John Blackwood's company in the Third Battalion dated 22 May 1758. Formerly in Clapham's Provincials.

Fleming, John, lieutenant in Lieutenant Colonel Francis Turbutt's Company in the Pennsylvania Regiment commanded by the Hon. J. Penn, Esqr., from 09 June 1764.

Fleming, Sir Collingwood, Bt., lieutenant from 03 May 1758 in Captain James Sharp's company in the Third Battalion. Lieutenant from 24 April 1759 in Captain James Sharp's company of Colonel William Clapham's Regiment of New Levies. Lieutenant in Captain Patrick Work's Company of the First Battalion of the Pennsylvania Regiment from 12 April 1760.

Fleming, Sir Collingwood, promoted to lieutenant after serving in the Pennsylvania Regiment of Three Battalions in 1758 and 1759. Reported as "dead".

Flemming, Archibald, lieutenant in the Middle Part of Mispillim Hundred company of Colonel John Vining's Regiment of Kent County Militia, Upon Delaware in 1756.

Flood, John, age 21, tailor, born Ireland, enlisted 15 July 1746 in Captain John Shannon's company of foot.

Flower, Samuel, lieutenant colonel in the Associated Regiment of Chester County in 1747.

Fluke, John Jacob, age 46, tailor, born Germany, enlisted 28 June 1746 in Captain John Deimer's company.

Foglesang, John Philip, private who enlisted 21 April 1756 in Captain Patrick Work's company in Colonel William Clapham's Regiment in 1756, the regiment in garrison at Fort Augusta, Shamokin, and listed in Shippen's Account Book.

Ford, Benjamin, Jun., lieutenant in the Brandy Wine Hundred company of Colonel William Armstrong's Upper Regiment of New Castle County in 1756.

Ford, Charles, lieutenant from 08 May 1759 in Captain Richard Gardiner's company of Colonel William Clapham's Regiment of New Levies.

Ford, Charles, promoted to lieutenant after serving in the Pennsylvania Regiment of Three Battalions in 1758 and 1759.

Forgerty, Patrick, age 31, laborer, born Ireland, enlisted 27 April 1759, private in Captain Joseph Richardson's company of the Third Battalion in the Pennsylvania Regiment. On a return of recruits dated 1759.

Forrest, Samuel, age 23, laborer, born England, enlisted 21 July 1746 in Captain John Shannon's company of foot.

Forrester, George, age 38, tailor, born Ireland, enlisted 08 May 1759 in Captain Robert Boyd's company [probably in the Third Battalion]. On a return dated May and June 1759.

Forster, James, an ensign stationed on the frontier in Lancaster County fifteen men at Fort Hunter, Paxtang Township, on 01 June 1764 as part of a unit under the command of Major Asher Clayton.

Forster, James, ensign in Captain Samuel Hunter's company in the First Battalion of the Pennsylvania Regiment from 04 August 1763.

Forster, John, lieutenant from 11 May 1759 in Captain James Armstrong's company of Colonel William Clapham's Regiment of New Levies.

Forster, John, promoted to lieutenant after serving in the Pennsylvania Regiment of Three Battalions in 1758 and 1759.

Forster, Thomas, a private in Captain Lieutenant Robert Callender's Company, Second Battalion in 1756; wounded at Kittanning.

Fortney, Samuel, age 23, butcher, born Germany, enlisted 07 July 1746 in Captain Samuel Perry's company.

Foster, Fucher, private, age 28, planter, born Rehoboth, Delaware, enlisted 20 April 1758 for the campaign in the lower counties.

On a return of Captain McClughan's company dated 17 May 1758.

Foster, John, private in Captain John Singleton's company in service between 01 May and 08 May 1758.

Foster, Thomas, lieutenant in the Associated Regiment of the West End of Lancaster County in 1747–8.

Foster, William, age 15, laborer, born Cavan, Ireland, enlisted 01 May 1759, private in Captain John Haslet's company in the Pennsylvania Regiment. On a list of recruits dated 20 May 1759.

Foster, William, age 25, born Chester, Pennsylvania, private in Captain John Singleton's company in service between 01 May and 08 May 1758.

Foster, William, age 28, born Maryland, private in Captain John Wright's company of the Lower County. On a muster dated 11 May 1759.

Foulk, Charles, captain in the provincial service in 1755 at Gnadenhutten.

Foulk, Charles, captain of company of the First Battalion in 1755/6.

Foulke, John, ensign from 04 May 1759 in Captain Samuel Price's company of Colonel William Clapham's Regiment of New Levies.

Foulke, John, ensign in Captain Samuel Mile's company of the First Battalion of the Pennsylvania Regiment from 22 April 1760.

Fouts, Conrad, age 25, laborer, born Zweibrucken, Germany, enlisted 12 June 1759, private in Captain John Mathers's company in the Pennsylvania Regiment. On a return dated 15 June 1759.

Fowler, Michael, age 40, laborer, born Germany, enlisted 02 July 1746 in Captain John Deimer's company.

Fox, Adam, age 20, laborer, born Germany, enlisted 02 July 1746 in Captain William Trent's company.

Fox, David, private who enlisted 28 April 1756 in Captain Joseph Shippen's company in Colonel William Clapham's Regiment in 1756, the regiment in garrison at Fort Augusta, Shamokin, and listed in Shippen's Account Book.

Fox, Jacob, age 20, laborer, born Pennsylvania, enlisted 04 May 1749 in Captain Richard Gardiner's company in Colonel William Denney's Pennsylvania Regiment.

Fox, Thomas, age 35, laborer, born Ireland, enlisted July 1746 in Captain William Trent's company.

Foy, James, enlisted 30 June 1746 in Captain William Trent's company, deserted 18 August 1746. [PA2:2 says Fay]

Foy, Matthew, age 40, laborer, born Ireland, enlisted 30 June 1746 in Captain William Trent's company. [PA2:2 says Fay]

Fraiss, Adam, a private in Captain Edward Jones's Independent Company of Horse, Philadelphia in 1756.

Franklin, Benjamin, General Dr., in command of several companies that were sent to Northampton in 1755, rendezvoused at Easton for some days until he was relieved by Clapham.

Franklin, William, Captain John Diemer's company, in winter quarters in Albany, N.Y., 1746–7, being discharged 31 October 1747.

Franks, David, a private in Captain Edward Jones's Independent Company of Horse, Philadelphia in 1756.

Franks, John Maus, a private in Captain Charles Batho's Independent Company of Foot, Philadelphia in 1756.

Frauberg, Andrew, captain, in the Christiana Hundred company of Colonel William Armstrong's Upper Regiment of New Castle County in 1756.

Frazier, Andrew, age 20, bricklayer, born Ireland, enlisted 26 July 1746 in Captain Samuel Perry's company.

Frazier, Robert, seaman on the provincial ship *Pennsylvania* on 17 August 1757.

Freburn, William, age 19, smith, born Pennsylvania, enlisted 07 July 1746 in Captain William Trent's company.

Frederick, George, age 20, laborer, born Worms, Germany, enlisted 29 May 1759, private in Captain John Mathers's company in the Pennsylvania Regiment. On a return dated 15 June 1759.

Fredericks, John, age 24, laborer, born Germany, enlisted 02 July 1746 in Captain John Deimer's company.

Free, Jacob, ensign in the Associated Regiment of Chester County in 1747.

Freeland, John, enlisted 13 May 1758 in Captain French Battell's company of Lower County Provincials.

Freestone, Isaac, a private in Captain Joseph Inslee's Company of Foot, Newtown, Bucks County, in 1756.

Freestone, John, mate of the provincial ship *Pennsylvania* on 17 August 1757.

Fretter, Casper, a private in Captain Edward Jones's Independent Company of Horse, Philadelphia in 1756.

Fretts, John George, a private in Captain John Kidd's Independent Company of Foot, Philadelphia in 1756.

Frew, John, lieutenant colonel, in the Associated Regiment of Chester County in 1747.

Friday, John Augustus, private, age 19, laborer, born Hanover, Germany, enlisted 23 April 1758 for the campaign in the lower counties. On a return of Captain McClughan's company dated 17 May 1758.

Froufalt, Jacob, a private in Captain Edward Jones's Independent Company of Horse, Philadelphia in 1756.

Fruit, Alexander, landsman on the provincial ship *Pennsylvania* on 17 August 1757.

Fry, John, age 26, laborer, born England, enlisted 13 July 1746 in Captain John Shannon's company of foot.

Fry, Peter, age 56, sailor, born England, enlisted 17 May 1759 in Captain Charles Stewart's company [probably one of the Associated Companies of Bucks County] on a return dated June 1759.

Frydel, Christopher, age 24, born Germany, enlisted 07 February 1758, private in Captain John Nicholas Weatherholt's company which enlisted for a term of three years and stationed in Heydelberg Township, Northampton County, in March and April 1758.

Fuchs, Adam, age 29, laborer, enlisted 30 June 1746 in Captain John Deimer's company.

Fulmer, John, ensign in Captain John Brady's company in Lieutenant Colonel Commandant Asher Clayton's Second Battalion of the Pennsylvania Regiment commanded by the Hon. J. Penn after 1763.

Fulton, James, lieutenant in Captain Samuel Postlewait's company of Colonel William Clapham's Regiment of New Levies.

Fulton, William, age 26, weaver, born Ireland, enlisted 22 May 1759 in Captain Robert Boyd's company [probably in the Third Battalion]. On a return dated May and June 1759.

Funniman, Henry, age 28, laborer, born Jersey, enlisted 28 April 1759, private in Captain John Haslet's company in the Pennsylvania Regiment. On a list of recruits dated 20 May 1759.

Furbe, Caleb, ensign in Captain Daniel James's company from the Lower District of Mother-Kill Hundred, Kent County, Delaware, vice Warren.

Furey, Michael, ensign in Captain William Clapham, Jr.'s company of the First Battalion of the Pennsylvania Regiment from 19 April 1760.

Furlong, Patrick, age 45, cooper, born Ireland, enlisted 28 April 1758. On a return of Captain John Blackwood's company in the Third Battalion dated 22 May 1758.

Furnantz, Anthony, private, age 31, laborer, born Madeira, Portugal, enlisted 01 May 1758 for the campaign in the lower counties. On a return of Captain McClughan's company dated 17 May 1758.

Futhey, Henry, age 21, laborer, born Ireland, enlisted 22 July 1746 in Captain John Shannon's company of foot.

Gaab, George Adam, quartermaster in Captain Edward Jones's Independent Company of Horse, Philadelphia in 1756.

Gaily, Samuel, private in Captain Patterson's company from 27 December 1757 stationed eastward of the Susquehanna. On a muster roll dated 08 March 1758.

Galbraith, James, captain, in the Associated Regiment of the West End of Lancaster County in 1747–8.

Galbraith, James, lieutenant colonel, in the Associated Regiment of the West End of Lancaster County in 1747–8.

Galbraith, John, captain, in the Associated Regiment of the West End of Lancaster County in 1747–8.

Galbreath, Nevin, sergeant in Captain Joseph Shippen's company in Colonel William Clapham's Regiment in 1756, the regiment in garrison at Fort Augusta, Shamokin, and listed in Shippen's Account Book. Enlisted 06 September 1756.

Gale, Nicholas, seaman on the provincial ship *Pennsylvania* on 17 August 1757.

Gallagher, Edward, age 17, born Chester, Pennsylvania, private in Captain John Haslett's company enlisted on 12 May 1758 and last paid on 21 May 1758.

Gallagher, Felix, age 22, laborer, born Ireland, enlisted 19 July 1746 in Captain John Shannon's company of foot.

Gallagher, Henry, age 25, sawyer, born Ireland, enlisted 27 June 1746 in Captain William Trent's company.

Gallagher, John, enlisted 09 May 1759, private in Captain Henry Van Bibber's company of the Lower County. On a return dated 04 June 1759.

Gallagher, John, hired 30 May 1757 as a battoe man, Master George Allen.

Gallagher, Michael, private in Captain Patterson's company from 01 December 1757 stationed eastward of the Susquehanna. On a muster roll dated 08 March 1758.

Gallagher, Thomas, age 23, laborer, born Ireland, enlisted 10 July 1746 in Captain Samuel Perry's company.

Gallery, George, a member of Captain Joseph Armstrong's Company on 07 August 1755, raised in Cumberland County.

Gallihan, Daniel, a private in Captain Joseph Inslee's Company of Foot, Newtown, Bucks County, in 1756.

Galt, Robert, *see* Robert Gates.

Gamell, James, landsman on the provincial ship *Pennsylvania* on 17 August 1757.

Gamm, Joseph, a private in Captain Joseph Inslee's Company of Foot, Newtown, Bucks County, in 1756.

Gandey, John, age 22, butcher, born Warrenton, England, enlisted 26 April 1759, private in Captain William Johnston's company in the Pennsylvania Regiment. On a return dated 12 May 1759.

Gano, Daniel, age 21, laborer, born Delaware, enlisted 29 April 1758 by Captain Benjamin Noxon.

Gano, George, captain in one of two regiments of New Castle County in 1747–8.

Gano, George, captain, in the Apoquinimink Hundred company of Colonel Jacob Van Bibber's Lower Regiment of New Castle County in 1756.

Gardiner, Richard, captain from 10 May 1759 in a company of Colonel William Clapham's Regiment of New Levies.

Gardner, _____, ensign in Captain David Jamison's company from 10 March 1758, stationed at Fort Augusta.

Gardner, Francis, ensign in the Associated Regiment of Chester County in 1747.

Gardner, Jacob, hired 30 May 1757 as a battoe man, Master George Allen.

Gardner, Mathew, age 18, carpenter, born Scotland, enlisted 11 May 1758. On a return of Captain John Blackwood's company in the Third Battalion dated 22 May 1758.

Gardner, Richard, promoted to captain after serving in the Pennsylvania Regiment of Three Battalions in 1758 and 1759. Reported as "discontinued".

Garnell, William, lieutenant in one of the Associated Companies of York County in 1756.

Garner, Samuel, age 19, laborer, born Bucks, Pennsylvania, enlisted 15 May 1759, private in Captain John Mathers's company in the Pennsylvania Regiment. On a return dated 15 June 1759.

Garraway, Charles, captain of a company from 23 December 1757 stationed eastward of the Susquehanna.

Garraway, lieutenant of Captain Joseph Shippen's Company, Third Battalion (known as the Augusta Regiment) from 15 April 1756. Captain in a company in the First Battalion from 23 December 1757. Appears to have been replaced by John Prentice in March 1759.

Garraway, William, ensign in one of two regiments of New Castle County in 1747–8.

Garrett, John, age 23, laborer, born Maryland, enlisted 24 April 1758 by Captain Benjamin Noxon.

Garrett, Richard, age 20, laborer, born Maryland, enlisted 01 May 1758 by Captain Benjamin Noxon.

Garrigue, Matthew, age 34, tailor, born St. Christopher's, enlisted 27 June 1746 in Captain William Trent's company.

Garrigues, Francis, ensign in the Associated Regiment of Foot of Philadelphia on 29 Dec 1747.

Garrison, Benjamin, age 22, laborer, born New Castle, Delaware, enlisted 25 April 1759, private in Captain James Armstrong's company in Colonel William Clapham's Pennsylvania Regiment. On a return dated 01 June 1759.

Garrison, John, age 19, laborer, born New Castle, Delaware, enlisted 20 May 1759, private in Captain James Armstrong's company in Colonel William Clapham's Pennsylvania Regiment. On a return dated 01 June 1759.

Garvin, Matthew, age 21, laborer, born Ireland, enlisted 03 May 1758. On a return of Captain John Bull's company dated 01 July 1758.

Gary, John, age 25, laborer, born Sussex, Delaware, enlisted 15 July 1746 in Captain John Shannon's company of foot.

Gass, John, a private in Captain Samuel Mifflin's Association Battery Company of Philadelphia in 1756.

Gates, Robert, on a list of men recruited by Captain Andrew McDowell's company in the Second Battalion, Pennsylvania Regiment dated 04 June 1759.

Gatte, George, age 31, tanner, born Germany, enlisted 05 May 1758. On a return of Captain John Blackwood's company in the Third Battalion dated 22 May 1758.

Geary, John, *see* Gary, John.

Gebhard, Jacob, a private in Captain Adam Heylman's Company, of the St. Vincent and Puke's Land Association on 10 May 1756.

Geiger, Henry, ensign in Captain Conrad Weiser's Company in the First Battalion from 20 December 1755. Lieutenant in Captain Edward Ward's company in the First Battalion from 21 December 1757 stationed westward of the Susquehanna.

Geiger, Henry, ensign on a List of Officers in the Province Pay, 1756 in the First Battalion of the Pennsylvania Regiment with a commission date of 20 December 1755. {PA5, I, 88}

Geiger, Henry, promoted to lieutenant after serving in the Pennsylvania Regiment of Three Battalions in 1758 and 1759.

Geisinger, Peter, shot and killed 22 June 1754 {See A Journal in 1754, A(1) 2, p. 160}

Gensal, Matthais, a private in Captain Edward Jones's Independent Company of Horse, Philadelphia in 1756.

George Thompson, ensign in Lieutenant Colonel Commandant Asher Clayton's Company of the Second Battalion of the Pennsylvania Regiment commanded by the Hon. J. Penn in 1764.

George, Adam, age 17, born Germany, enlisted 01 September 1757, private in Captain John Nicholas Weatherholt's company which enlisted for a term of three years and stationed in Heydelberg Township, Northampton County, in March and April 1758.

Gesser, John Adam, age 40, laborer, born Germany, enlisted 12 July 1746 in Captain Samuel Perry's company.

Gethins, Daniel, age 28, trader, born Ireland, enlisted 07 August 1746 in Captain William Trent's company.

Getz, Andreas, *see* Andreas, Gitz.

Ghilin, Cæsar, a private in Captain John Kidd's Independent Company of Foot, Philadelphia in 1756.

Gibbin, Daniel, age 21, laborer, born Ireland, enlisted 03 May 1758 by Captain Benjamin Noxon.

Gibbin, Thomas, private in Captain Patterson's company from 14 January 1758 stationed eastward of the Susquehanna. On a muster roll dated 08 March 1758.

Gibbons, John, private, age 28, laborer, born Devon, England, enlisted 26 April 1758 for the campaign in the lower counties. On a return of Captain McClughan's company dated 17 May 1758.

Gibbony, John, ensign in one of the Associated Companies of Lancaster County in 1756.

Gibson, William, age 30, laborer, born Ireland, enlisted 27 April 1759, private in Captain James Armstrong's company in Colonel William Clapham's Pennsylvania Regiment. On a return dated 01 June 1759.

Gibson, William, captain, in one of the Associated Companies of York County in 1756.

Gilbert, Bernard, born Germany, enlisted 14 July 1746 in Captain Samuel Perry's company.

Gilbert, Frederick, private who enlisted 20 April 1756 in Captain Joseph Shippen's company in Colonel William Clapham's Regiment in 1756, the regiment in garrison at Fort Augusta, Shamokin, and listed in Shippen's Account Book. Deserted with arms, regimentals, and blanket on 14 October 1756.

Gilburat, George Christopher, a private in Captain John Kidd's Independent Company of Foot, Philadelphia in 1756.

Gilchrist, James, lieutenant in the Associated Regiment of the West End of Lancaster County in 1747–8.

Gill, James, age 35, cooper, born England, enlisted 04 May 1749 in Captain Richard Gardiner's company in Colonel William Denney's Pennsylvania Regiment.

Gillespie, Abel, age 21, cooper, born Ireland, enlisted 16 July 1746 in Captain Samuel Perry's company.

Gillespie, James, captain then lieutenant colonel, in the Associated Regiment of the West End of Lancaster County in 1747–8.

Gillespie, James, colonel in the Regiment of the West End of Lancaster County in 1747–8.

Gillespie, Peter, private in Captain Patterson's company from 20 December 1757 stationed eastward of the Susquehanna. On a muster roll dated 08 March 1758.

Gillis, John, seaman on the provincial ship *Pennsylvania* on 17 August 1757.

Gilmor, William, age 17, born Kent, Delaware, tailor, private in Captain John Haslett's company enlisted on 10 May 1758 and last paid on 21 May 1758.

Giltner, Conrad, age 35, born Germany, enlisted 16 May 1759, private in Captain Robert Curry's company in Colonel William

Clapham's Pennsylvania Regiment. On a return dated June 1759.

Gips, Nicholas, age 20, born Germany, enlisted 01 September 1757, private in Captain John Nicholas Weatherholt's company which enlisted for a term of three years and stationed in Heydelberg Township, Northampton County, in March and April 1758.

Gitz, Andreas, private who enlisted 27 April 1756 in Captain Joseph Shippen's company in Colonel William Clapham's Regiment in 1756, the regiment in garrison at Fort Augusta, Shamokin, and listed in Shippen's Account Book.

Givens, Samuel, on a return of Captain David Hunter's Company [probably from York County] in Colonel William Clapham's Regiment of New Levies dated 26 May 1759.

Glassford, Henry, captain in the Associated Regiment of Chester County in 1747.

Gleghorn, Matthew, age 34, laborer, born Ireland, enlisted 08 May 1758 by Captain Benjamin Noxon.

Glen, Thomas, age 30, laborer, born Pennsylvania, enlisted 09 May 1749 in Captain Richard Gardiner's company in Colonel William Denney's Pennsylvania Regiment.

Glin, Thomas, *see* Glen, Thomas.

Godfrey, Thomas, ensign from 02 May 1758 in Captain John Blackwood's company in the Third Battalion. On a return dated 22 May 1758.

Goff, Ephraim, age 25, mariner, born New England, enlisted 08 May 1758. On a weekly return of Captain Samuel Jones's company in 1758.

Goggin, John, gunner's mate of the provincial ship *Pennsylvania* on 17 August 1757.

Golden, Anthony, ensign in one of two regiments of New Castle County in 1747–8.

Golden, Eleazer, private, age 34, sailor, born Cape May, New Jersey, enlisted 25 April 1758 for the campaign in the lower counties. On a return of Captain McClughan's company dated 17 May 1758.

Gollerthon, William, age 25, laborer, born Virginia, enlisted 07 August 1746 in Captain William Trent's company.

Good, George, a private in Captain Adam Heylman's Company, of the St. Vincent and Puke's Land Association on 10 May 1756.

Good, Jacob, a private in Captain Adam Heylman's Company, of the St. Vincent and Puke's Land Association on 10 May 1756.

Goodfellow, Daniel, age 20, laborer, born Ireland, enlisted 21 July 1746 in Captain John Shannon's company of foot.

Goodhouse, Peter, age 19, laborer, 08 July 1746 in Captain John Deimer's company.

Gooding, Isaac, ensign in the St. George's Hundred company of Colonel Jacob Van Bibber's Lower Regiment of New Castle County in 1756.

Gooding, Jacob, captain in one of two regiments of New Castle County in 1747–8.

Gooding, Jacob, captain in the Red Lyon Hundred company of Colonel Jacob Van Bibber's Lower Regiment of New Castle County in 1756.

Gooding, Jacob, Jr., first lieutenant from April 18, 1758, promoted to captain 13 June 1758, vice Noxon,. On a list of officers of the lower government on Delaware, 1758/9.

Gooding, John, Sen., colonel, in one of two regiments of New Castle County in 1747–8.

Gooding, William, age 25, laborer, born Ireland, enlisted 07 May 1759 in Captain Robert Boyd's company [probably in the Third Battalion]. On a return dated May and June 1759. Died 03 June 1759.

Goodman, Conrad, age 22, laborer, born Germany, enlisted 20 July 1746 in Captain Samuel Perry's company.

Goodwin, Abraham, age 41, carpenter, born Pennsylvania, enlisted 06 May 1758. On a return of Captain John Blackwood's company in the Third Battalion dated 22 May 1758.

Goodwin, John, age 30, laborer, born England, enlisted 14 July 1746 in Captain William Trent's company.

Gordon, Lewis, captain stationed on the frontier in Northampton County with one sergeant and eleven men at Easton on 01 June

1764 as part of a unit under the command of Major Asher Clayton.

Gordon, Philip, age 20, laborer, born Bucks, Pennsylvania, enlisted 08 May 1759, private in Captain Joseph Richardson's company of the Third Battalion in the Pennsylvania Regiment. On a return of recruits dated 1759.

Gordon, Samuel, captain in one of the Associated Companies of York County in 1756.

Gordon, Thomas, a private in Captain Edward Jones's Independent Company of Horse, Philadelphia in 1756.

Gorley, Henry, age 30, laborer, born Donegal, Ireland, enlisted 22 May 1759, private in Captain John Mathers's company in the Pennsylvania Regiment. On a return dated 15 June 1759.

Gorrel, John, age 16, laborer, born Chester, Pennsylvania, enlisted 08 June 1759, private in Captain John Mathers's company in the Pennsylvania Regiment. On a return dated 15 June 1759.

Goshean, Peter, a private in Captain John Kidd's Independent Company of Foot, Philadelphia in 1756.

Goudy, James, hired 28 May 1757 as a battoe man, Master George Allen.

Goudy, Samuel, hired 10 June 1757 as a battoe man, Master George Allen.

Gower, John Nicholas, age 23, tailor, enlisted 12 July 1746 in Captain John Deimer's company.

Grace, Robert, captain in the Associated Regiment of Chester County in 1747.

Grace, William, age 30, laborer, born Ireland, enlisted 21 July 1746 in Captain William Trent's company.

Graff, John George, age 23, laborer, enlisted 14 July 1746 in Captain John Deimer's company.

Graham, Francis, age 35, laborer, born Ireland, enlisted 26 April 1758 by Captain Benjamin Noxon. Formerly with Sir William Pepperal.

Graham, Francis, ensign in one of two regiments of New Castle County in 1747–8.

Graham, James, captain in the Associated Regiment of Chester County in 1747.

Graham, James, captain in the Associated Regiment of the West End of Lancaster County in 1747–8.

Graham, John, private, age 21, laborer, born Slator Neck, Delaware, enlisted 24 April 1758 for the campaign in the lower counties. On a return of Captain McClughan's company dated 17 May 1758.

Graham, William, age 23, laborer, born Derry, Ireland, enlisted 03 May 1759, corporal in Captain John Haslet's company in the Pennsylvania Regiment. On a list of recruits dated 20 May 1759.

Granshaar, John, age 21, born Germany, house-carpenter, enlisted 05 December 1757, private in Captain John Nicholas Weatherholt's company which enlisted for a term of three years and stationed in Heydelberg Township, Northampton County, in March and April 1758.

Grant, John, a private in Captain Joseph Inslee's Company of Foot, Newtown, Bucks County, in 1756.

Grant, John, age 31, clothier, born Ireland, enlisted 11 August 1746 in Captain William Trent's company.

Grantham, Charles, lieutenant in Captain Samuel West's company of the First Battalion of the Pennsylvania Regiment from 02 May 1760.

Grantlet, John, age 23, laborer, born Maryland, enlisted 29 April 1758 by Captain Benjamin Noxon.

Gray, Benjamin, age 18, miller, born New Castle, Delaware, enlisted 07 May 1759, private in Captain James Armstrong's company in Colonel William Clapham's Pennsylvania Regiment. On a return dated 01 June 1759.

Gray, George, Jun., lieutenant in the Associated Regiment of Foot of Philadelphia on 29 Dec 1747.

Gray, George, lieutenant in the Associated Regiment of Bucks County in 1748.

Gray, Joseph, enlisted 28 June 1746 in Captain William Trent's company, deserted 12 July 1746.

Gray, Joseph, landsman on the provincial ship *Pennsylvania* on 17 August 1757.

Gray, Thomas, captain in the Miln Creek Hundred company of Colonel William Armstrong's Upper Regiment of New Castle County in 1756.

Graydon, Alexander, Captain then Colonel, in the Associated Regiment of Bucks County in 1748. Captain in one of the Associated Companies of Bucks County in 1756. Captain in one of the new levies in May 1758.

Graydon, Caleb, ensign in Captain Caleb Graydon's company from 13 December 1757, stationed at Fort Augusta. Ensign from 02 December 1757 in Captain James Burd's company in the Second Battalion. Lieutenant from 13 November 1758 in the same company, vice Hayes. Promoted to captain after serving in the Pennsylvania Regiment of Three Battalions in 1758 and 1759. Reported to have "Joined Colonel Francis". Quartermaster of the First Battalion in 1760. Captain of a company in the First Battalion of the Pennsylvania Regiment from 21 August 1763.

Grebs, Simon, age 42, tailor, enlisted 28 June 1746 in Captain John Deimer's company.

Green, James, age 29, laborer, born Ireland, enlisted 01 May 1758. On a weekly return of Captain Samuel Jones's company in 1758.

Green, Thomas, midshipman of the provincial ship *Pennsylvania* on 17 August 1757.

Green, Timothy, captain stationed on the frontier in Lancaster County with one sergeant and fifteen men at John Cameron's, Hanover Township, on 01 June 1764 as part of a unit under the command of Major Asher Clayton.

Green, Timothy, captain of a company in Lieutenant Colonel Commandant Asher Clayton's Second Battalion of the Pennsylvania Regiment commanded by the Hon. J. Penn from 18 July 1763.

Green, William, a private in Captain Samuel Mifflin's Association Battery Company of Philadelphia in 1756.

Green, William, age 22, carpenter, born Sussex, Delaware, sergeant in Captain John Wright's company of the Lower County. On a muster dated 11 May 1759.

Green, William, ensign in one of the Associated Companies of Kent County in June 1748.

Greenwood, Joseph, enlisted 18 May 1758 in Captain French Battell's company of Lower County Provincials.

Greer, John, landsman on the provincial ship *Pennsylvania* on 17 August 1757.

Gregan, Edward, age 40, laborer, born Ireland, enlisted 03 July 1746 in Captain John Deimer's company.

Gregg, Andrew, captain in the Associated Regiment of the West End of Lancaster County in 1747–8.

Gregory, George, *see* George Creekery.

Gribbin, James, age 27, laborer, born Maryland, enlisted 29 April 1758 by Captain Benjamin Noxon.

Griffin, Evan, age 30, laborer, born Ireland, 14 July 1746 in Captain John Deimer's company.

Griffith, John, age 23, laborer, born Wales, enlisted 30 April 1759, private in Captain Joseph Richardson's company of the Third Battalion in the Pennsylvania Regiment. On a return of recruits dated 1759.

Griffith, Richard, age 41, farmer, born Wales, enlisted 03 May 1759, private in Captain William Johnston's company in the Pennsylvania Regiment. On a return dated 12 May 1759.

Griffith, Timothy, captain in one of two regiments of New Castle County in 1747–8.

Griffith, William, age 30, shoemaker, born England, enlisted 30 June 1746 in Captain William Trent's company.

Griffiths, Griffith, 1st lieutenant in the Associated Regiment in the County of Philadelphia in 1748.

Grigan, Edward, *see* Gregan, Edward.

Grim, Charles, age 26, laborer, born Germany, enlisted 07 July 1746 in Captain John Deimer's company.

Grim, George, age 42, weaver, born Germany, enlisted 10 July 1746 in Captain John Deimer's company.

Grim, Jacob, age 23, smith, born Germany, enlisted 09 July 1746 in Captain John Deimer's company.

Grimes, William, age 20, laborer, born Ireland, enlisted 18 May 1758 by Lieutenant William McClay for Captain John Montgomery's company.

Grissal, William, private, age 32, scribler, born Stroud, England, enlisted 12 May 1758 for the campaign in the lower counties. On a return of Captain McClughan's company dated 17 May 1758.

Grissy, Anthony, a private in Captain George Armstrong's Company, Second Battalion in 1756; missing at the capture of Kittanning.

Grist Francis, a private in Captain Samuel Mifflin's Association Battery Company of Philadelphia in 1756.

Groghan, George, captain in the provincial service in 1755 at Aughwick.

Groin, Robert, a member of Captain Joseph Armstrong's Company on 07 August 1755, raised in Cumberland County.

Gross, Frederick, age 21, cooper, born Germany, enlisted 01 May 1758. On a return of Captain John Blackwood's company in the Third Battalion dated 22 May 1758.

Ground, Nicholas, age 18, laborer, born Germany, enlisted 30 April 1759, private in Captain Joseph Richardson's company of the Third Battalion in the Pennsylvania Regiment. On a return of recruits dated 1759.

Grove, Anthony, private who enlisted 08 May 1756 in Captain Joseph Shippen's company in Colonel William Clapham's Regiment in 1756, the regiment in garrison at Fort Augusta, Shamokin, and listed in Shippen's Account Book.

Groves, Jonathan, private, age 20, laborer, born New Castle, Delaware, enlisted 21 April 1758 for the campaign in the lower counties. On a return of Captain McClughan's company dated 17 May 1758.

Groves, Thomas, master-of-arms of the provincial ship *Pennsylvania* on 17 August 1757.

Grubb, Emanuel, captain in the Brandy Wine Hundred company of Colonel William Armstrong's Upper Regiment of New Castle County in 1756.

Grubb, John, private, age 26, tanner, born Brandywine Hundred, Delaware, enlisted 11 May 1758 for the campaign in the lower counties. On a return of Captain McClughan's company dated 17 May 1758.

Grubb, Samuel, captain from 07 May 1759 of a company of Colonel William Clapham's Regiment of New Levies.

Grubb, Samuel, promoted to captain after serving in the Pennsylvania Regiment of Three Battalions in 1758 and 1759. Reported as "dead".

Grubb, Thomas, ensign in one of the Associated Companies of Lancaster County in 1756.

Grubb, Thomas, ensign in the Associated Regiment of the West End of Lancaster County in 1747–8.

Gruber, Anthony, age 34, laborer, born Germany, enlisted 08 May 1758. On a return of Captain John Bull's company dated 01 July 1758. Formerly in Pennsylvania Regiment.

Grundy, Thomas, private, age 33, bricklayer, born Liverpool, England, enlisted 27 April 1758 for the campaign in the lower counties. On a return of Captain McClughan's company dated 17 May 1758.

Grunnet, Christopher, age 30, saddler, born Germany, enlisted 01 May 1759, private in Captain James Armstrong's company in Colonel William Clapham's Pennsylvania Regiment. On a return dated 01 June 1759.

Guinop, Joseph, ensign in Captain John Lytle's company of the Second Battalion of the Pennsylvania Regiment from 24 April 1760.

Guinop, Thomas, a private in Captain Joseph Inslee's Company of Foot, Newtown, Bucks County, in 1756.

Gumry, Samuel, age 20, weaver, born England, enlisted 02 May 1758 by Captain Benjamin Noxon.

Gunning, Alexander, age 20, laborer, born Ireland, enlisted 07 May 1759 in Captain Robert Boyd's company [probably in the Third Battalion]. On a return dated May and June 1759.

Gunter, William, age 20, laborer, born England, enlisted 19 August 1746 in Captain William Trent's company.

Guthrie, James, a member of Captain Joseph Armstrong's Company on 07 August 1755, raised in Cumberland County.

Guthry, John, age 24, weaver, born Down, Ireland, enlisted 19 May 1759, sergeant in Captain John Haslet's company in the Pennsylvania Regiment. On a list of recruits dated 20 May 1759.

Gutton, Matthew, a member of Captain David Jameson's Company at McCord's Fort on 02 April 1756 when he was wounded.

Guttrey, Samuel, private in Captain John Singleton's company in service between 01 May and 08 May 1758.

Guy, Nicholas, age 21, born Virginia, private in Captain John Wright's company of the Lower County. On a muster dated 11 May 1759.

Gwinnup, Joseph, age 22, cordwainer, born Pennsylvania, enlisted 03 May 1758. On a return of Captain John Bull's company dated 01 July 1758.

Gwinnup, William, age 39, laborer, born Pennsylvania, enlisted 17 May 1758. On a return of Captain John Bull's company dated 01 July 1758.

Hadden, William, ensign from 25 April 1758 in Captain David Hunter's company in the First Battalion.

Hadden, William, promoted to lieutenant after serving in the Pennsylvania Regiment of Three Battalions in 1758 and 1759. Reported as "left the Province".

Haddon, John, ensign from 06 June 1758 in Captain John Montgomery's company in the Third Battalion.

Hagard, William, age 20, cordwainer, born Ulster, Ireland, enlisted 29 April 1759, private in Captain James Armstrong's company in Colonel William Clapham's Pennsylvania Regiment. On a return dated 01 June 1759.

Hall, Abraham, on a list of men recruited by Captain Andrew McDowell's company in the Second Battalion, Pennsylvania Regiment dated 04 June 1759.

Hall, David, captain in the Northern District of Lewes and Rehoboth Hundred company of Colonel Jacob Kollock's

Regiment of Sussex County in 1756. Described as Lewes District Company in 1758.

Hall, George, private, age 22, cooper, born Milford Hundred, Delaware, enlisted 10 May 1758 for the campaign in the lower counties. On a return of Captain McClughan's company dated 17 May 1758.

Hall, Hugh, ensign from 04 May 1758 in Captain Adam Read's company of the Third Battalion. Reported to be of a reputable and good family in Lancaster County.

Hall, Isaac, ensign in the Lower Part of Mispillim Hundred company of Colonel John Vining's Regiment of Kent County Militia, Upon Delaware in 1756.

Hall, Jacob, captain in the Associated Regiment in the County of Philadelphia in 1748.

Hall, Jacob, ensign in one of the companies of Colonel Jacob Duché's Philadelphia Regiment in 1756.

Hall, John, captain in the Associated Regiment in the County of Philadelphia in 1748.

Hall, John, ensign in the Associated Regiment of Bucks County in 1748.

Hall, John, ensign in the Northern District of Lewes and Rehoboth Hundred Captain David Hall's company of Colonel Jacob Kollock's Regiment of Sussex County in 1756. Reported dead in 1758. Described as Lewes District Company in 1758.

Hall, Jonas, age 25, blacksmith, born Ireland, enlisted 14 July 1746 in Captain John Shannon's company of foot.

Hall, Moses, age 28, born Maryland, private in Captain John Wright's company of the Lower County. On a muster list dated 11 May 1759.

Hall, Thomas, age 25, mariner, born England, enlisted 06 May 1758. On a weekly return of Captain Samuel Jones's company in 1758.

Hall, Thomas, enlisted 20 May 1758 in Captain French Battell's company of Lower County Provincials.

Hall, William, enlisted 21 May 1759, private in Captain Henry Van Bibber's company of the Lower County. On a return dated 04 June 1759.

Haller, Henry, ensign from 15 December 1757 in Joseph Shippen's company in the Second Battalion, stationed at Fort Augusta. Reported missing at Grant's defeat near Fort Duquesne, 14 September 1758.

Haller, Henry, promoted to lieutenant after serving in the Pennsylvania Regiment of Three Battalions in 1758 and 1759.

Halms, William, *see* Holmes, William.

Hambel, Adam, promoted to lieutenant after serving in the Pennsylvania Regiment of Three Battalions in 1758 and 1759. Reported as "doubtful".

Hambright, John, Captain from 02 May 1758 in a troop of Light Horse in the Second Battalion.

Hambright, John, Captain from 14 December 1757 of a company stationed at Fort Augusta.

Hambright, John, ensign in the Associated Regiment of Chester County in 1747. Captain of a company of the Third Battalion (known as the Augusta Regiment) from 12 June 1756. Captain in a company in the Second Battalion from 14/15 December 1757 stationed at Fort Augusta.

Hambright, John, promoted to captain after serving in the Pennsylvania Regiment of Three Battalions in 1758 and 1759.

Hamiltoin, Robert, age 35, weaver, born Ireland, enlisted 27 May 1759 in Captain Charles Stewart's company [probably one of the Associated Companies of Bucks County] on a return dated June 1759.

Hamilton, Alexander, hired 17 June 1757 as a battoe man, Master George Allen.

Hamilton, Hance, lieutenant colonel of the First Battalion (John Armstrongs's) of Colonel William Denny's Regiment, 31 May 1758; replaced by Patrick Work in March 1759.

Hamilton, Hans (or Hance), captain in the provincial service in 1755. Captain of a company in the Second Battalion from 16 January 1756. Captain of a company from 06 December 1757 stationed westward of the Susquehanna. Stationed at Fort Bedford, 12 April 1759.

Hamilton, Hans, promoted to the rank of lieutenant colonel after having served in the Pennsylvania Regiment of Three Battalions, 1758 and 1759.

Hamilton, Hugh, ensign in the Associated Regiment in the County of Philadelphia in 1748.

Hamilton, James, age 21, hunter, born Pennsylvania, enlisted 02 May 1758 by Captain Benjamin Noxon.

Hamilton, James, age 21, laborer, born Chester, Pennsylvania, enlisted 21 May 1759 in Captain Robert Boyd's company [probably in the Third Battalion]. On a return dated May and June 1759.

Hamilton, James, age 24, laborer, born Ireland, enlisted 21 July 1746 in Captain Samuel Perry's company.

Hamilton, James, Esq., lieutenant governor and commander-in-chief in 1749.

Hamilton, Samuel, age 20, born Lancaster, Pennsylvania, private in Captain John Singleton's company in service between 01 May and 08 May 1758.

Hamilton, Thomas, captain from 16 May 1758 of a company in the Third Battalion. Captain from 01 May 1759 of a company of Colonel William Clapham's Regiment of New Levies.

Hamilton, Thomas, hired 02 June 1757 as a battoe man, Master George Allen.

Hamilton, Thomas, promoted to captain after serving in the Pennsylvania Regiment of Three Battalions in 1758 and 1759.

Hammon, John, age 30, laborer, born Ireland, enlisted 22 July 1746 in Captain John Shannon's company of foot.

Hammond, Lawrence, enlisted 19 May 1758 in Captain French Battell's company of Lower County Provincials.

Hamper, Joseph, ensign in Captain John Kidd's Independent Company of Foot, Philadelphia in 1756.

Hank, John, age 21, farmer, born Pennsylvania, enlisted 21 May 1759 in Captain Charles Stewart's company [probably one of the Associated Companies of Bucks County] on a return dated June 1759.

Hanna, John, age 23, laborer, born Ireland, enlisted 09 May 1758. On a return of Captain John Bull's company dated 01 July 1758. Formerly in Pennsylvania Regiment.

Hannagin, Dennis, age 15, laborer, born Ireland, enlisted 13 June 1759 in Captain Charles Stewart's company [probably one of the Associated Companies of Bucks County] on a return dated June 1759.

Hannow, Alexander, private in Captain John Singleton's company in service between 01 May and 08 May 1758.

Hanzer, Samuel, age 24, born Sussex, Delaware, private in Captain John Wright's company of the Lower County. On a muster dated 11 May 1759.

Hanzer, Thomas, age 19, born Sussex, Delaware, private in Captain John Wright's company of the Lower County. On a muster dated 11 May 1759.

Hapnor, John, age 23, born Philadelphia, baker, "pock pitted, a Dutchman", private in Captain John Singleton's company in service between 01 May and 08 May 1758.

Haragan, Conrad, age 18, laborer, born Ireland, enlisted 16 May 1758 by Lieutenant William McClay for Captain John Montgomery's company.

Haragon, Cornelius, *see* Cornelius Harigan.

Harbadge, Edward, private, age 24, brushmaker, born London, England, enlisted 26 April 1758 for the campaign in the lower counties. On a return of Captain McClughan's company dated 17 May 1758.

Harbaugh, Francis, age 34, laborer, born Germany, enlisted 09 May 1758. On a return of Captain John Bull's company dated 01 July 1758.

Harder, Henry, age 24, laborer, born Holland, enlisted 30 April 1759, private in Captain John Haslet's company in the Pennsylvania Regiment. On a list of recruits dated 20 May 1759.

Harding, William, age 27, watchmaker, born England, enlisted 10 May 1759 in Captain Charles Stewart's company [probably one of the Associated Companies of Bucks County] on a return dated June 1759.

Harford, David, on a list of men recruited by Captain Andrew McDowell's company in the Second Battalion, Pennsylvania Regiment dated 04 June 1759.

Harigan, Cornelius, age 28, laborer, born Ireland, enlisted 25 April 1758 by Captain Benjamin Noxon.

Harkins, Edward, age 30, laborer, born Ireland, enlisted 03 May 1758. On a return of Captain John Bull's company dated 01 July 1758.

Harkins, James, age 34, laborer, born Ireland, enlisted 22 July 1746 in Captain John Shannon's company of foot.

Harman, Job, age 21, laborer, born Sussex, Delaware, enlisted 14 July 1746 in Captain John Shannon's company of foot.

Harper, Josiah, ensign from 30 April 1759 in Captain Joseph Richard's company of Colonel William Clapham's Regiment of New Levies. From Lancaster County. Recommended by Thomas Boude and James Arbuckle.

Harragan, Cornelius, enlisted 09 May 1759, private in Captain Henry Van Bibber's company of the Lower County. On a return dated 04 June 1759.

Harris, David, ensign not assigned in the First Battalion of the Pennsylvania Regiment from 10 May 1760.

Harris, Henry, age 30, laborer, born Wales, enlisted 24 July 1746 in Captain John Shannon's company of foot.

Harris, James, age 33, laborer, born Ireland, enlisted 13 July 1746 in Captain William Trent's company.

Harris, John, ensign to captain on 04 August 1748, in the Associated Regiment of the West End of Lancaster County in 1747–8.

Harris, Thomas, captain in the Associated Regiment of the West End of Lancaster County in 1747–8.

Harris, Walter, age 20, mariner, born England, enlisted 01 May 1758. On a weekly return of Captain Samuel Jones's company in 1758.

Harris, William, age 25, laborer, born Wales, enlisted 15 May 1758. On a return of Captain John Blackwood's company in the Third Battalion dated 22 May 1758.

Harris, William, age 26, laborer, born England, enlisted 10 May 1758. On a weekly return of Captain Samuel Jones's company in 1758.

Harry, Daniel, ensign, commander of Fort Henry in 1754. {See A Journal in 1754, A(1) 2: 159}, provincial officer from June 1754 at Fort Lebanon. Ensign in Captain John Nicholas Wetterholt's company of the First Battalion from 26 January 1756. Left out in the reorganization of December 1757, but appears to be an ensign in Captain Jacob Morgan's company in the Second Battalion on 06/07 December 1757, stationed eastward of the Susquehanna. Appears to have been replaced in the company by Joseph Armstrong by 22 February 1758.

Harry, George, age 19, laborer, enlisted 08 July 1746 in Captain John Deimer's company.

Hart, Henry, age 24, shoemaker, born Germany, enlisted 29 April 1758. On a return of Captain John Blackwood's company in the Third Battalion dated 22 May 1758.

Hart, Hugh, age 23, born Armagh, Ireland, laborer, private in Captain John Haslett's company enlisted on 22 May 1758 and last paid on 21 May 1758.

Hart, Hugh, age 29, laborer, born Ireland, enlisted 30 April 1759, private in Captain John Haslet's company in the Pennsylvania Regiment. On a list of recruits dated 20 May 1759.

Hart, James, lieutenant in the Associated Regiment of Bucks County in 1748.

Hart, John, lieutenant, a member of Captain Adam Heylman's Company, of the St. Vincent and Puke's Land Association on 10 May 1756.

Hart, Joseph, ensign in the Associated Regiment of Bucks County in 1748.

Hart, William, age 34, sawyer, born England, enlisted 22 July 1746 in Captain John Deimer's company.

Hart, William, ensign in the Associated Regiment of Bucks County in 1748.

Hartman, John, private in Captain Adam Heylman's Company, of the St. Vincent and Puke's Land Association on 10 May 1756.

Hartman, Moses, private in Captain Edward Jones's Independent Company of Horse, Philadelphia in 1756.

Hartz, George, private in Captain Adam Heylman's Company, of the St. Vincent and Puke's Land Association on 10 May 1756.

Harvey, Benjamin, private in Captain Joseph Inslee's Company of Foot, Newtown, Bucks County, in 1756.

Harvey, Thomas, age 17, born Chester, Pennsylvania, private in Captain John Haslett's company enlisted on 12 May 1758 and last paid on 21 May 1758.

Harvey, Thomas, age 24, born New England, cordwainer, private in Captain John Shannon's Company, enlisted 10 July 1746. On a roll of deserters dated 22 July 1746. [B3:422:18]

Harvey, Thomas, private in Captain John Singleton's company in service between 01 May and 08 May 1758.

Haslet, James, age 18, laborer, born Pennsylvania, enlisted 27 May 1759 in Captain Charles Stewart's company [probably one of the Associated Companies of Bucks County]. On a return dated June 1759.

Haslet, John, age 25, laborer, born Pennsylvania, enlisted 05 May 1759 in Captain Charles Stewart's company [probably one of the Associated Companies of Bucks County]. On a return dated June 1759.

Haslett, John, promoted to captain after serving in the Pennsylvania Regiment of Three Battalions in 1758 and 1759.

Haslett, John, captain from 28 April 1758 of a company in the Second Battalion and last paid on 21 May 1758. Captain from 24 April 1759 of a company in Colonel William Clapham's Regiment of New Levies.

Hasserus, Frederick, a private in Captain Adam Heylman's Company, of the St. Vincent and Puke's Land Association on 10 May 1756.

Hassey, Joseph, cadet in 1758 of the Second Battalion.

Hatfield, Whitly, age 18, born Maryland, private in Captain John Wright's company of the Lower County. a muster dated 11 May 1759.

Hathorn, Daniel, a private in Captain John Kidd's Independent Company of Foot, Philadelphia in 1756.

Haverloe, John, captain in the Northern District of Broad Kiln Hundred company of Colonel Jacob Kollock's Regiment of Sussex County in 1756/8.

Haviland, Bryan, *see* Bryan Havlin.

Havlin, Bryan, age 25, laborer, born Derry, Ireland, enlisted 01 May 1759, private in Captain John Haslet's company in the Pennsylvania Regiment. On a list of recruits dated 20 May 1759.

Hawke, George, hired 07 June 1757 as a battoe man, Master George Allen.

Hawkins, James, age 22, laborer, born Tyrone, Ireland, enlisted 01 May 1759, private in Captain John Haslet's company in the Pennsylvania Regiment. On a list of recruits dated 20 May 1759.

Hay, John, on a list of men recruited by Captain Andrew McDowell's company in the Second Battalion, Pennsylvania Regiment dated 04 June 1759.

Hay, William, lieutenant in the Christiana Hundred company of Colonel William Armstrong's Upper Regiment of New Castle County in 1756.

Hayes, Adam, ensign in the Associated Regiment of Lancaster County over the Susquehanna in 1747–8.

Hayes, James, lieutenant in Captain Hugh Mercer's Company, Second Battalion from 22 May 1756. Lieutenant from 03 December 1757 in Captain James Burd's company in the Second Battalion. Wounded at Grant's defeat near Fort Duquesne on 14 September 1758. Resigned 13 November 1758.

Hayes, Thomas, ensign from 02 December 1757 in Captain William Thompson's company of the First Battalion stationed westward of the Susquehanna.

Hays, James, a lieutenant stationed on the frontier in Northampton County with one sergeant and seventeen men at Emanuel Consauly's, Upper Smithfield, on 01 June 1764 as part of a unit under the command of Major Asher Clayton.

Hays, James, lieutenant in the provincial service in 1755. Lieutenant in Captain Jacob Orndt's company from 03

December 1757 stationed eastward of the Susquehanna. Lieutenant in Captain John Webb's company in the First Battalion of the Pennsylvania Regiment from 29 November 1763. Obtained land for his service in 1764 at Beech Creek, Clinton County, where he is buried in the Hays graveyard.

Hays, James, private who enlisted 22 April 1756 in Captain Joseph Shippen's company in Colonel William Clapham's Regiment in 1756, the regiment in garrison at Fort Augusta, Shamokin, and listed in Shippen's Account Book.

Hays, Patrick, ensign in one of the Associated Companies of Lancaster County in 1756.

Hays, Thomas, ensign commissioned on 02 December 1757, stationed at Fort Augusta.

Hayshill, Leonard, age 36, born Germany, enlisted 04 December 1757, drummer in Captain John Nicholas Weatherholt's company which enlisted for a term of three years and stationed in Heydelberg Township, Northampton County, in March and April 1758.

Hazlem, Mark, age 24, laborer, born Derry, Ireland, enlisted 06 May 1759, drummer in Captain John Haslet's company in the Pennsylvania Regiment. On a list of recruits dated 20 May 1759.

Hazlet, Andrew, on a return of Captain David Hunter's Company [probably from York County] in Colonel William Clapham's Regiment of New Levies dated 26 May 1759.

Hazzard, Cord., captain in the Northern District of Indian River Hundred company of Colonel Jacob Kollock's Regiment of Sussex County in 1756. Reported in 1758 to be captain of a company from the Angola District.

Heah, Andrew, age 24, laborer, born Germany, enlisted 28 April 1759, private in Captain Joseph Richardson's company of the Third Battalion in the Pennsylvania Regiment. On a return of recruits dated 1759.

Heidler, Martin, ensign, from 16 March 1758 in Captain John Hambright's company in the Second Battalion, stationed westward of Susquehanna.

Heiser, Henry, age 21, laborer, born Germany, enlisted 25 April 1759, private in Captain Joseph Richardson's company of the Third Battalion in the Pennsylvania Regiment. On a return of recruits dated 1759.

Hela, Lodowick, age 30, physician, born Germany, enlisted 14 May 1749 in Captain Richard Gardiner's company in Colonel William Denney's Pennsylvania Regiment.

Hellings, Robert, a private in Captain Joseph Inslee's Company of Foot, Newtown, Bucks County, in 1756.

Hemmins, James, age 17, born Sussex, Delaware, private in Captain John Wright's company of the Lower County. On a muster dated 11 May 1759.

Hemmins, John, age 22, born Maryland, private in Captain John Wright's company of the Lower County. On a muster dated 11 May 1759.

Hemphill, Edward, age 38, laborer, born Ireland, enlisted 24 May 1759 in Captain Robert Boyd's company [probably in the Third Battalion] on a return dated May and June 1759.

Henderson, James, age 24, tailor, born Scotland, enlisted 11 July 1746 in Captain John Shannon's company of foot.

Henderson, James, private, age 30, laborer, born Antrim, Ireland, enlisted 08 May 1758 for the campaign in the lower counties. On a return of Captain McClughan's company dated 17 May 1758.

Henderson, John, age 18, cordwainer, born Pennsylvania, enlisted 14 May 1749 in Captain Richard Gardiner's company in Colonel William Denney's Pennsylvania Regiment.

Henderson, John, age 19, laborer, born Pennsylvania, enlisted 08 May 1759 in Captain Charles Stewart's company [probably one of the Associated Companies of Bucks County]. On a return dated June 1759.

Hendricks, James, captain in a company in the First Battalion of the Pennsylvania Regiment during or after 1763.

Hendricks, Tobias, lieutenant in the Associated Regiment of Lancaster County over the Susquehanna in 1747–8.

Hendrickson, John, ensign in the Christiana Hundred company of Colonel William Armstrong's Upper Regiment of New Castle County in 1756.

Hennan, James, age 17, born Armagh, Ireland, private in Captain John Haslett's company enlisted on 10 May 1758 and last paid on 21 May 1758.

Henry, Adam, ensign from 6/14 December 1757 in Captain Thomas Lloyd's company in the Second Battalion, stationed at Fort Augusta.

Henry, George, age 35, born Germany, enlisted 25 October 1757, private in Captain John Nicholas Weatherholt's company which enlisted for a term of three years and stationed in Heydelberg Township, Northampton County, in March and April 1758.

Henry, Godlip, a private in Captain John Kidd's Independent Company of Foot, Philadelphia in 1756.

Henry, Henry, age 19, laborer, born Ireland, enlisted 20 July 1746 in Captain John Shannon's company of foot.

Henry, James, a member of Captain David Jameson's Company at McCord's Fort on 02 April 1756 when he was wounded.

Henry, Robert of the provincial ship *Pennsylvania* on 17 August 1757.

Henry, Valentine, a private in Captain Adam Heylman's Company, of the St. Vincent and Puke's Land Association on 10 May 1756.

Henry, William, 1st lieutenant in Captain William Vanderspeigle's Philadelphia Company in 1760.

Henry, William, a private in Captain Adam Heylman's Company, of the St. Vincent and Puke's Land Association on 10 May 1756.

Hensler, George, age 22, cooper, born Germany, enlisted 26 April 1758. On a weekly return of Captain Samuel Jones's company in 1758.

Herlock, Isaac, age 19, born Kent on Delaware, laborer, private in Captain John Shannon's Company, enlisted 17 July 1746. On a roll of deserters dated 22 July 1746. [B3:422:18]

Herlock, Isaac, age 19, laborer, born Kent, Delaware, enlisted 17 July 1746 in Captain John Shannon's company of foot.

Hern, Michael, hired 04 June 1757 as a battoe man, Master George Allen.

Hernold, Henry, private who enlisted 16 April 1756 in Captain Joseph Shippen's company in Colonel William Clapham's Regiment in 1756, the regiment in garrison at Fort Augusta, Shamokin, and listed in Shippen's Account Book.

Hero, Thomas, on a list of men recruited by Captain Andrew McDowell's company in the Second Battalion, Pennsylvania Regiment dated 04 June 1759.

Hersfield, Timothy, lieutenant colonel in the provincial service in 1755.

Hervey, Thomas, age 38, shoemaker, born New York, enlisted 05 May 1759 in Captain Robert Boyd's company [probably in the Third Battalion]. On a return dated May and June 1759.

Hervill, John, enlisted 16 May 1758 in Captain French Battell's company of Lower County Provincials.

Hess, Abel, a private in Captain Edward Jones's Independent Company of Horse, Philadelphia in 1756.

Heylman, Adam, captain of a company of the St. Vincent and Puke's Land Association on 10 May 1756.

Heylman, Balthazer, a private in Captain Adam Heylman's Company, of the St. Vincent and Puke's Land Association on 10 May 1756.

Heylman, John Adam, a private in Captain Adam Heylman's Company, of the St. Vincent and Puke's Land Association on 10 May 1756.

Heylman, John, a private in Captain Adam Heylman's Company, of the St. Vincent and Puke's Land Association on 10 May 1756.

Heylman, Michael, a private in Captain Adam Heylman's Company, of the St. Vincent and Puke's Land Association on 10 May 1756.

Heyster, Andreas, a private in Captain Charles Batho's Independent Company of Foot, Philadelphia in 1756.

Hiese, Casper, age 39, smith, born Germany, enlisted 04 May 1758. On a return of Captain John Blackwood's company in the Third Battalion dated 22 May 1758.

Higgins, James, a private in Captain George Armstrong's Company, Second Battalion in 1756; killed at Kittanning.

Higgins, Richard, age 23, born England, laborer, private in Captain John Shannon's Company, enlisted 16 July 1746. On a roll of deserters dated 22 July 1746. [B3:422:18]

Highlands, Fergain, private in Captain Patterson's company from 18 June 1757 stationed eastward of the Susquehanna. On a muster roll dated 08 March 1758.

Hildebrand, John, age 28, laborer, born Germany, enlisted 13 July 1746 in Captain Samuel Perry's company.

Hill, Arthur, enlisted 17 May 1758 in Captain French Battell's company of Lower County Provincials.

Hill, Jonathan, age 18, born Sussex, Delaware, private in Captain John Wright's company of the Lower County. On a muster dated 11 May 1759.

Hill, William, Keeper of the Powder House on 25 July 1745 in Philadelphia.

Hillyard, Charles, captain in the Lower Part of Duck Creek Hundred company of Colonel John Vining's Regiment of Kent County Militia, Upon Delaware in 1756.

Hillyard, Charles, lieutenant in the Murder Kiln [or Mother-Kill] Hundred company of Colonel John Vining's Regiment of Kent County Militia, Upon Delaware in 1756. Lieutenant in Captain Daniel Robinson's company from the Lower District of Mother-Kill Hundred, Kent County, Delaware. Resigned before 29 March 1758.

Hilyear, Stoneman, a private in Captain Joseph Inslee's Company of Foot, Newtown, Bucks County, in 1756.

Hinckle, John, age 21, smith, born Maryland, enlisted 09 May 1758. On a return of Captain John Bull's company dated 01 July 1758.

Hindman, John, a member of Captain Joseph Armstrong's Company on 07 August 1755, which was raised in Cumberland County.

Hinds, John, age 23, blacksmith, born England, enlisted 07 July 1746 in Captain William Trent's company.

Hipshar, Lawrence, age 20, born Germany, enlisted 20 May 1759, private in Captain Robert Curry's company in Colonel William Clapham's Pennsylvania Regiment. On a return dated June 1759.

Hirons, Mark, ensign in one of the Associated Companies of Kent County in 1747–8.

Hirons, William, lieutenant in one of the Associated Companies of Kent County in 1747–8.

Hitchcock, John, carpenter's yeoman of the provincial ship *Pennsylvania* on 17 August 1757.

Hitchley, George, age 26, laborer, born England, enlisted 09 July 1746 in Captain William Trent's company.

Hodgson, Joseph, ensign in one of the Associated Companies of Kent County in 1747–8.

Hodgson, Robert, Second lieutenant from 23 April 1758 in Captain Richard Well's company raised for the campaign in the lower counties.

Hoffmaster, Albright, age 19, laborer, born Germany, enlisted 04 May 1758. On a weekly return of Captain Samuel Jones's company in 1758.

Hogans, Richard, private in Captain Patterson's company from 01 December 1757 stationed eastward of the Susquehanna. On a muster roll dated 08 March 1758.

Hogg, James, lieutenant in Captain George Armstrong's Company, Second Battalion from May 1756; killed at Kittanning.

Holer, Jacob, age 24, potter, born Germany, enlisted 08 May 1759 in Captain Charles Stewart's company [probably one of the Associated Companies of Bucks County]. On a return dated June 1759.

Holgate, John, age 40, laborer, enlisted 07 July 1746 in Captain John Deimer's company.

Holkins, William, age 22, born Wiltshire, England, private in Captain John Haslett's company enlisted on 09 May 1758 and last paid on 21 May 1758.

Holland, Charles, age 27, weaver, born Ireland, enlisted 17 July 1746 in Captain Samuel Perry's company.

Holliday, James, lieutenant in Captain John Steel's Company, Second Battalion from 25 March 1756

Holloway, John, age 19, laborer, born Pennsylvania, enlisted 02 May 1749 in Captain Richard Gardiner's company in Colonel William Denney's Pennsylvania Regiment.

Holmes, James, age 30, cooper, born Antrim, Ireland, enlisted 08 May 1759, private in Captain John Haslet's company in the Pennsylvania Regiment. On a list of recruits dated 20 May 1759.

Holmes, Jonathan, lieutenant in the Associated Regiment of Lancaster County over the Susquehanna in 1747–8.

Holmes, William, landsman on the provincial ship *Pennsylvania* on 17 August 1757.

Holstein, Frederick, ensign in the Associated Regiment of Foot of Philadelphia on 29 Dec 1747.

Holstein, Matthias, lieutenant in the Associated Regiment of Foot of Philadelphia on 29 Dec 1747.

Holston, William, private, age 22, shoemaker, born Pocomock, Maryland, enlisted 10 May 1758 for the campaign in the lower counties. On a return of Captain McClughan's company dated 17 May 1758.

Holt, Ryves, Jr., ensign from 23 May 1759 of Captain John Wright's company from the Lower County. On a muster rolled dated 11 May 1559.

Holt, Ryves, lieutenant colonel in Colonel Jacob Kollock's Regiment of Sussex County in 1756/8.

Holton, Francis, captain in one of the Associated Companies of York County in 1756.

Holton, Patrick, landsman on the provincial ship *Pennsylvania* on 17 August 1757.

Honey, George, age 34, weaver, born Germany, enlisted 07 July 1746 in Captain Samuel Perry's company.

Honnog, Francis, age 25, born Ireland, enlisted 25 May 1759, private in Captain Robert Curry's company in Colonel William

Clapham's Pennsylvania Regiment. On a return dated June 1759.

Hood, Thomas, landsman on the provincial ship *Pennsylvania* on 17 August 1757.

Hooper, Thomas, enlisted June 1746 in Captain William Trent's company, deserted 28 July 1746.

Hoopes, Adam, captain of commissary in the provincial service in 1755.

Hoopes, Adam, commissary of provisions for the Second Battalion in 1756.

Hope, Thomas, lieutenant in the Associated Regiment of Chester County in 1747.

Hopkins, Thomas, on a return of Captain David Hunter's Company [probably from York County] in Colonel William Clapham's Regiment of New Levies dated 26 May 1759.

Horley, Jacob, age 38, vintner, born Wirtemberg [Wurttemberg], Germany, enlisted 21 May 1759, private in Captain John Mathers's company in the Pennsylvania Regiment. On a return dated 15 June 1759.

Horn, George, age 19, born New Jersey, "a Dutchman", private in Captain John Singleton's company in service between 01 May and 08 May 1758.

Horstem, John, age 22, laborer, born Germany, enlisted 13 July 1746 in Captain Samuel Perry's company.

Hotham, Joseph, ensign in one of two regiments of New Castle County in 1747–8.

Hotkins, William, age 24, laborer, born Sussex, England, enlisted 27 April 1759, private in Captain John Haslet's company in the Pennsylvania Regiment. On a list of recruits dated 20 May 1759.

Housegger, Nicholas, captain stationed on the frontier in Berks County with Ensign William McMeen, one sergeant, and twenty-six men in Heidelberg Township on 01 June 1764 as part of a unit under the command of Major Asher Clayton.

Housegger, Nicholas, lieutenant in Captain Samuel J. Atlee's company of the First Battalion of the Pennsylvania Regiment from 19 April 1760. Captain in a company in the First

Battalion of the Pennsylvania Regiment from 11 November 1763.

Houser, Casper, age 22, laborer, born Germany, enlisted 05 May 1758. On a return of Captain John Bull's company dated 01 July 1758.

Houston, Alexander, private, age 25, laborer, born Toboyne, Ireland, enlisted 01 May 1758 for the campaign in the lower counties. On a return of Captain McClughan's company dated 17 May 1758.

Houston, George, a private in Captain Samuel Mifflin's Association Battery Company of Philadelphia in 1756.

How, Frederick, age 50, musician, born Nassau, Germany, enlisted 06 June 1759, private in Captain John Mathers's company in the Pennsylvania Regiment. On a return dated 15 June 1759.

Howell, Charles, age 20, laborer, born Ireland, enlisted 31 May 1759 in Captain Robert Boyd's company [probably in the Third Battalion]. On a return dated May and June 1759.

Howell, David, ensign in one of two regiments of New Castle County in 1747–8.

Howell, David, ensign in the Red Lyon Hundred company of Colonel Jacob Van Bibber's Lower Regiment of New Castle County in 1756.

Howell, Rees, ensign from 29 April 1759 in Captain Samuel Grubb's company of Colonel William Clapham's Regiment of New Levies.

Howell, William, age 34, laborer, born Ireland, enlisted 22 July 1746 in Captain John Deimer's company.

Howell, William, age 35, cooper, born Wales, enlisted 02 July 1746 in Captain John Shannon's company of foot.

Howell, William, age 36, laborer, born Monmouth, Wales, enlisted 12 June 1759, private in Captain John Mathers's company in the Pennsylvania Regiment. On a return dated 15 June 1759.

Hown, Henry, private who enlisted 27 April 1756 in Captain Nathaniel Miles's company in Colonel William Clapham's Regiment in 1756, the regiment in garrison at Fort Augusta, Shamokin, and listed in Shippen's Account Book.

Hoy, Richard, age 21, weaver, born Ireland, enlisted 21 May 1759 in Captain Charles Stewart's company [probably one of the Associated Companies of Bucks County]. On a return dated June 1759.

Hubert, Thomas, Jun., captain in the Associated Regiment of Chester County in 1747. [CR,V, 325]

Hudson, Richard, age 27, laborer, born Ireland, enlisted May 1758. On a return of Captain John Bull's company dated 01 July 1758. Formerly in the Pennsylvania Regiment.

Hugg, John, age 35, cooper, born West Jersey, enlisted 11 July 1746 in Captain John Shannon's company of foot.

Hughes, Barnabas, age 40, laborer, born Maryland, enlisted 12 June 1758 by Lieutenant William McClay for Captain John Montgomery's company.

Hughes, George, captain in the Associated Regiment of Bucks County in 1748.

Hughes, Henry, age 23, ropemaker, born London, enlisted 06 May 1758. On a return of Captain John Bull's company dated 01 July 1758.

Hughes, James, ensign in Captain Patrick Davis's company from 04 December 1757 stationed eastward of the Susquehanna, but is also reported on the same date as an ensign in Captain Charles Garraway's company, also stationed eastward of the Susquehanna. Appears to have been replaced by William Work on 15 March 1758 in Captain Davis's company.

Hughes, James, ensign of what appears to be the headquarters company of Colonel William Denny's Regiment, 04 December 1757. Promoted to lieutenant on 17 March 1758 in Captain David Jamison's company in the Second Battalion, vice Reynolds. This company was originally Smith's Company stationed east of the Susquehanna.

Hughes, James, promoted to lieutenant after serving in the Pennsylvania Regiment of Three Battalions in 1758 and 1759. Reported as in the "Regular Service".

Hughes, John, captain in the Associated Regiment of Foot of Philadelphia on 29 Dec 1747.

Hughes, Matthew, lieutenant colonel.

Hughes, Memucan, ensign from 02 May 1759 in Captain William Johnston's company of Colonel William Clapham's Regiment of New Levies. Also identified as a lieutenant from the same date following the resignation of Lieutenant David McAllister.

Hugons, John, age 25, weaver, born Cecil, Maryland, enlisted 11 May 1759, private in Captain John Haslet's company in the Pennsylvania Regiment. On a list of recruits dated 20 May 1759.

Hume, John, captain in one of the Associated Companies of Kent County in 1747–8.

Humphreys, James, a private in Captain Charles Batho's Independent Company of Foot, Philadelphia in 1756.

Humphreys, Samuel, lieutenant from 26 January 1756 in Captain Christian Bussé's company in the First Battalion. Lieutenant from 11 December 1757 in Captain Jacob Morgan's company in Second Battalion, stationed eastward of the Susquehanna.

Humphreys, William, a private in Captain Charles Batho's Independent Company of Foot, Philadelphia in 1756.

Humphreys, William, age 25, laborer, born Maryland, enlisted 02 May 1758 by Captain Benjamin Noxon.

Humphrys, Samuel, lieutenant on a List of Officers in the Province Pay, 1756 in the First Battalion of the Pennsylvania Regiment with a commission date of 25 January 1756. {PA5, I, 88}

Hunsicker, Daniel, a lieutenant stationed on the frontier in Northampton County with one sergeant and seventeen men at Brinker's Mill, Hamilton Township, on 01 June 1764 as part of a unit under the command of Major Asher Clayton.

Hunsicker, Daniel, lieutenant in Captain James Irvine's company in the First Battalion of the Pennsylvania Regiment from 19 July 1763.

Hunt, _____, landsman on the provincial ship *Pennsylvania* on 17 August 1757.

Hunt, Roger, captain in the Associated Regiment of Chester County in 1747.

Hunter, Alexander, captain in the Associated Regiment of Bucks County in 1748.

Hunter, David, captain in one of the Associated Companies of York County in 1756. Captain from 25 April 1758 of a company in the First Battalion of Col. William Denny's Regiment. Captain from 30 April 1759 of a company of Colonel William Clapham's Regiment of New Levies.

Hunter, David, promoted to captain after serving in the Pennsylvania Regiment of Three Battalions in 1758 and 1759.

Hunter, James, age 21, laborer, born Ireland, enlisted 04 May 1749 in Captain Richard Gardiner's company in Colonel William Denney's Pennsylvania Regiment.

Hunter, James, captain in the Associated Regiment of Chester County in 1747.

Hunter, James, landsman on the provincial ship *Pennsylvania* on 17 August 1757.

Hunter, John, on a return of Captain David Hunter's Company [probably from York County] in Colonel William Clapham's Regiment of New Levies dated 26 May 1759.

Hunter, John, on a return of Captain David Hunter's Company [probably from York County] in Colonel William Clapham's Regiment of New Levies dated 26 May 1759.

Hunter, Peter, master of the provincial ship *Pennsylvania* on 17 August 1757.

Hunter, Robert, lieutenant in Captain James Hendrick's company in the First Battalion of the Pennsylvania Regiment during or after 1763.

Hunter, Samuel, on a return of Captain David Hunter's Company [probably from York County] in Colonel William Clapham's Regiment of New Levies dated 26 May 1759.

Hunter, Samuel, lieutenant in Captain Joseph Scott's company of the Second Battalion of the Pennsylvania Regiment from 02 May 1760. Promoted to captain after serving in the Pennsylvania Regiment of Three Battalions in 1758 and 1759. Reported to have "Joined Colonel Francis". Captain in a company in the First Battalion of the Pennsylvania Regiment from 10 November 1763. Stationed on the frontier in Lancaster County with one sergeant and fifteen men at David Patten's,

Paxtang Township, 01 June 1764 under the command of Major Asher Clayton.

Hunter, Thomas, on a return of Captain David Hunter's Company [probably from York County] in Colonel William Clapham's Regiment of New Levies dated 26 May 1759.

Hunter, William, a member of Captain David Jameson's Company at McCord's Fort on 02 April 1756 when he was wounded.

Hunter, William, a private in Captain George Armstrong's Company, Second Battalion in 1756; missing at the capture of Kittanning.

Hunter, William, age 22, laborer, born England, enlisted 08 May 1758 by Captain Benjamin Noxon.

Hurst, Thomas, a private in Captain Joseph Inslee's Company of Foot, Newtown, Bucks County, in 1756.

Hurst, William, a private in Captain Joseph Inslee's Company of Foot, Newtown, Bucks County, in 1756.

Hurton, Michael, a private in Captain Edward Jones's Independent Company of Horse, Philadelphia in 1756.

Husk, John, age 25, born Germany, enlisted 30 April 1759, private in Captain Robert Curry's company in Colonel William Clapham's Pennsylvania Regiment. On a return dated June 1759.

Husk, Thomas, age 30, drummer, born Scotland, enlisted 10 May 1749 in Captain Richard Gardiner's company in Colonel William Denney's Pennsylvania Regiment.

Husley, Jacob, age 23, born Germany, enlisted 01 September 1757, private in Captain John Nicholas Weatherholt's company which enlisted for a term of three years and stationed in Heydelberg Township, Northampton County, in March and April 1758.

Huston, Alexander, a private in Captain Edward Jones's Independent Company of Horse, Philadelphia in 1756.

Huston, James, captain in the Associated Regiment of Bucks County in 1748.

Huston, Robert, age 30, cordwainer, born Ireland, enlisted 22 April 1758 by Captain Benjamin Noxon.

Huston, William, age 20, saddler, born Ireland, enlisted 07 July 1746 in Captain Samuel Perry's company.

Hutchins, Thomas, lieutenant in Captain Robert Callender's company in the First Battalion from 18 December 1757 stationed westward of the Susquehanna. Quartermaster from 07 June 1758 of the Third Battalion.

Hutchins, Thomas, promoted to lieutenant after serving in the Pennsylvania Regiment of Three Battalions in 1758 and 1759. Reported as in the "Regular Service".

Hutchinson, John, age 28, laborer, born Ireland, enlisted 26 May 1759 in Captain Robert Boyd's company [probably in the Third Battalion]. On a return dated May and June 1759.

Hutchinson, Joseph, lieutenant in the Lower Part of Murder Kiln [or Mother-Kill] Hundred company of Colonel John Vining's Regiment of Kent County Militia, Upon Delaware in 1756.

Hydler, Martin, lieutenant not assigned in the First Battalion of the Pennsylvania Regiment from 22 April 1760.

Hyndshaw, James, captain of a company of the Second Battalion of the Pennsylvania Regiment from 15 April 1760.

Hyndshaw, James, lieutenant in Captain John Nicholas Wetterholt's company of the First Battalion from 21 December 1755. Lieutenant from 10 December 1757 in Captain Samuel Weiser's company stationed eastward of the Susquehanna. Also reported as being a lieutenant in Captain Charles Garraway's company from 10 December 1757. Captain in one of the new levies in May 1758. Captain from 15 May 1759 of a company in the Old Levies.

Hyndshaw, James, lieutenant in the provincial service in 1755.

Hyndshaw, James, lieutenant on a List of Officers in the Province Pay, 1756 in the First Battalion of the Pennsylvania Regiment with a commission date of 12 January 1756. {PA5, I, 88}

Hyndshaw, James, promoted to captain after serving in the Pennsylvania Regiment of Three Battalions in 1758 and 1759.

Hynes, William, landsman on the provincial ship *Pennsylvania* on 17 August 1757.

Imholt, Henry, age 21, laborer, born Germany, enlisted 08 May 1759, private in Captain Joseph Richardson's company of the

Third Battalion in the Pennsylvania Regiment. On a return of recruits dated 1759.

Imhook, Christian, a private in Captain Charles Batho's Independent Company of Foot, Philadelphia in 1756.

Ingelman, Jeremiah, landsman on the provincial ship *Pennsylvania* on 17 August 1757.

Inglis, John, a private in Captain Samuel Mifflin's Association Battery Company of Philadelphia in 1756.

Inglis, John, captain in the Associated Regiment of Foot of Philadelphia on 29 Dec 1747.

Innis, John, landsman on the provincial ship *Pennsylvania* on 17 August 1757.

Innis, Timothy, private, age 30, tailor, born Kildare, Ireland, enlisted 09 May 1758 for the campaign in the lower counties. On a return of Captain McClughan's company dated 17 May 1758.

Inslee, Joseph, Jun, ensign in Captain Joseph Inslee's Company of Foot, Newtown, Bucks County, in 1756.

Inslee, Joseph, captain in the Associated Regiment of Bucks County in 1748.

Inslee, Joseph, captain of a Company of Foot, Newtown, Bucks County, in 1756.

Irish, Richard, age 24, laborer, born England, enlisted 30 July 1746 in Captain William Trent's company.

Irvine, James, captain stationed on the frontier in Northampton County with Ensign Nicholas Kern, one sergeant, and twenty-five men at Nicholas Kern's, Lehigh Gap on 01 June 1764 as part of a unit under the command of Major Asher Clayton.

Irvine, James, ensign in Captain Samuel J. Atlee's company of the First Battalion of the Pennsylvania Regiment from 02 May 1760. Captain of a company in the First Battalion of the Pennsylvania Regiment from 30 December 1763.

Irvine, John, age 23, laborer, enlisted 11 July 1746 in Captain John Deimer's company.

Irvine, Joseph, *see* Irwin, Joseph.

Irwin, Abram, a member of Captain Joseph Armstrong's Company on 07 August 1755, raised in Cumberland County.

Irwin, Archibald, ensign in Captain John Steel's Company, Second Battalion from April 1756

Irwin, Christopher, a member of Captain Joseph Armstrong's Company on 07 August 1755, raised in Cumberland County.

Irwin, John, a member of Captain Joseph Armstrong's Company on 07 August 1755, raised in Cumberland County.

Irwin, John, age 34, born Ireland, enlisted 25 May 1759, private in Captain Robert Curry's company in Colonel William Clapham's Pennsylvania Regiment. On a return dated June 1759.

Irwin, Joseph, ensign in the Associated Regiment of Lancaster County over the Susquehanna in 1747–8.

Irwin, Moses, captain in one of the Associated Companies of Lancaster County in 1756.

Irwin, Moses, lieutenant in one of the new levies in May 1758.

Irwin, Robert, wagonmaster of Colonel William Denny's Regiment, 1758

Iser, Jacob, age 28, laborer, born Germany, enlisted 22 July 1746 in Captain John Deimer's company.

Isgate, John, age 20, laborer, born Maryland, enlisted 20 July 1746 in Captain John Shannon's company of foot.

Isles, James, age 22, tanner, born England, enlisted 27 June 1746 in Captain William Trent's company.

Jack, James, lieutenant in the Associated Regiment of Lancaster County over the Susquehanna in 1747–8.

Jack, Patrick, lieutenant in Captain Christopher Lemms's company in Lieutenant Colonel Commandant Asher Clayton's Second Battalion of the Pennsylvania Regiment commanded by the Hon. J. Penn from 21 July 1763.

Jackson, Benjamin, enlisted 23 May 1758 in Captain French Battell's company of Lower County Provincials.

Jackson, Charles, age 45, laborer, born England, enlisted 21 July 1746 in Captain John Shannon's company of foot.

Jackson, Daniel, age 25, laborer, born Pennsylvania, enlisted 27 June 1746 in Captain William Trent's company.

Jackson, George, age 28, born Maryland, private in Captain John Wright's company of the Lower County. On a muster dated 11 May 1759.

Jackson, Paul, captain from 11 May 1758 in a company in the Third Battalion. Professor of Latin in the Academy.

Jackson, Southey, private, age 20, shoemaker, born Indian River, Maryland, enlisted 19 April 1758 for the campaign in the lower counties. On a return of Captain McClughan's company dated 17 May 1758.

Jacobs, Thomas, age 19, laborer, born Pennsylvania, enlisted 07 May 1758. On a weekly return of Captain Samuel Jones's company in 1758.

Jacquet, Peter, ensign in one of two regiments of New Castle County in 1747–8.

Jake, Robert, enlisted 23 May 1759, private in Captain Henry Van Bibber's company of the Lower County. On a return dated 04 June 1759.

Jamely, James, midshipman on the provincial ship *Pennsylvania* on 17 August 1757.

Jameon, David, *see* David Jamison.

James, Daniel, captain from 29 March 1758 of a company from the Lower District of Mother-Kill Hundred, Kent County, Delaware, vice Robinson.

James, James, ensign in one of the Associated Companies of Kent County in August 1748.

James, Thomas, lieutenant colonel in one of two regiments of New Castle County in 1747–8.

James, Thomas, major in Colonel Jacob Van Bibber's Lower Regiment of New Castle County in 1756.

Jameson, _____, captain of a company of men at McCord's Fort on 02 April 1756.

Jamison, David, captain from 19 May 1756 of a company of the Third Battalion (known as the Augusta Regiment). Captain from 09 December 1757 of a company in the Second Battalion, stationed at Fort Augusta. Major from 03 June 1758 of the Second Battalion. Major with a brevet dated 24 April 1759 of the Second Battalion of the Pennsylvania Regiment. Major of the First Battalion of the Pennsylvania Regiment from 12 April 1760.

Jamison, Dr., surgeon in the Second Battalion, killed by Indians near McCord's Fort, April 1756.

January, Benjamin, age 42, shoemaker, born Pennsylvania, enlisted 30 April 1758. On a return of Captain John Blackwood's company in the Third Battalion dated 22 May 1758.

January, Benjamin, age 43, shoemaker, born New Castle, Delaware, enlisted 24 April 1759, private in Captain William Johnston's company in the Pennsylvania Regiment. On a return dated 12 May 1759.

January, Benjamin, landsman on the provincial ship *Pennsylvania* on 17 August 1757.

Janvier, Francis, lieutenant in one of two regiments of New Castle County in 1747–8.

Jeffreys, William, age 22, laborer, born Pennsylvania, enlisted 02 May 1749 in Captain Richard Gardiner's company in Colonel William Denney's Pennsylvania Regiment.

Jemison, George, a private in Captain Joseph Inslee's Company of Foot, Newtown, Bucks County, in 1756.

Jemison, Robert, captain in the Associated Regiment of Bucks County in 1748.

Jemison, Samuel, ensign in the Associated Regiment of the West End of Lancaster County in 1747–8.

Jemison, Samuel, lieutenant in one of the Associated Companies of Lancaster County in 1756.

Jenkins, Thomas, age 32, laborer, born England, enlisted 05 July 1746 in Captain William Trent's company.

Jenkins, Thomas, age 35, laborer, born England, enlisted 03 May 1759, private in Captain John Haslet's company in the Pennsylvania Regiment. On a list of recruits dated 20 May 1759.

Jenkins, Thomas, age 38, born London, England, watchmaker, private in Captain John Haslett's company enlisted on 18 May 1758 and last paid on 21 May 1758.

Jenkinson, Henry, a private in Captain John Kidd's Independent Company of Foot, Philadelphia in 1756.

Jennings, Henry, age 40, laborer, born Ireland, enlisted 04 May 1759 in Captain Robert Boyd's company [probably in the Third Battalion]. On a return dated May and June 1759.

Jester, John, enlisted 16 May 1758 in Captain French Battell's company of Lower County Provincials.

Joans, James, private in Captain John Singleton's company in service between 01 May and 08 May 1758.

Joans, Zachariah, age 22, born King William, Virginia, "thin visaged Welshman", private in Captain John Singleton's company in service between 01 May and 08 May 1758.

John Deimer's company.

John, Daniel, private, age 27, laborer, born Pencador, Delaware, enlisted 08 May 1758 for the campaign in the lower counties. On a return of Captain McClughan's company dated 17 May 1758.

John, David, lieutenant in one of two regiments of New Castle County in August 1748.

John, Samuel, promoted to captain after serving in the Pennsylvania Regiment of Three Battalions in 1758 and 1759. Reported as "dead".

Johns, Joseph, enlisted in Captain William Trent's company, 29 July 1746, died.

Johnson, _____, ensign of Captain Nathan Mile's Company, Third Battalion (known as the Augusta Regiment) in 1756.

Johnson, James, age 27, laborer, born Ireland, enlisted 29 April 1759 in Captain Charles Stewart's company [probably one of the Associated Companies of Bucks County]. On a return dated June 1759.

Johnson, John, ensign in the Associated Regiment of Chester County in 1747.

Johnson, John, lieutenant in one of the Associated Companies of Bucks County in 1756.

Johnson, Martin Gill, enlisted 15 May 1759, private in Captain Henry Van Bibber's company of the Lower County. On a return dated 04 June 1759.

Johnson, William, ensign in Captain Christian Bussé's company of the First Battalion from 12 March 1756.

Johnson, William, lieutenant from 02 May 1758 in Captain John Blackwood's company in the Third Battalion. On a return dated 22 May 1758.

Johnston, Francis, captain of a company of the Second Battalion of the Pennsylvania Regiment from 29 April 1760.

Johnston, Francis, ensign from 10 December 1757 in Captain David Jamison's company in the Second Battalion. Also seen as an ensign in Captain George Armstrong's company from 15 December 1757 until his transfer before 04 January 1758, stationed westward of the Susquehanna.

Johnston, Francis, promoted to captain after serving in the Pennsylvania Regiment of Three Battalions in 1758 and 1759.

Johnston, James Jun., age 22, laborer, born England, enlisted 13 August 1746 in Captain Samuel Perry's company.

Johnston, James, age 20, laborer, born Ireland, enlisted 16 July 1746 in Captain Samuel Perry's company.

Johnston, John, age 23, laborer, born Ulster, Ireland, enlisted 02 May 1759, private in Captain James Armstrong's company in Colonel William Clapham's Pennsylvania Regiment. On a return dated 01 June 1759.

Johnston, John, age 27, born Lancaster, Pennsylvania, "marked well with the Smallpox", private in Captain John Singleton's company in service between 01 May and 08 May 1758.

Johnston, John, enlisted 11 July 1746 in Captain William Trent's company, deserted 01 August 1746.

Johnston, William, age 17, laborer, born Tyrone, Ireland, enlisted 27 May 1759, private in Captain John Mathers's company in the Pennsylvania Regiment. On a return dated 15 June 1759.

Johnston, William, captain from 11 May 1759 of a company of Colonel William Clapham's Regiment of New Levies. Also identified as a captain from 12 May 1759 in a company in Colonel William Denny's Pennsylvania Regiment.

Johnston, William, promoted to captain after serving in the Pennsylvania Regiment of Three Battalions in 1758 and 1759.

Jones, Abel, age 29, joiner, enlisted 01 May 1759, private in Captain James Armstrong's company in Colonel William Clapham's Pennsylvania Regiment. On a return dated 01 June 1759.

Jones, Abraham, ensign in the Associated Regiment of Foot of Philadelphia on 29 Dec 1747.

Jones, Christopher, private, age 25, miller, born West Meath, Ireland, enlisted 26 April 1758 for the campaign in the lower counties. On a return of Captain McClughan's company dated 17 May 1758.

Jones, Edward, captain in the Independent Company of Horse, Philadelphia in 1756.

Jones, Edward, captain then colonel on 04 August 1748, in the Associated Regiment in the County of Philadelphia in 1748.

Jones, Evan, age 38, laborer, born Chester, Pennsylvania, enlisted 27 May 1759, private in Captain John Mathers's company in the Pennsylvania Regiment. On a return dated 15 June 1759.

Jones, John, a member of Captain Joseph Armstrong's Company on 07 August 1755, raised in Cumberland County.

Jones, John, age 22, cordwainer, born New England, enlisted 26 June 1746 in Captain John Shannon's company of foot.

Jones, John, age 25, laborer, born Wales, enlisted May 15 April 1758 by Captain Benjamin Noxon.

Jones, John, age 39, cooper, born Bucks, Pennsylvania, enlisted 27 April 1759, private in Captain Joseph Richardson's company of the Third Battalion in the Pennsylvania Regiment. On a return of recruits dated 1759.

Jones, John, age 39, mariner, born Wales, enlisted 15 May 1758. On a weekly return of Captain Samuel Jones's company in 1758.

Jones, John, captain in the St. George's Hundred company of Colonel Jacob Van Bibber's Lower Regiment of New Castle County in 1756.

Jones, John, ensign from 29 April 1758 in Captain John Singleton's company in the Second Battalion in service between 01 May and 08 May 1758.

Jones, John, lieutenant in Captain Samuel Mile's company of the First Battalion of the Pennsylvania Regiment from 17 April 1760.

Jones, John, promoted to lieutenant after serving in the Pennsylvania Regiment of Three Battalions in 1758 and 1759. Reported as "dead".

Jones, John, seaman on the provincial ship *Pennsylvania* on 17 August 1757.

Jones, John, sergeant in Captain Joseph Shippen's company in Colonel William Clapham's Regiment in 1756, the regiment in garrison at Fort Augusta, Shamokin, and listed in Shippen's Account Book. Enlisted 14 April 1756 and discharged 13 August 1756.

Jones, John, sergeant, age 20, barber, born Pennsylvania, enlisted 19 April 1758 for the campaign in the lower counties. On a return of Captain McClughan's company dated 17 May 1758.

Jones, Joseph, age 20, laborer, born Wales, enlisted 24 April 1758 by Captain Benjamin Noxon.

Jones, Rees, captain in the White Clay Creek Hundred company of Colonel William Armstrong's Upper Regiment of New Castle County in 1756.

Jones, Robert, age 34, bricklayer, born Ireland, enlisted 30 June 1746 in Captain John Shannon's company of foot.

Jones, Samuel, age 21, laborer, born Bristol, enlisted 01 May 1758. On a return of Captain John Bull's company dated 01 July 1758.

Jones, Samuel, captain of a company in 1758. Captain from 05 May 1759 of a company of Colonel William Clapham's Regiment of New Levies.

Jones, Samuel, ensign from 14 May 1758 in Captain William Biles's company in the Third Battalion.

Jones, Thomas, age 22, laborer, born Wales, enlisted May 1758 by Captain Benjamin Noxon.

Jones, Thomas, age 24, sadker, born Pennsylvania, enlisted 01 July 1746 in Captain William Trent's company.

Jones, Thomas, private in Captain Patterson's company from 01 December 1757 stationed eastward of the Susquehanna. On a muster roll dated 08 March 1758.

Jourdain, John, a private in Captain John Kidd's Independent Company of Foot, Philadelphia in 1756.

Judge, Rowland, enlisted 10 July 1746 in Captain William Trent's company.

Kain, Daniel, private, age 29, shoemaker, born Antrim, Ireland, enlisted 20 April 1758 for the campaign in the lower counties. On a return of Captain McClughan's company dated 17 May 1758.

Kain, John, age 22, tanner, born Ireland, enlisted 07 July 1746 in Captain Samuel Perry's company.

Kain, Miles, age 21, laborer, born Ireland, enlisted 15 July 1746 in Captain Samuel Perry's company.

Kaizer, Jacob, age 30, bricklayer, 08 August 1746 in Captain John Deimer's company.

Kanedy, James, *see* James Kennedy.

Karrigar, John Philip, age 26, laborer, born Germany, enlisted 06 July 1746 in Captain John Deimer's company.

Kaup, John, age 25, born Germany, enlisted 01 September 1757, fifer in Captain John Nicholas Weatherholt's company which enlisted for a term of three years and stationed in Heydelberg Township, Northampton County, in March and April 1758.

Kayle, Thomas, private, age 30, carpenter, enlisted 12 May 1758 for the campaign in the lower counties. On a return of Captain McClughan's company dated 17 May 1758.

Kayser, Henry, age 25, bricklayer, 17 July 1746 in Captain John Deimer's company.

Kearn, Jacob, ensign on a List of Officers in the Province Pay, 1756 in the First Battalion of the Pennsylvania Regiment with a commission date of 5 January 1756. {PA5, I, 88}

Kearsley, John, Jr., a private in Captain Edward Jones's Independent Company of Horse, Philadelphia in 1756.

Kearsley, John, a private in Captain John Kidd's Independent Company of Foot, Philadelphia in 1756.

Keaton, Edward, *see* Cayton, Edward.

Kecholar, Charles, landsman on the provincial ship *Pennsylvania* on 17 August 1757.

Keech, John, age 24, saddler, born Pennsylvania, enlisted 08 July 1746 in Captain Samuel Perry's company.

Keen, John, a private in Captain Joseph Inslee's Company of Foot, Newtown, Bucks County, in 1756.

Keene, Matthias, lieutenant in one of the Associated Companies of Bucks County in 1756.

Kehl, George, age 24, laborer, born Pennsylvania, enlisted 07 July 1746 in Captain John Deimer's company.

Keis, Andrew, age 27, laborer, born Ireland, enlisted 25 May 1759, private in Captain Robert Curry's company in Colonel William Clapham's Pennsylvania Regiment. On a return dated June 1759.

Keis, Andrew, age 35, cooper, born Pennsylvania, enlisted 13 June 1759, private in Captain Robert Curry's company in Colonel William Clapham's Pennsylvania Regiment. On a return dated June 1759.

Keith, Charles, enlisted 28 May 1759, private in Captain Henry Van Bibber's company of the Lower County. On a return dated 04 June 1759.

Keith, George, age 23, laborer, born Germany, enlisted 28 April 1759, private in Captain Joseph Richardson's company of the Third Battalion in the Pennsylvania Regiment. On a return of recruits dated 1759.

Kellam, Benjamin, ensign in the Brandy Wine Hundred company of Colonel William Armstrong's Upper Regiment of New Castle County in 1756.

Kellar, Jacob, drummer in Captain Joseph Shippen's company in Colonel William Clapham's Regiment in 1756, the regiment in garrison at Fort Augusta, Shamokin, and listed in Shippen's Account Book. Enlisted 20 April 1756.

Kelles, Johan Jost, *see* Kelly, Johan Jost.

Kelley, Edward, private in Captain Patterson's company from 29 December 1757 stationed eastward of the Susquehanna. On a muster roll dated 08 March 1758.

Kelley, James, seaman on the provincial ship *Pennsylvania* on 17 August 1757.
Kelley, John, landsman on the provincial ship *Pennsylvania* on 17 August 1757.
Kelley, John, private, age 28, laborer, born Down, Ireland, enlisted 20 April 1758 for the campaign in the lower counties. On a return of Captain McClughan's company dated 17 May 1758.
Kelley, Nathaniel, private in Captain Patterson's company from 27 February 1758 stationed eastward of the Susquehanna. On a muster roll dated 08 March 1758.
Kelley, Thomas, lieutenant in the Associated Regiment of Bucks County in 1748.
Kelliah, John, private in Captain Patterson's company from 26 December 1757 stationed eastward of the Susquehanna. On a muster roll dated 08 March 1758.
Kelly, Daniel, enlisted 12 July 1746 in Captain Samuel Perry's company.
Kelly, Johan Jost, age 18, laborer, enlisted 13 July 1746 in Captain John Deimer's company.
Kelly, John, a private in Captain Hance Hamilton's Company, Second Battalion in 1756; killed at Kittanning.
Kelly, Matthew, age 25, laborer, born Ireland, enlisted 24 April 1758 by Captain Benjamin Noxon.
Kelly, Peter, age 36, tanner, born Ireland, enlisted 02 July 1746 in Captain John Shannon's company of foot.
Kelse, Richard, enlisted 21 May 1759, private in Captain Henry Van Bibber's company of the Lower County. On a return dated 04 June 1759.
Kelsean, Joseph, on a return of Captain David Hunter's Company [probably from York County] in Colonel William Clapham's Regiment of New Levies dated 26 May 1759.
Kemmey, Job, enlisted 19 May 1758 in Captain French Battell's company of Lower County Provincials.
Kemmey, John, enlisted 22 May 1758 in Captain French Battell's company of Lower County Provincials.
Kemp, Christian, a private in Captain John Kidd's Independent Company of Foot, Philadelphia in 1756.

Kendy, Abraham, a private in Captain Edward Jones's Independent Company of Horse, Philadelphia in 1756.

Kennedy, Alexander, a private in Captain Samuel Mifflin's Association Battery Company of Philadelphia in 1756.

Kennedy, Hugh, age 21, laborer, born Ireland, enlisted 14 July 1746 in Captain Samuel Perry's company.

Kennedy, James, age 24, laborer, enlisted 06 May 1759, private in Captain James Armstrong's company in Colonel William Clapham's Pennsylvania Regiment. On a return dated 01 June 1759.

Kennedy, John, ensign in Captain Samuel Weiser's company from 13 December 1757 stationed eastward of the Susquehanna. Also reported as an ensign in Captain Charles Garraway's company from 13 December 1757.

Kennedy, John, promoted to lieutenant after serving in the Pennsylvania Regiment of Three Battalions in 1758 and 1759. Reported as "discontinued".

Kennedy, Robert, age 19, laborer, born Ireland, enlisted 24 April 1758. On a weekly return of Captain Samuel Jones's company in 1758.

Kennedy, Thomas, age 24, born Monaghan, Ireland, private in Captain John Haslett's company enlisted on 09 May 1758 and last paid on 21 May 1758.

Kennedy, Thomas, landsman on the provincial ship *Pennsylvania* on 17 August 1757.

Kennedy, William, age 25, born Chester, Pennsylvania, weaver, private in Captain John Singleton's company in service between 01 May and 08 May 1758.

Kent, John, age 22, laborer, born Kent, Delaware, enlisted 14 July 1746 in Captain John Shannon's company of foot.

Kent, John, lieutenant in the Associated Regiment of Chester County in 1747.

Kern, Jacob, captain stationed on the frontier in Berks County with one sergeant and fourteen men at Kaufman's Mill, Bern Township, on 01 June 1764 as part of a unit under the command of Major Asher Clayton.

Kern, Jacob, ensign in Captain Jacob Morgan's company of the First Battalion from 05 December 1755. Lieutenant in Captain Christian Bussè's company and adjutant of the Second Battalion from 23 December 1757, stationed eastward of the Susquehanna. Promoted to captain after serving in the Pennsylvania Regiment of Three Battalions in 1758 and 1759. Reported to have "Joined Colonel Francis". Captain of a company of the Second Battalion of the Pennsylvania Regiment from 20 April 1760. Captain of a company in the First Battalion of the Pennsylvania Regiment from 13 July 1763.

Kern, Nicholas, an ensign stationed on the frontier in Northampton County with Captain James Irvine, one sergeant, and twenty-five men at Nicholas Kern's, Lehigh Gap on 01 June 1764 as part of a unit under the command of Major Asher Clayton.

Kern, Nicholas, ensign in Captain James Irvine's company in the First Battalion of the Pennsylvania Regiment from 18 July 1763. Resigned.

Kerner, Baltzer, a private in Captain John Kidd's Independent Company of Foot, Philadelphia in 1756.

Kerr, George, *see* Carr, George.

Ketchmore, Thomas, age 22, blacksmith, born England, enlisted 19 April 1758 by Captain Benjamin Noxon.

Keutzer, Nichoas, age 40, carpenter, enlisted 06 August 1746 in Captain John Deimer's company.

Keys, William, enlisted 17 May 1758 in Captain French Battell's company of Lower County Provincials.

Keysey, James, age 21, born Meath, Ireland, weaver, private in Captain John Haslett's company enlisted on 13 May 1758 and last paid on 21 May 1758.

Kickler, Philip, age 17, laborer, born Germany, enlisted 09 May 1758. On a return of Captain John Bull's company dated 01 July 1758.

Kidd, John, Captain of an Independent Company of Foot, Philadelphia in 1756.

Kiezer, Jacob, *see* Jacob Kuzer.

Killen, Robert, captain in the Middle Part of Mispillim Hundred company of Colonel John Vining's Regiment of Kent County Militia, Upon Delaware in 1756.

Kilpatrick, Dennis, a private in Captain Hugh Mercer's Company, Second Battalion in 1756; killed at Kittanning.

Kilpatrick, Hugh, captain in the Associated Regiment of Chester County in 1747.

Kilpatrick, Patrick, private, age 24, weaver, born Faughboyne, Ireland, enlisted 24 April 1758 for the campaign in the lower counties. On a return of Captain McClughan's company dated 17 May 1758.

Kimble, William, landsman on the provincial ship *Pennsylvania* on 17 August 1757.

Kincaid [Kingeade], Robert, hired 20 May 1757 as a battoe man, Master George Allen.

King, James, lieutenant in one of two regiments of New Castle County in 1747–8.

King, Michael, age 25, shoemaker, born Pennsylvania, enlisted 03 May 1758. On a return of Captain John Bull's company dated 01 July 1758.

King, Victor, lieutenant from 16 May 1758 in Captain Thomas Hamilton's company in the Third Battalion.

King, Victor, promoted to lieutenant after serving in the Pennsylvania Regiment of Three Battalions in 1758 and 1759.

King, William, age 31, mariner, born Barbadoes, enlisted 07 August 1746 in Captain William Trent's company.

Kingeade, Robert, *see* Robert Kincaid.

Kinght, Peter, lieutenant in the Associated Regiment in the County of Philadelphia in 1748.

Kinkannon, Patrick, private who enlisted 24 April 1756 in Captain Joseph Shippen's company in Colonel William Clapham's Regiment in 1756, the regiment in garrison at Fort Augusta, Shamokin, and listed in Shippen's Account Book.

Kinnard, William, private in Captain Patterson's company from 04 March 1757 stationed eastward of the Susquehanna. On a muster roll dated 08 March 1758.

Kinsey, Gilbert, age 44, cordwainer, born England, enlisted 16 July 1746 in Captain John Shannon's company of foot.

Kirgan, Jacob, age 19, weaver, born Chester, Pennsylvania, enlisted 11 May 1759, private in Captain John Mathers's company in the Pennsylvania Regiment. On a return dated 15 June 1759.

Kirkpatrick, David, second lieutenant from 25 April 1758 in Captain John McClughan's company raised for the campaign in the lower counties. Reported as dead.

Kirkpatrick, John, age 25, laborer, born Ireland, enlisted 23 May 1758 by Captain Benjamin Noxon.

Kirkpatrick, John, ensign in one of the new levies in May 1758.

Kirth, James, age 30, gentleman, born Scotland, enlisted 05 May 1749 in Captain Richard Gardiner's company in Colonel William Denney's Pennsylvania Regiment.

Kirts, Henry, age 16, skinner, born Germany, enlisted 04 May 1759, private in Captain William Johnston's company in the Pennsylvania Regiment. On a return dated 12 May 1759.

Kitson, Thomas, private, age 34, laborer, born Worcester, England, enlisted 24 April 1758 for the campaign in the lower counties. On a return of Captain McClughan's company dated 17 May 1758.

Klemm, William, lieutenant in the Associated Regiment of Foot of Philadelphia on 29 Dec 1747.

Kline, John, age 24, born Germany, enlisted 01 September 1757, private in Captain John Nicholas Weatherholt's company which enlisted for a term of three years and stationed in Heydelberg Township, Northampton County, in March and April 1758.

Kline, Philip, age 34, born Germany, enlisted 14 June 1757, private in Captain John Nicholas Weatherholt's company which enlisted for a term of three years and stationed in Heydelberg Township, Northampton County, in March and April 1758.

Kneffely, Philip Valentine, private who enlisted 19 April 1756 in Captain Elisha Saltar's company in Colonel William

Clapham's Regiment in 1756, the regiment in garrison at Fort Augusta, Shamokin, and listed in Shippen's Account Book.

Knight, George, age 22, mariner, born England, enlisted 15 May 1758. On a weekly return of Captain Samuel Jones's company in 1758.

Knight, Joseph, age 30, laborer, born England, enlisted 10 July 1746 in Captain John Deimer's company.

Knipal, Christopher, age 18, laborer, born Germany, enlisted 27 May 1758 by lieutenant William McClay for Captain John Montgomery's company.

Knoll, Peter, a private in Captain Charles Batho's Independent Company of Foot, Philadelphia in 1756.

Knowles, John, ensign in Captain Charles Batho's Independent Company of Foot, Philadelphia on 12 March 1756.

Knowles, John, ensign, Lower Delaware in the room of Buckridge Sims, 16 March 1756 {B6:1074:304}

Knowles, Peter, *see* Peter Nouls.

Koch, William, age 25, born Pennsylvania, enlisted 06 September 1757, private in Captain John Nicholas Weatherholt's company which enlisted for a term of three years and stationed in Heydelberg Township, Northampton County, in March and April 1758.

Kochenderfer, Andrew, age 33, carpenter, enlisted 14 July 1746 in Captain John Deimer's company.

Kollock, Jacob, Jun., lieutenant in the Northern District of Lewes and Rehoboth Hundred Captain David Hall's company of Colonel Jacob Kollock's Regiment of Sussex County in 1756/8. Described as Lewes District Company in 1758.

Kollock, Jacob, colonel of a Regiment of Sussex County in 1756/8.

Kollock, Jacob, lieutenant in Captain John Shannon's company from 25 June 1746, in winter quarters in Albany, N.Y., 1746–7, being discharged 31 October 1747.

Kornman, Conrad, *see* Cornman, Conrad.

Kough, Conrad, age 28, laborer, born Germany, enlisted 28 April 1759, private in Captain Joseph Richardson's company of the

Third Battalion in the Pennsylvania Regiment. On a return of recruits dated 1759.

Kountz, Henry, age 28, laborer, born Germany, enlisted 17 July 1746 in Captain Samuel Perry's company.

Kreamer, Jacob, *see* Jacob Cremer.

Kreider, Jacob, ensign in Captain Jacob Orndt's company of the First Battalion from 19 April 1756.

Kreusen, Henry, captain in one of the Associated Companies of Bucks County in 1756.

Krist, Michael, *see* Christ, Michael.

Krith, James, age 30, baker, born England, enlisted 09 May 1749 in Captain Richard Gardiner's company in Colonel William Denney's Pennsylvania Regiment.

Krumbach, Peter, age 23, blacksmith, born Germany, enlisted 17 July 1746 in Captain Samuel Perry's company.

Kumly, Conrad, a private in Captain Edward Jones's Independent Company of Horse, Philadelphia in 1756.

Kunrad, Peter, *see* Peter Conrad.

Kuntz, John, a private in Captain Edward Jones's Independent Company of Horse, Philadelphia in 1756.

Kurtz, Henry, *see* Henry Kirts.

Kuzer, Jacob, age 22, miler, born Germany, enlisted 10 May 1758. On a return of Captain John Blackwood's company in the Third Battalion dated 22 May 1758.

Laciter, Edward, landsman on the provincial ship *Pennsylvania* on 17 August 1757.

Lackey, James, age 21, laborer, enlisted 22 July 1746 in Captain John Deimer's company.

Lacy, James, age 22, carpenter, born Pennsylvania, enlisted 25 April 1758. On a weekly return of Captain Samuel Jones's company in 1758.

Laferty, John, age 25, laborer, born Antrim, Ireland, enlisted 29 April 1759, private in Captain John Haslet's company in the Pennsylvania Regiment. On a list of recruits dated 20 May 1759.

Lafferdson, Laffert, ensign in one of the Associated Companies of Bucks County in 1756.

Lake, John, private, age 30, butcher, born Great Hornet, England, enlisted 06 May 1758 for the campaign in the lower counties. On a return of Captain McClughan's company dated 17 May 1758.

Lalley, Thomas, enlisted 03 July 1746 in Captain William Trent's company, deserted 31 August 1746.

Lanagan, Patrick, seaman on the provincial ship *Pennsylvania* on 17 August 1757.

Lancaster, Henry, age 23, laborer, born Maryland, enlisted 29 April 1758 by Captain Benjamin Noxon.

Lancaster, Sinclair, age 21, cordwainer, born Maryland, enlisted 25 April 1758 by Captain Benjamin Noxon.

Landsgrove, John, age 49, gardener, born Brunswick, Hanover, enlisted 16 May 1759, private in Captain John Mathers's company in the Pennsylvania Regiment. On a return dated 15 June 1759.

Lane, Joseph, age 24, laborer, enlisted 09 July 1746 in Captain John Deimer's company.

Lang, Josh, age 35, mariner, born England, enlisted 16 May 1749 in Captain Richard Gardiner's company in Colonel William Denney's Pennsylvania Regiment.

Langley, Thomas, landsman on the provincial ship *Pennsylvania* on 17 August 1757.

Lappin, Paul, age 19, laborer, born Ireland, enlisted 21 July 1746 in Captain John Shannon's company of foot.

Lardner, Lyford, lieutenant in the Associated Regiment of Foot of Philadelphia on 29 Dec 1747.

Lardner, Lynford, lieutenant in Edward Jones's Independent Company of Horse, Philadelphia in 1756.

Larey, John, age 21, laborer, born Ireland, enlisted 26 June 1746 in Captain William Trent's company.

Larimore, Hugh, age 35, weaver, born Ireland, enlisted 03 May 1758 by Captain Benjamin Noxon.

Larkins, John, enlisted 22 May 1758 in Captain French Battell's company of Lower County Provincials.

Lasson, John, a private in Captain George Armstrong's Company, Second Battalion in 1756; killed at Kittanning.

Lastly, Barnabas, age 24, laborer, born Ireland, enlisted 23 July 1746 in Captain John Shannon's company of foot.

Latimer, James, captain in the Christiana Hundred company of Colonel William Armstrong's Upper Regiment of New Castle County in 1756.

Lattimore, Robert, promoted to lieutenant after serving in the Pennsylvania Regiment of Three Battalions in 1758 and 1759.

Laughman, John, age 19, laborer, born Ireland, enlisted 19 May 1758 by Lieutenant William McClay for Captain John Montgomery's company.

Laughrey, _____, ensign from 26 April 1758 in Captain William McKnight's company in the First Battalion.

Laughrey, James, commissioned 20 December 1757, lieutenant in Captain John Nicholas Weatherholt's company, which enlisted for a term of three years and was stationed in Heydelberg Township, Northampton County, in March and April 1758. Resigned 17 March 1759.

Laughrey, James, lieutenant in Captain John Nicholas Wetherholt's company from 20 December 1757 stationed eastward of the Susquehanna.

Laughry, Dennis, age 20, born Ireland, enlisted 01 February 1758, private in Captain John Nicholas Weatherholt's company which enlisted for a term of three years and was stationed in Heydelberg Township, Northampton County, in March and April 1758.

Launtz, Baltzer, private who enlisted 28 April 1756 in Captain Joseph Shippen's company in Colonel William Clapham's Regiment in 1756, the regiment in garrison at Fort Augusta, Shamokin, and listed in Shippen's Account Book.

Laurence, Edward, age 34, laborer, born Pennsylvania, enlisted 15 May 1749 in Captain Richard Gardiner's company in Colonel William Denney's Pennsylvania Regiment.

Laury, Michael, private in Captain Charles Foulk's company of the First Battalion in 1755/6.

Lavel, David, age 15, laborer, born Newcastle, enlisted 07 May 1759, private in Captain John Haslet's company in the

Pennsylvania Regiment. On a list of recruits dated 20 May 1759.

Laverty, Patrick, age 22, weaver, born Ireland, enlisted 18 July 1746 in Captain Samuel Perry's company.

Lawell, David, ensign in the Associated Regiment of Bucks County in 1748.

Lawrence, Thomas, a private in Captain Charles Batho's Independent Company of Foot, Philadelphia in 1756.

Lawrence, Thomas, age 36, saddler, born Ireland, enlisted 10 May 1758. On a weekly return of Captain Samuel Jones's company in 1758.

Lawrence, Thomas, Jun., ensign in the Associated Regiment of Foot of Philadelphia on 29 Dec 1747.

Lawrie, James, lieutenant in Captain Samuel Perry's company, in winter quarters in Albany, N.Y., 1746–7, being discharged 31 October 1747.

Lawson, Moses, ensign in one of the Associated Companies of York County in 1756.

Layans, Robert, age 17, laborer, born Pennsylvania, enlisted 08 May 1758. On a return of Captain John Bull's company dated 01 July 1758.

Layland, Thomas, a private in Captain Joseph Inslee's Company of Foot, Newtown, Bucks County, in 1756.

Leas, Bartley, on a list of men recruited by Captain Andrew McDowell's company in the Second Battalion, Pennsylvania Regiment dated 04 June 1759.

Lecompt, Peter, enlisted 24 May 1758 in Captain French Battell's company of Lower County Provincials.

Lee, James, age 30, laborer, born Ireland, enlisted 07 July 1746 in Captain John Shannon's company of foot.

Lee, Robert, age 28, laborer, born Ireland, enlisted 01 August 1746 in Captain Samuel Perry's company.

Lee, Thomas, age 18, laborer, born Ireland, enlisted 19 July 1746 in Captain Samuel Perry's company.

Leech, Jacob, lieutenant, then Captain on 04 August 1748, in the Associated Regiment in the County of Philadelphia in 1748. Elected captain in the room of Thomas York. [CR,V, 325]

Leech, James, age 18, laborer, born Maryland, enlisted 09 May 1758 by Captain Benjamin Noxon.

Leech, James, enlisted 28 May 1758 in Captain French Battell's company of Lower County Provincials.

Leech, Joseph, lieutenant in one of the companies of Colonel Jacob Duché's Philadelphia Regiment in 1756.

Leech, Thomas, Junr., second lieutenant of the provincial ship *Pennsylvania* on 17 August 1757.

Leeper, James, lieutenant in one of the new levies in May 1758.

Leggitt, George, captain in the Associated Regiment of Chester County in 1747. [CR,V,325]

Leggitt, Thomas, lieutenant in the Associated Regiment of Chester County in 1747. [CR,V,325]

Lemie, Abraham, *see* Abraham Lemy.

Lemms, Christopher, captain of a company in Lieutenant Colonel Commandant Asher Clayton's Second Battalion of the Pennsylvania Regiment commanded by the Hon. J. Penn from 22 July 1763.

Lemy, Abraham, on a list of men recruited by Captain Andrew McDowell's company in the Second Battalion, Pennsylvania Regiment dated 04 June 1759.

Leopold, Albert, age 23, cooper, enlisted 08 July 1746 in Captain John Deimer's company.

Lester, Thomas, age 29, mariner, born New England, enlisted 20 May 1749 in Captain Richard Gardiner's company in Colonel William Denney's Pennsylvania Regiment.

Leston, Ebenezer, age 25, laborer, born Delaware, enlisted 03 May 1758 by Captain Benjamin Noxon.

Letbe, John, age 21, laborer, born Germany, enlisted 01 May 1758. On a return of Captain John Bull's company dated 01 July 1758.

Levis, Joseph, lieutenant in the Associated Regiment in the County of Philadelphia in 1748.

Lewis, Charles, age 27, laborer, born York, England, enlisted 16 May 1759, private in Captain John Mathers's company in the Pennsylvania Regiment. On a return dated 15 June 1759.

Lewis, Daniel, age 27, fiddle maker, born England, enlisted 25 April 1758. On a weekly return of Captain Samuel Jones's company in 1758.

Lewis, Evan, ensign from 29 March 1758 in Captain John Caton's company from Upper District of Mother-Kill Hundred, Kent County, Delaware.

Lewis, James, lieutenant in one of the Associated Companies of Kent County in August 1748.

Lewis, James, lieutenant in one of the new levies in May 1758.

Lewis, John, a private in Captain George Armstrong's Company, Second Battalion in 1756; missing at the capture of Kittanning.

Lewis, Philip, a private in Captain Adam Heylman's Company, of the St. Vincent and Puke's Land Association on 10 May 1756.

Lewis, William, age 40, laborer, born Chester, Pennsylvania, enlisted 10 May 1759, private in Captain James Armstrong's company in Colonel William Clapham's Pennsylvania Regiment. On a return dated 01 June 1759.

Lieser, Frederick, age 19, born Germany, enlisted 21 June 1757, private in Captain John Nicholas Weatherholt's company which enlisted for a term of three years and was stationed in Heydelberg Township, Northampton County, in March and April 1758.

Likens, John, lieutenant in Captain Samuel Hunter's company in the First Battalion of the Pennsylvania Regiment from 15 July 1763.

Lillis, William, age 18, laborer, born Ireland, enlisted 25 May 1758 by Lieutenant William McClay for Captain John Montgomery's company.

Lindon, Patrick, age 35, laborer, born Ireland, enlisted 05 July 1746 in Captain William Trent's company.

Lindsay, James, lieutenant in Captain David McAllister's company of the First Battalion of the Pennsylvania Regiment from 25 April 1760.

Lindsay, John, private who enlisted 20 April 1756 in Captain Joseph Shippen's company in Colonel William Clapham's Regiment in 1756, the regiment in garrison at Fort Augusta, Shamokin, and listed in Shippen's Account Book.

Lindsay, Robert, age 26, laborer, born Ireland, enlisted 27 April 1759 in Captain Charles Stewart's company [probably one of the Associated Companies of Bucks County]. On a return dated June 1759.

Lindsay, Samuel, captain of a company in Lieutenant Colonel Commandant Asher Clayton's Second Battalion of the Pennsylvania Regiment commanded by the Hon. J. Penn from 13 July 1763.

Lindsey, George, enlisted 24 May 1758 in Captain French Battell's company of Lower County Provincials.

Lindsey, Samuel, ensign from 03 May 1758 in Captain James Sharp's company of the Third Battalion. Ensign from 21 April 1759 in Captain James Sharp's company of Colonel William Clapham's Regiment of New Levies.

Lindsey, Samuel, promoted to captain after serving in the Pennsylvania Regiment of Three Battalions in 1758 and 1759. Reported to have "joined Colonel Francis".

Lindsey, Walter, age 28, laborer, born Ireland, enlisted 24 July 1746 in Captain Samuel Perry's company.

Linegar, William, age 28, private in Captain John Wright's company of the Lower County. On a muster dated 11 May 1759.

Lings, Archibald, age 17, born Virginia, private in Captain John Wright's company of the Lower County. On a muster dated 11 May 1759.

Linings, John, private who enlisted 15 April 1756 in Captain Joseph Shippen's company in Colonel William Clapham's Regiment in 1756, the regiment in garrison at Fort Augusta, Shamokin, and listed in Shippen's Account Book.

Littell, Absalom, ensign in Captain Joseph Cord's Company from the Southern District of Broad-Kill Hundred, Sussex County, Delaware, in Colonel Jacob Killock's Regiment in 1758.

Little, Absalom, ensign in the Southern District of Broad Kiln Hundred company of Colonel Jacob Kollock's Regiment of Sussex County in 1756.

Little, Casper, ensign in one of the Associated Companies of York County in 1756.

Little, John, captain of a company under Commandant James Potter on the Northern Frontier on 02 October 1764.
Little, John, ensign in one of the Associated Companies of York County in 1756.
Little, Nathaniel, ensign in the Associated Regiment of the West End of Lancaster County in 1747–8.
Little, Richard, private, age 26, schoolmaster, born Ireland, enlisted 21 April 1758 for the campaign in the lower counties. On a return of Captain McClughan's company dated 17 May 1758.
Littles, William, ensign in the Associated Regiment of Chester County in 1747.
Lloyd, Thomas was promoted to the rank of lieutenant colonel after having served in the Pennsylvania Regiment of Three Battalions, 1758 and 1759 and left the province.
Lloyd, Thomas, captain of a company of the Third Battalion (known as the Augusta Regiment) promoted to aid-de-camp on 02 April 1756. Captain of a company in the Second Battalion from 07 December 1757 and from 22 February 1758 stationed at Fort Augusta. Lieutenant colonel from 30 May 1758 in the Second Battalion. Lieutenant colonel of the First Battalion of the Pennsylvania Regiment in 1759.
Loan, Swain, age 22, mariner, born Sweedland, enlisted 01 May 1758. On a weekly return of Captain Samuel Jones's company in 1758.
Locke, Jacob, age 22, blacksmith, born Pennsylvania, enlisted 05 May 1758. On a weekly return of Captain Samuel Jones's company in 1758.
Logan, George, a private in Captain Joseph Inslee's Company of Foot, Newtown, Bucks County, in 1756.
Logan, Hugh, age 24, born Scotland, private in Captain John Haslett's company enlisted on 08 May 1758 and last paid on 21 May 1758.
Logan, James, age 26, laborer, born Ireland, enlisted 01 May 1759 in Captain Charles Stewart's company [probably one of the Associated Companies of Bucks County]. On a return dated June 1759.

Logan, William, private in Captain Joseph Inslee's Company of Foot, Newtown, Bucks County, in 1756.

Lollar, Andrew, *see* Sollar, Andrew.

Long, Hendy, on a return of Captain David Hunter's Company [probably from York County] in Colonel William Clapham's Regiment of New Levies dated 26 May 1759.

Long, John, age 24, born Chester, Pennsylvania, private in Captain John Singleton's company in service between 01 May and 08 May 1758.

Long, John, on a return of Captain David Hunter's Company [probably from York County] in Colonel William Clapham's Regiment of New Levies dated 26 May 1759.

Long, John, landsman on the provincial ship *Pennsylvania* on 17 August 1757.

Long, Killian, in Captain Charles Foulk's company of the First Battalion in 1755/6.

Long, Richard, ensign in Captain Joseph Armstrong's company in Lieutenant Colonel Commandant Asher Clayton's Second Battalion of the Pennsylvania Regiment commanded by the Hon. J. Penn from 17 July 1763.

Long, Solomon, age 30, laborer, born Ireland, enlisted 15 May 1758 by Captain Benjamin Noxon. Formerly with the Royal Americans.

Longshore, Robert, a private in Captain Joseph Inslee's Company of Foot, Newtown, Bucks County, in 1756.

Longwill, James, private, age 22, laborer, born St. Johnson, Ireland, enlisted 27 April 1758 for the campaign in the lower counties. On a return of Captain McClughan's company on 17 May 1758.

Lorne, Charles, age 25, weaver, born Ireland, enlisted 21 July 1746 in Captain William Trent's company.

Losch, Jacob, a private in Captain Adam Heylman's Company, of the St. Vincent and Puke's Land Association on 10 May 1756.

Lott, Henry, captain in one of the Associated Companies of Bucks County in 1756.

Loudoun, Richard, private in Captain John Singleton's company in service between 01 May and 08 May 1758.

Loughrey, Archibald, ensign in Captain Christopher Lemms' company in Lieutenant Colonel Commandant Asher Clayton's Second Battalion of the Pennsylvania Regiment commanded by the Hon. J. Penn 18 July 1763.

Loughrey, Jeremiah, lieutenant in Captain John Proctor's company in the First Battalion of the Pennsylvania Regiment during or after 1763.

Love, Robert, age 20, born New Castle, "bold looking, a Scotchman", private in Captain John Singleton's company in service between 01 May and 08 May 1758.

Love, Samuel, ensign in the Associated Regiment of Chester County in 1747.

Low, Matthias, age 20, laborer, born Germany, enlisted 15 May 1758. On a return of Captain John Bull's company dated 01 July 1758.

Lowdon, John, ensign in Captain Edward Ward's Company, Second Battalion from 19 April 1756, living at Susquehanna.

Lower, William, age 19, laborer, enlisted 01 July 1746 in Captain John Deimer's company.

Lowermore, Hugh, a private in Captain Joseph Inslee's Company of Foot, Newtown, Bucks County, in 1756.

Lowrie, William, seaman on the provincial ship *Pennsylvania* on 17 August 1757.

Lowry, David, age 31, born Antrim, Ireland, private in Captain John Haslett's company enlisted on 13 May 1758 and last paid on 21 May 1758.

Lowry, Robert, ensign from 27 April 1759 in Captain John Clark's company of Colonel William Clapham's Regiment of New Levies.

Luff, Caleb, ensign in the Dover Hundred company of Colonel John Vining's Regiment of Kent County Militia, Upon Delaware in 1756.

Lutz, John, age 25, born Germany, tailor, enlisted 01 September 1757, corporal in Captain John Nicholas Weatherholt's company which enlisted for a term of three years and was stationed in Heydelberg Township, Northampton County, in March and April 1758.

Lycans, John, a lieutenant stationed on the frontier in Lancaster County with one sergeant and fifteen men at Monody Gap, Hanover Township, on 01 June 1764 as part of a unit under the command of Major Asher Clayton.

Lyon, William, ensign in Captain Hugh Mercer's Company, Second Battalion, resigned before 22 May 1756. Lieutenant from 06 December 1757 in Captain William Thompson's company stationed westward of the Susquehanna. Resigned 17 March 1758.

Lytle, John, captain of a company of the Second Battalion of the Pennsylvania Regiment from 27 April 1760.

Lytle, John, commissioned 11 December 1757, ensign in Captain George Armstrong's Company of the First Battalion. Ensign in Captain John Nicholas Weatherholt's company which enlisted for a term of three years and was stationed in Heydelberg Township, Northampton County, in March and April 1758.

Lyttle, John, *see* John Lytle.

Lyttle, John, second lieutenant from 01 May 1758 in Captain William Thompson's troop of Light Horse in the First Battalion.

Lyttle, John, ensign in Captain John Nicholas Wetherholt's company from 11 December 1757 stationed eastward of the Susquehanna.

Lyttle, John, Jr., promoted to captain after serving in the Pennsylvania Regiment of Three Battalions in 1758 and 1759.

Lyttle, John, promoted to captain after serving in the Pennsylvania Regiment of Three Battalions in 1758 and 1759.

Maag, Jacob, a private in Captain Edward Jones's Independent Company of Horse, Philadelphia in 1756.

Machan, John, a member of Captain Joseph Armstrong's Company on 07 August 1755, raised in Cumberland County.

Mack, Frederick, a private in Captain Adam Heylman's Company, of the St. Vincent and Puke's Land Association on 10 May 1756.

Mackaning, William, age 21, born Maryland, private in Captain John Wright's company of the Lower County. On a muster dated 11 May 1759.

Mackey, Daniel, a member of Captain David Jameson's Company at McCord's Fort on 02 April 1756 when he was killed.

Mackey, Robert, lieutenant in the Associated Regiment of Chester County in 1747.

Mackey, William, seaman on the provincial ship *Pennsylvania* on 17 August 1757.

Maclay, William, lieutenant from 07 May 1758 in Captain John Montgomery's company in the Third Battalion.

Maclay, William, lieutenant in Lieutenant Colonel Commandant Asher Clayton's Company of the Second Battalion of the Pennsylvania Regiment commanded by the Hon. J. Penn from 04 July 1764.

Maclay, William, promoted to lieutenant after serving in the Pennsylvania Regiment of Three Battalions in 1758 and 1759.

Madden, Daniel, seaman on the provincial ship *Pennsylvania* on 17 August 1757.

Maddin, Patrick, private in Captain Patterson's company from 13 February 1758 stationed eastward of the Susquehanna. On a muster roll dated 08 March 1758.

Maddox, Joshua, a private in Captain John Kidd's Independent Company of Foot, Philadelphia in 1756.

Maffet, John, on a list of men recruited by Captain Andrew McDowell's company in the Second Battalion, Pennsylvania Regiment dated 04 June 1759.

Magraw, James, age 21, tailor, born Maryland, private in Captain John Wright's company of the Lower County. On a muster dated 11 May 1759.

Mahan, Owen, age 36, laborer, born Ireland, enlisted 13 August 1746 in Captain William Trent's company.

Mahan, Thomas, age 27, chair maker, born Ireland, enlisted 02 May 1758 by Captain Benjamin Noxon.

Mahany, William, landsman on the provincial ship *Pennsylvania* on 17 August 1757.

Mahood, John, age 21, carpenter, born Delaware, enlisted 20 May 1758 by Captain Benjamin Noxon.

Major, William, age 30, born Ireland, private in Captain John Haslett's company enlisted on 04 May 1758 and last paid on 21 May 1758.

Maloney, Ber., age 34, laborer, born Ireland, enlisted 01 May 1758. On a return of Captain John Blackwood's company in the Third Battalion dated 22 May 1758.

Malony, John Berry, age 30, laborer, born Ireland, enlisted 07 May 1758. On a weekly return of Captain Samuel Jones's company in 1758.

Malvain, William, age 30, laborer, born Ireland, enlisted 29 July 1746 in Captain Samuel Perry's company.

Man, William, age 17, born Sussex, Delaware, private in Captain John Wright's company of the Lower County. On a muster dated 11 May 1759.

Mangan, John, age 22, laborer, born Ireland, enlisted 14 July 1746 in Captain Samuel Perry's company.

Mann, Jacob, a private in Captain Adam Heylman's Company, of the St. Vincent and Puke's Land Association on 10 May 1756.

Mann, William, private, age 17, farmer, born Angola Hundred, Delaware, enlisted 22 April 1758 for the campaign in the lower counties. On a return of Captain McClughan's company dated 17 May 1758.

Mannerly, William, enlisted 17 May 1758 in Captain French Battell's company of Lower County Provincials.

Mar, John Peter, age 25, laborer, born Germany, enlisted 12 July 1746 in Captain John Deimer's company.

Marrat, Joseph, ensign in the Upper Part of Mispillim Hundred company of Colonel John Vining's Regiment of Kent County Militia, Upon Delaware in 1756.

Marsh, Peter, ensign in the Southern District of Lewes and Rehoboth Hundred Captain John Newbold's company of Colonel Jacob Kollock's Regiment of Sussex County in 1756/8. Described as Rehobeth District Company in 1758.

Marshal, William, age 30, laborer, born Ireland, enlisted 03 May 1758. On a return of Captain John Bull's company dated 01 July 1758. Formerly in Pennsylvania Regiment.

Marshall, Adam, a private in Captain Edward Jones's Independent Company of Horse, Philadelphia in 1756.

Marshall, David, captain in one of the Associated Companies of Kent County in June 1748.

Marshall, William, landsman on the provincial ship *Pennsylvania* on 17 August 1757.

Marsloff, Philip, lieutenant in Captain Jacob Orndt's company of the First Battalion from 27 April 1756; left out of the reorganization of December 1757.

Marsloff, Philip, lieutenant on a List of Officers in the Province Pay, 1756 in the First Battalion of the Pennsylvania Regiment with a commission date of 27 April 1756. {PA5, I, 88}

Martin, Daniel, private in Captain Patterson's company from 08 January 1758 stationed eastward of the Susquehanna. On a muster roll dated 08 March 1758.

Martin, George, captain in one of the Associated Companies of Kent County in 1747–8.

Martin, Hugh, on a list of men recruited by Captain Andrew McDowell's company in the Second Battalion, Pennsylvania Regiment dated 04 June 1759.

Martin, Hugh, private, age 30, weaver, born Tyrone, Ireland, enlisted 29 April 1758 for the campaign in the lower counties. On a return of Captain McClughan's company dated 17 May 1758.

Martin, James, *see* Mortin, James.

Martin, James, lieutenant in the Associated Regiment of Bucks County in 1748.

Martin, John, private who enlisted 16 April 1756 in Captain Joseph Shippen's company in Colonel William Clapham's Regiment in 1756, the regiment in garrison at Fort Augusta, Shamokin, and listed in Shippen's Account Book.

Martin, Patrick, age 30, laborer, born Ireland, enlisted 19 July 1746 in Captain William Trent's company.

Martin, Samuel, ensign in the Associated Regiment of Bucks County in 1748.

Marvin, Henry, age 24, born Ireland, piper, private in Captain John Shannon's Company, enlisted 9 July 1746. On a roll of deserters dated 22 July 1746. [B3:422:18]

Mason, Abraham, ensign in the Associated Regiment of Foot of Philadelphia on 29 Dec 1747.

Mason, Elias, age 19, born Kent, Delaware, private in Captain John Wright's company of the Lower County. On a muster dated 11 May 1759.

Massey, James, lieutenant from 06 May 1759 in Captain Samuel Grubb's company of Colonel William Clapham's Regiment of New Levies.

Massey, James, promoted to lieutenant after serving in the Pennsylvania Regiment of Three Battalions in 1758 and 1759.

Mather, John, captain from 22 April 1759 of a company in Colonel William Clapham's Regiment of New Levies.

Mather, John, major in the Associated Regiment of Chester County in 1747.

Mather, John, promoted to captain after serving in the Pennsylvania Regiment of Three Battalions in 1758 and 1759. Reported as "dead".

Mathers, James, lieutenant in the Associated Regiment of Chester County in 1747.

Mathers, John, captain in the Associated Regiment of Chester County in 1747.

Matthews, _____, sergeant in Captain Jacob Morgan's company stationed eastward of the Susquehanna in December 1757.

Matthews, Edmund, ensign in Captain James Patterson's company of the First Battalion from 14 March 1758 stationed eastward of the Susquehanna. On a muster roll dated 08 March 1758.

Matthews, Edmund, lieutenant in Captain Francis Johnston's company of the Second Battalion of the Pennsylvania Regiment from 16 April 1760.

Matthews, Edmund, promoted to lieutenant after serving in the Pennsylvania Regiment of Three Battalions in 1758 and 1759. Reported as "discontinued".

Matthews, George, age 23, blacksmith, born Ireland, enlisted 20 July 1746 in Captain Samuel Perry's company.
Matthews, Hugh, age 45, laborer, born Nichliff, Ireland, enlisted 22 May 1759, private in Captain John Mathers's company in the Pennsylvania Regiment. On a return dated 15 June 1759.
Matthews, John, on a return of Captain David Hunter's Company [probably from York County] in Colonel William Clapham's Regiment of New Levies dated 26 May 1759.
Matthias, George, age 18, laborer, born Chester, Pennsylvania, enlisted 02 June 1759 in Captain Robert Boyd's company [probably in the Third Battalion]. On a return dated May and June 1759.
Matthias, William, age 22, laborer, born Ireland, enlisted 11 June 1759 in Captain Robert Boyd's company [probably in the Third Battalion] on a return dated May and June 1759.
Maxwell, James, ensign in one of the new levies in May 1758.
Maxwell, Richard, age 23, cordwainer, born New England, enlisted 12 June 1758 by Lieutenant William McClay for Captain John Montgomery's company.
Maxwell, William, captain, 1745
Maxwell, William, captain in the Associated Regiment of Lancaster County over the Susquehanna in 1747–8.
Maxwell, William, major in the Associated Regiment of Lancaster County over the Susquehanna in 1747–8.
Maxwell, William, on a list of men recruited by Captain Andrew McDowell's company in the Second Battalion, Pennsylvania Regiment dated 04 June 1759.
Maybe, Edward, age 30, laborer, born England, enlisted 29 May 1749 in Captain Richard Gardiner's company in Colonel William Denney's Pennsylvania Regiment.
Mayor, Ludowick, on a return of Captain David Hunter's Company [probably from York County] in Colonel William Clapham's Regiment of New Levies dated 26 May 1759.
McAdoe, Ezekiel, private in Captain Patterson's company from 01 December 1757 stationed eastward of the Susquehanna. On a muster roll dated 08 March 1758.

McAfee, John, age 21, born Chester, Pennsylvania, laborer, private in Captain John Haslett's company enlisted on 08 May 1758 and last paid on 21 May 1758.

McAfee, John, age 25, born Long Island, private in Captain John Wright's company of the Lower County. On a muster dated 11 May 1759.

McAfee, Robert, age 22, cooper, born Ireland, enlisted 05 July 1746 in Captain John Shannon's company of foot.

McAlca, Mark, a private in Captain Joseph Inslee's Company of Foot, Newtown, Bucks County, in 1756.

McAlevy, William, private in Captain Patterson's company from 10 January 1758 stationed eastward of the Susquehanna. On a muster roll dated 08 March 1758.

McAllister, Alexander, age 24, laborer, born Donegal, Ireland, enlisted 06 May 1759, private in Captain John Haslet's company in the Pennsylvania Regiment. On a list of recruits dated 20 May 1759.

McAllister, David, captain of a company of the First Battalion of the Pennsylvania Regiment from 19 April 1760.

McAllister, David, lieutenant in Captain William McKnight's company in the First Battalion. Lieutenant from 20 April 1759 in Captain William Johnston's company of Colonel William Clapham's Regiment of New Levies. On a return dated 12 May 1759 listed as resigned.

McAllister, David, promoted to captain after serving in the Pennsylvania Regiment of Three Battalions in 1758 and 1759. Reported as "dead".

McAllister, James, lieutenant in Captain Joseph Armstrong's company in Lieutenant Colonel Commandant Asher Clayton's Second Battalion of the Pennsylvania Regiment commanded by the Hon. J. Penn from 17 July 1763.

McAllister, Patrick, age 26, laborer, born Donegal, Ireland, enlisted 27 April 1759, private in Captain John Haslet's company in the Pennsylvania Regiment. On a list of recruits dated 20 May 1759.

McAllister, Patrick, age 27, born Longford, Ireland, laborer, private in Captain John Haslett's company enlisted on 09 May 1758 and last paid on 21 May 1758.

McAnulty, John, private, age 28, farmer, born Derry, Ireland, enlisted 22 April 1758 for the campaign in the lower counties. On a return of Captain McClughan's company dated 17 May 1758.

McAteer, James, captain in the Associated Regiment of Lancaster County over the Susquehanna in 1747–8.

McBride, Francis, hired 02 June 1757 as a battoe man, Master George Allen.

McCabe, Alexander, age 28, laborer, born Ireland, enlisted 03 July 1746 in Captain John Shannon's company of foot.

McCadden, Henry, age 23, cordwainer, born Ireland, enlisted 03 May 1758. On a return of Captain John Bull's company dated 01 July 1758.

McCafferty, Bartholomew, a private in Captain John Potter's Company, Second Battalion; killed near McDowell's Fort in November 1756.

McCall, Archibald, a private in Captain Samuel Mifflin's Association Battery Company of Philadelphia in 1756.

McCall, George, a private in Captain John Kidd's Independent Company of Foot, Philadelphia in 1756.

McCall, John, captain in the Associated Regiment of Chester County in 1747.

McCall, John, ensign in one of the Associated Companies of York County in 1756.

McCall, Samuel Jr., a private in Captain Charles Batho's Independent Company of Foot, Philadelphia in 1756.

McCalla, Charles, age 31, laborer, born Ireland, enlisted 22 July 1746 in Captain John Shannon's company of foot.

McCalla, George, a private in Captain Samuel Mifflin's Association Battery Company of Philadelphia in 1756.

McCalla, James, age 24, born Derry, Ireland, "a Scotchman", private in Captain John Haslett's company enlisted on 16 May 1758 and last paid on 21 May 1758.

McCalley, Edward, private who enlisted 01 April 1756 in Captain Joseph Shippen's company in Colonel William Clapham's Regiment in 1756, the regiment in garrison at Fort Augusta, Shamokin, and listed in Shippen's Account Book.

McCamant, Charles, a member of Captain Joseph Armstrong's Company on 07 August 1755, raised in Cumberland County.

McCamant, James, Jun., a member of Captain Joseph Armstrong's Company on 07 August 1755, raised in Cumberland County.

McCamant, James, Sr., a member of Captain Joseph Armstrong's Company on 07 August 1755, raised in Cumberland County.

McCamish, James, a member of Captain Joseph Armstrong's Company on 07 August 1755, raised in Cumberland County.

McCamish, William, a member of Captain Joseph Armstrong's Company on 07 August 1755, raised in Cumberland County.

McCane, Alexander, promoted to lieutenant after serving in the Pennsylvania Regiment of Three Battalions in 1758 and 1759.

McCanna, Patrick, private who enlisted 10 May 1756 in Captain Joseph Shippen's company in Colonel William Clapham's Regiment in 1756, the regiment in garrison at Fort Augusta, Shamokin, and listed in Shippen's Account Book.

McCarrick, Patrick, age 25, laborer, born Ireland, enlisted 27 April 1759 in Captain Charles Stewart's company [probably one of the Associated Companies of Bucks County]. On a return dated June 1759.

McCarroll, Thomas, seaman on the provincial ship *Pennsylvania* on 17 August 1757.

McCarter, John, ensign in one of the Associated Companies of Lancaster County in 1756.

McCartney, John, a private in Captain Hugh Mercer's Company, Second Battalion in 1756; killed at Kittanning.

McCarty, Bartholomew, age 22, laborer, born Ireland, enlisted 07 August 1746 in Captain William Trent's company.

McCarty, Cornelius, age 26, mariner, born Ireland, enlisted 10 July 1746 in Captain William Trent's company.

McCarty, Jeremiah, age 22, born Scotland, wigmaker, private in Captain John Haslett's company enlisted on 10 May 1758 and last paid on 21 May 1758.

McCarty, John, age 24, laborer, born Ireland, enlisted 30 June 1746 in Captain William Trent's company.

McCarvey, Jeremiah, age 25, laborer, born Ireland, enlisted 17 July 1746 in Captain John Deimer's company.

McCastle, William, age 26, laborer, born Antrim, Ireland, enlisted 30 April 1759, private in Captain James Armstrong's company in Colonel William Clapham's Pennsylvania Regiment. On a return dated 01 June 1759.

McCawley, Andrew, private in Captain Patterson's company from 06 January 1758 stationed eastward of the Susquehanna. On a muster roll dated 08 March 1758.

McCay, David, lieutenant from 30 April 1759 in Captain John Haslet's company in Colonel William Clapham's Regiment of New Levies.

McCay, David, promoted to lieutenant after serving in the Pennsylvania Regiment of Three Battalions in 1758 and 1759.

McClackran, Thomas, landsman on the provincial ship *Pennsylvania* on 17 August 1757.

McClavran, John, age 20, born Argyle, Scotland, private in Captain John Haslett's company enlisted on 10 May 1758 and last paid on 21 May 1758.

McClavran, John, age 25, laborer, born Scotland, enlisted 03 May 1759, private in Captain John Haslet's company in the Pennsylvania Regiment. On a list of recruits dated 20 May 1759.

McClean, Anthony, ensign in Captain Samuel Nelson's company of the First Battalion of the Pennsylvania Regiment from April 1760.

McClean, John, age 35, weaver, born Ireland, enlisted 15 July 1746 in Captain John Shannon's company of foot.

McClearn, James, private, age 27, laborer, born Londonderry, Ireland, enlisted 01 May 1758 for the campaign in the lower counties. On a return of Captain McClughan's company dated 17 May 1758.

McCleary, Robert, age 18, tailor, born Pennsylvania, enlisted 05 May 1759, private in Captain John Haslet's company in the

Pennsylvania Regiment. On a list of recruits dated 20 May 1759.

McClellan, James, private, age 29, laborer, born Antrim, Ireland, enlisted 29 April 1758 for the campaign in the lower counties. On a return of Captain McClughan's company dated 17 May 1758.

McCloskey, Henry, age 19, laborer, born Ireland, enlisted 17 July 1746 in Captain Samuel Perry's company.

McCloud, John, enlisted 18 May 1758 in Captain French Battell's company of Lower County Provincials.

McClowley, James, landsman on the provincial ship *Pennsylvania* on 17 August 1757.

McCluan, John, age 22, born Armagh, Ireland, weaver, private in Captain John Haslett's company enlisted on 13 May 1758 and last paid on 21 May 1758.

McClue, John, ensign in Major Thomas Smallman's company of the Second Battalion of the Pennsylvania Regiment from 03 May 1760.

McClughan, John, Captain from 16 April 1758 of a company raised for the campaign in the lower counties. On a return of his company dated 17 May 1758. Captain from 21 May 1759 of a company from the Lower County. Commission revoked.

McClung, Charles, captain from 09 May 1758 of a company in the Third Battalion.

McClure, David, captain in the Associated Regiment of the West End of Lancaster County in 1747–8.

McClure, John, age 26, born Antrim, Ireland, "well made, a good woodsman", private in Captain John Haslett's company enlisted on 18 May 1758 and last paid on 21 May 1758.

McClure, Samuel, age 26, laborer, born Ulster, Ireland, enlisted 30 April 1759, private in Captain James Armstrong's company in Colonel William Clapham's Pennsylvania Regiment. On a return dated 01 June 1759.

McClure, William, ensign not assigned in the First Battalion of the Pennsylvania Regiment from 11 May 1760.

McConnell, James, private in Captain John Singleton's company in service between 01 May and 08 May 1758.

McConnell, Robert, a member of Captain Joseph Armstrong's Company on 07 August 1755, raised in Cumberland County.

McCord, John, age 18, laborer, born Lancaster, Pennsylvania, enlisted 02 May 1759, private in Captain John Mathers's company in the Pennsylvania Regiment. On a return dated 15 June 1759.

McCord, William, a member of Captain Joseph Armstrong's Company on 07 August 1755, raised in Cumberland County.

McCord, William, age 30, laborer, born Ireland, enlisted 24 July 1746 in Captain Samuel Perry's company.

McCormick, David, enlisted 28 May 1759, private in Captain Henry Van Bibber's company of the Lower County. On a return dated 04 June 1759.

McCormick, John, a private in Captain Lieutenant Robert Callender's County, Second Battalion in 1756; killed at Kittanning.

McCormick, John, age 22, laborer, born Ireland, enlisted 28 April 1759 in Captain Charles Stewart's company [probably one of the Associated Companies of Bucks County]. On a return dated June 1759.

McCormick, John, lieutenant in the Associated Regiment of Lancaster County over the Susquehanna in 1747–8.

McCormick, Thomas, age 21, weaver, born Ireland, enlisted 18 July 1746 in Captain Samuel Perry's company.

McCotter, John, private in Captain Patterson's company from 02 January 1758 stationed eastward of the Susquehanna. On a muster roll dated 08 March 1758.

McCowen, Patrick, *see* McGowen, Patrick.

McCowey, Francis, age 35, born Armagh, Ireland, enlisted 22 May 1759, private in Captain John Mathers's company in the Pennsylvania Regiment. On a return dated 15 June 1759.

McCoy, Francis, hired 27 May 1757 as a battoe man, Master George Allen.

McCrea, William, captain then major in one of two regiments of New Castle County in 1747–8.

McCrinnel, William, age 30, laborer, born Scotland, enlisted 27 July 1746 in Captain Samuel Perry's company.

McCryne, Dominick, private who enlisted 04 May 1756 in Captain Joseph Shippen's company in Colonel William Clapham's Regiment in 1756, the regiment in garrison at Fort Augusta, Shamokin, and listed in Shippen's Account Book. Described as being of Hunter's Fort. May have been in Captain Elisha Slatar's company instead of Captain Shippen's.

McCuen, John, captain in the Associated Regiment of the West End of Lancaster County in 1747–8.

McCulloch, George, lieutenant in one of the new levies in May 1758.

McCullough, George, ensign in the Associated Regiment of Chester County in 1747.

McCullough, Miles, private in Captain Patterson's company from 01 January 1758 stationed eastward of the Susquehanna. On a muster roll dated 08 March 1758.

McCullough, Thomas, lieutenant in one of two regiments of New Castle County in 1747–8.

McCully, Hugh, age 26, cordwainer, born Monaghan, Ireland, enlisted 25 April 1759, private in Captain James Armstrong's company in Colonel William Clapham's Pennsylvania Regiment. On a return dated 01 June 1759.

McCully, Matthew, on a list of men recruited by Captain Andrew McDowell's company in the Second Battalion, Pennsylvania Regiment dated 04 June 1759.

McCully, Samuel, age 21, laborer, born Ireland, enlisted 23 May 1758 by Captain Benjamin Noxon.

McCurdy, _____, sergeant in Captain Nathan Mile's Company, Third Battalion (known as the Augusta Regiment) from 20 August 1756.

McCutchin, James, private in Captain John Singleton's company in service between 01 May and 08 May 1758.

McCutchin, John, age 20, born Cecil, Maryland, private in Captain John Singleton's company in service between 01 May and 08 May 1758.

McDael, John, landsman on the provincial ship *Pennsylvania* on 17 August 1757.

McDaniel, Daniel, private in Captain Patterson's company from 29 December 1757 stationed eastward of the Susquehanna. On a muster roll dated 08 March 1758.

McDaniel, Dennis, age 25, laborer, born Ireland, enlisted 14 July 1746 in Captain John Shannon's company of foot.

McDaniel, Henry, age 36, cooper, born Ireland, enlisted 10 June 1759, private in Captain Robert Curry's company in Colonel William Clapham's Pennsylvania Regiment. On a return dated June 1759.

McDaniel, James, age 30, laborer, born Tyrone, Ireland, enlisted 28 April 1759, private in Captain Joseph Richardson's company of the Third Battalion in the Pennsylvania Regiment. On a return of recruits dated 1759.

McDaniel, John, age 27, born Ireland, enlisted 23 May 1759, private in Captain Robert Curry's company in Colonel William Clapham's Pennsylvania Regiment. On a return dated June 1759.

McDaniel, John, private in Captain Patterson's company from 13 January 1758 stationed eastward of the Susquehanna. On a muster roll dated 08 March 1758.

McDavid, Neill, age 30, shoemaker, born Ireland, enlisted 01 May 1759, private in Captain James Armstrong's company in Colonel William Clapham's Pennsylvania Regiment. On a return dated 01 June 1759.

McDonald, Arthur, age 24, laborer, born Ireland, enlisted 08 August 1746 in Captain John Deimer's company.

McDonald, Bryan, age 18, laborer, born Ireland, enlisted 25 May 1758 by Lieutenant William McClay for Captain John Montgomery's company.

McDonald, Henry, age 40, cooper, born Scotland, enlisted 10 May 1759, private in Captain Robert Curry's company in Colonel William Clapham's Pennsylvania Regiment. On a return dated June 1759.

McDonald, James, a private in Captain John Potter's Company, Second Battalion; killed near McDowell's Fort in November 1756.

McDonald, John, a member of Captain David Jameson's Company at McCord's Fort on 02 April 1756 when he was wounded.

McDonald, Minass, age 30, laborer, born Ireland, enlisted 07 August 1746 in Captain William Trent's company.

McDonald, Peter, age 21, smith, born Scotland, enlisted 29 June 1746 in Captain William Trent's company.

McDonald, Richard, ensign in the Associated Regiment of the West End of Lancaster County in 1747–8.

McDonald, William, a private in Captain John Potter's Company, Second Battalion; killed near McDowell's Fort in November 1756.

McDonnell, John, age 40, laborer, born Ulster, Ireland, enlisted 26 April 1759, private in Captain James Armstrong's company in Colonel William Clapham's Pennsylvania Regiment. On a return dated 01 June 1759.

McDoran, John, age 49, groom, born Belfast, Ireland, enlisted 05 May 1759, private in Captain John Mathers's company in the Pennsylvania Regiment. On a return dated 15 June 1759.

McDougall, Henry Allen, first lieutenant of the provincial ship *Pennsylvania* on 17 August 1757.

McDowell, Alexander, Rev., chaplain of the Second Battalion of the Pennsylvania Regiment from April 1760.

McDowell, Andrew, captain in the Associated Regiment of Chester County in 1747.

McDowell, Andrew, colonel in the Associated Regiment of Chester County in 1747.

McDowell, Andrew, ensign from 30 April 1759 in Captain John Haslet's company in Colonel William Clapham's Regiment of New Levies. Captain from 06 May 1759 of a company of Colonel William Clapham's Regiment of New Levies.

McDowell, Andrew, promoted to captain after serving in the Pennsylvania Regiment of Three Battalions in 1758 and 1759.

McDowell, George, ensign from 24 April 1759 in Captain John Singleton's company of Colonel William Clapham's Regiment of New Levies.

McDowell, Thomas, lieutenant in the Associated Regiment of the West End of Lancaster County in 1747–8.

McDowell, William, promoted to lieutenant after serving in the Pennsylvania Regiment of Three Battalions in 1758 and 1759.

McDowell, William, sergeant in Captain Hance Hamilton's Company, Second Battalion in 1756 at the capture of Kittanning. Ensign from 16 May 1758 in Captain Thomas Hamilton's company in the Third Battalion. Lieutenant from 24 April 1759 in Captain John Singleton's company of Colonel William Clapham's Regiment of New Levies.

McDugald, Daniel, *see* McDugald, Donald.

McDugald, Donald, seaman on the provincial ship *Pennsylvania* on 17 August 1757.

McEanet, Daniel, captain in one of the companies of Colonel Jacob Duché's Philadelphia Regiment in 1756.

McEldemar, John, enlisted 01 July 1746 in Captain William Trent's company, deserted 19 August 1746.

McFarran, Matthias, age 20, laborer, born Pennsylvania, enlisted 28 May 1759 in Captain Robert Boyd's company [probably in the Third Battalion]. On a return dated May and June 1759.

McFetridge, William, private who enlisted 22 April 1756 in Captain Joseph Shippen's company in Colonel William Clapham's Regiment in 1756, the regiment in garrison at Fort Augusta, Shamokin, and listed in Shippen's Account Book.

McGarragh, John, on a return of Captain David Hunter's Company [probably from York County] in Colonel William Clapham's Regiment of New Levies dated 26 May 1759.

McGarrity, Michael, private who enlisted 11 May 1756 in Captain Joseph Shippen's company in Colonel William Clapham's Regiment in 1756, the regiment in garrison at Fort Augusta, Shamokin, and listed in Shippen's Account Book.

McGarvey, Francis, age 26, laborer, born Derry, Ireland, enlisted 12 May 1759, private in Captain John Mathers's company in the Pennsylvania Regiment. On a return dated 15 June 1759.

McGarvey, James, age 23, laborer, born Ireland, enlisted 10 July 1746 in Captain John Shannon's company of foot.

McGarvin, James, age 34, laborer, born Ireland, enlisted 23 May 1758 by Captain Benjamin Noxon.

McGaughy, John, age 40, laborer, born Ireland, enlisted 21 July 1746 in Captain Samuel Perry's company.

McGaughy, William, age 24, laborer, born Ireland, enlisted 22 July 1746 in Captain Samuel Perry's company.

McGee, Thomas, age 21, laborer, born Ireland, enlisted 01 August 1746 in Captain William Trent's company.

McGill, Andrew, age 24, born Maryland, private in Captain John Wright's company of the Lower County. On a muster dated 11 May 1759. Described as an Indian.

McGill, Charles, lieutenant in the Associated Regiment of Lancaster County over the Susquehanna in 1747–8.

McGill, Michael, age 26, miller, born Ireland, enlisted 09 May 1759, private in Captain Robert Curry's company in Colonel William Clapham's Pennsylvania Regiment. On a return dated June 1759.

McGill, Patrick, age 30, laborer, born Armagh, Ireland, enlisted 25 April 1759, private in Captain James Armstrong's company in Colonel William Clapham's Pennsylvania Regiment. On a return dated 01 June 1759.

McGill, Patrick, private, age 26, weaver, born Kilmore, Ireland, enlisted 30 April 1758 for the campaign in the lower counties. On a return of Captain McClughan's company dated 17 May 1758.

McGinnis, Cornelius, a private in Captain Hugh Mercer's Company, Second Battalion in 1756; killed at Kittanning.

McGinnis, James, age 20, shoemaker, born New Jersey, enlisted 30 April 1758. On a return of Captain John Blackwood's company in the Third Battalion dated 22 May 1758.

McGlen, John, a private in Captain Joseph Inslee's Company of Foot, Newtown, Bucks County, in 1756.

McGonigle, James, age 23, laborer, born Derry, Ireland, enlisted 04 May 1759, private in Captain John Haslet's company in the Pennsylvania Regiment. On a list of recruits dated 20 May 1759.

McGoun, Patrick, age 35, laborer, born Ireland, enlisted 30 June 1746 in Captain William Trent's company.

McGowan, Felix, age 23, laborer, born Cavan, Ireland, enlisted 29 April 1759, private in Captain John Haslet's company in the Pennsylvania Regiment. On a list of recruits dated 20 May 1759.

McGowen, Patrick, landsman on the provincial ship *Pennsylvania* on 17 August 1757.

McGown, James, age 24, laborer, born Glasgow, enlisted 07 May 1759, private in Captain John Haslet's company in the Pennsylvania Regiment. On a list of recruits dated 20 May 1759.

McGray, George, age 22, born Sussex, Delaware, private in Captain John Wright's company of the Lower County. On a muster dated 11 May 1759.

McGrew, Archibald, lieutenant in one of the Associated Companies of York County in 1756. Captain from 15 May 1758 in a company in the Third Battalion.

McGrew, Archibald, promoted to captain after serving in the Pennsylvania Regiment of Three Battalions in 1758 and 1759.

McGuire, Nicholas, age 45, laborer, born Ireland, enlisted 05 July 1746 in Captain John Shannon's company of foot.

McGwier, Phillip, age 36, carpenter, born Ireland, enlisted 01 May 1758. On a weekly return of Captain Samuel Jones's company in 1758.

McHarg, Thomas, age 36, tailor, born Scotland, enlisted 06 May 1759, private in Captain Robert Curry's company in Colonel William Clapham's Pennsylvania Regiment. On a return dated June 1759.

McHatten, Alexander, age 20, born Derry, Ireland, private in Captain John Haslett's company enlisted on 12 May 1758 and last paid on 21 May 1758.

McHatten, James, age 23, born Derry, Ireland, private in Captain John Haslett's company enlisted on 22 May 1758 and last paid on 21 May 1758.

McIlhenny, Dennis, hired 29 May 1757 as a battoe man, Master George Allen.

McIlhenny, James, age 22, cooper, born Ireland, enlisted 03 June 1758 by Lieutenant William McClay for Captain John Montgomery's company.

McIlvaine William, a private in Captain John Kidd's Independent Company of Foot, Philadelphia in 1756.

McIlvaine, Joseph, age 23, laborer, born Ireland, enlisted 02 August 1746 in Captain Samuel Perry's company.

McIlvaine, Joseph, age 35, laborer, born Ireland, enlisted 15 May 1759 in Captain Robert Boyd's company [probably in the Third Battalion]. On a return dated May and June 1759.

McIntee, Arthur, landsman on the provincial ship *Pennsylvania* on 17 August 1757.

McInteger, John, hired 28 May 1757 as a battoe man, Master George Allen.

McIntire, Archibald, age 20, laborer, born Ayr, Scotland, enlisted 05 May 1759, private in Captain John Haslet's company in the Pennsylvania Regiment. On a list of recruits dated 20 May 1759.

McIntire, John, landsman on the provincial ship *Pennsylvania* on 17 August 1757.

McIntosh, Hugh, private, age 35, laborer, born Perth, Scotland, enlisted 08 May 1758 for the campaign in the lower counties. On a return of Captain McClughan's company dated 17 May 1758.

McIntosh, John, private, age 19, laborer, born Indian River, Delaware, enlisted 09 May 1758 for the campaign in the lower counties. On a return of Captain McClughan's company dated 17 May 1758.

McKean, Alexander, lieutenant from 15 May 1758 in Captain Archibald McGrew's company in the Third Battalion.

McKean, Daniel, age 30, laborer, born Antrim, Ireland, enlisted 24 April 1759, private in Captain James Armstrong's company in Colonel William Clapham's Pennsylvania Regiment. On a return dated 01 June 1759.

McKean, Hugh, ensign from 01 May 1759 in Captain Thomas Hamilton's company of Colonel William Clapham's Regiment of New Levies.

McKearney, Jonathan, a member of Captain Joseph Armstrong's Company on 07 August 1755, raised in Cumberland County.

McKee, Alexander, ensign in Captain Elisha Salter's Company, Third Battalion (known as the Augusta Regiment) from 17 August 1756. Commissioned a captain lieutenant 01 December 1757 Late Clapham's Company stationed at Fort Augusta. Lieutenant from 17 December 1757 in Captain Charles Garraway's company stationed eastward of the Susquehanna. Also reported as lieutenant from 17 December 1757 in Captain Asher Clayton's company in the Second Battalion.

McKee, Alexander, promoted to lieutenant after serving in the Pennsylvania Regiment of Three Battalions in 1758 and 1759.

McKee, Andrew, age 25, laborer, born Ireland, enlisted 14 July 1746 in Captain John Shannon's company of foot.

McKee, Thomas, captain in the Associated Regiment of the West End of Lancaster County in 1747–8.

McKee, Thomas, captain in the provincial service in 1755 at Hunter's Mill.

McKee, William, age 26, laborer, born Ireland, enlisted 17 July 1746 in Captain William Trent's company.

McKeen, Hugh, *see* Hugh McKean.

McKeis, William, *see* McKee, William.

McKenney, Amos, enlisted 20 May 1758 in Captain French Battell's company of Lower County Provincials.

McKenny, Charles, age 20, cooper, born Ireland, enlisted 01 May 1758 by Captain Benjamin Noxon.

McKeown, Felix, age 21, born Cavan, Ireland, laborer, private in Captain John Haslett's company enlisted on 15 May 1758 and last paid on 21 May 1758.

McKim, Thomas, lieutenant in the Brandy Wine Hundred company of Colonel William Armstrong's Upper Regiment of New Castle County in 1756.

McKinley, John of the Upper Regiment of New Castle County in 1756.

McKinley, John, lieutenant in one of two regiments of New Castle County in 1747–8.

McKinley, William, private who enlisted 16 April 1756 in Captain Joseph Shippen's company in Colonel William Clapham's Regiment in 1756, the regiment in garrison at Fort Augusta, Shamokin, and listed in Shippen's Account Book.

McKinney, Alexander, age 30, weaver, born Ireland, enlisted 29 July 1746 in Captain Samuel Perry's company.

McKinny, James, age 40, tailor, born Ireland, enlisted 03 August 1746 in Captain Samuel Perry's company.

McKnight, George, lieutenant from 05 May 1759 in Captain Samuel Jones's company of Colonel William Clapham's Regiment of New Levies.

McKnight, George, promoted to lieutenant after serving in the Pennsylvania Regiment of Three Battalions in 1758 and 1759. Reported as "dead".

McKnight, James, age 25, born Ireland, enlisted 05 June 1759, private in Captain Robert Curry's company in Colonel William Clapham's Pennsylvania Regiment. On a return dated June 1759.

McKnight, John, promoted to captain after serving in the Pennsylvania Regiment of Three Battalions in 1758 and 1759.

McKnight, William, captain from 26 April 1758 in a company in the First Battalion of Col. William Denny's Regiment.

McKnight, William, captain in the Associated Regiment of Chester County in 1747.

McLachlan, John, age 30, laborer, born Ireland, enlisted 16 May 1759 in Captain Robert Boyd's company [probably in the Third Battalion]. On a return dated May and June 1759.

McLaughlin, James, captain in the Associated Regiment of Bucks County in 1748.

McLaughlin, James, captain in the provincial service in 1755.

McLaughlin, Neal, hired 10 June 1757 as a battoe man, Master George Allen.

McLaughlin, Thomas, age 19, weaver, born Derry, Ireland, enlisted 10 May 1759, private in Captain John Mathers's company in the Pennsylvania Regiment. On a return dated 15 June 1759.

McLease, Neal, age 28, sawyer, born Derry, Ireland, enlisted 10 May 1759, private in Captain John Mathers's company in the Pennsylvania Regiment. On a return dated 15 June 1759.

McLees, Archibald, age 25, laborer, born Ireland, enlisted 28 July 1746 in Captain Samuel Perry's company.

McLees, James, age 20, weaver, born Ireland, enlisted 20 July 1746 in Captain Samuel Perry's company.

McLoy, John, age 26, weaver, born Ireland, enlisted 08 May 1758 by Captain Benjamin Noxon.

McLuskey, Henry, *see* McCloskey, Henry.

McMahon, Redmond, age 20, laborer, born Ireland, enlisted 13 July 1746 in Captain Samuel Perry's company.

McMakin, James, lieutenant in the Associated Regiment of Chester County in 1747.

McManus, James, age 20, laborer, born Ireland, enlisted 26 June 1746 in Captain William Trent's company.

McMath, James, age 17, born Monaghan, Ireland, private in Captain John Haslett's company enlisted on 10 May 1758 and last paid on 21 May 1758.

McMeehan, William, second lieutenant from 03 October 1758 in Captain John McClughan's company raised for the campaign in the lower counties. Ensign from 21 May 1759 of a company from the Lower County.

McMeehan, William, surgeon from 20 April 1758. On a list of officers of the lower government on Delaware, 1758/9. Surgeon from 07 May 1759 of Colonel William Clapham's Regiment of New Levies.

McMeehen, James, captain in one of two regiments of New Castle County in 1747–8.

McMeen, William, an ensign stationed on the frontier in Berks County with Captain Nicholas Housegger, one sergeant, and twenty-six men in Heidelberg Township on 01 June 1764 as part of a unit under the command of Major Asher Clayton.

McMeen, William, ensign in Captain Nicholas Housegger's company in the First Battalion of the Pennsylvania Regiment from 10 December 1763.

McMehan, William, lieutenant in the Miln Creek Hundred company of Colonel William Armstrong's Upper Regiment of New Castle County in 1756.

McMullen, Charles, lieutenant in one of the Associated Companies of York County in 1756.

McMullen, Robert, lieutenant in the Associated Regiment of Chester County in 1747.

McMullen, Samuel, on a list of men recruited by Captain Andrew McDowell's company in the Second Battalion, Pennsylvania Regiment dated 04 June 1759.

McMullin, Alexander, private in Captain Patterson's company from 01 December 1757 stationed eastward of the Susquehanna. On a muster roll dated 08 March 1758.

McMullin, Patrick, age 24, born Ireland, laborer, private in Captain John Shannon's Company, enlisted 21 July 1746. On a roll of deserters dated 22 July 1746. [B3:422:18]

McMullin, Samuel, age 23, laborer, born Ireland, enlisted 14 May 1759 in Captain Charles Stewart's company [probably one of the Associated Companies of Bucks County]. On a return dated June 1759.

McMullin, William, ensign in the Associated Regiment of the West End of Lancaster County in 1747–8.

McMurphy, Archibald, age 27, laborer, born Scotland, enlisted 22 April 1758 by Captain Benjamin Noxon.

McNally, Adam, a private in Captain Adam Heylman's Company, of the St. Vincent and Puke's Land Association on 10 May 1756.

McNally, John, a private in Captain Adam Heylman's Company, of the St. Vincent and Puke's Land Association on 10 May 1756.

McNamara, Peter, enlisted 09 May 1758 for the campaign in the lower counties. On a return of Captain McClughan's company dated 17 May 1758.

McNealis, Charles, private in Captain Patterson's company from 27 December 1757 stationed eastward of the Susquehanna. On a muster roll dated 08 March 1758.

McNeely, James, ensign in one of the Associated Companies of Lancaster County in 1756.
McNoarth, Andrew, landsman on the provincial ship *Pennsylvania* on 17 August 1757.
McPeak, James [John], age 21, laborer, born Ireland, enlisted 30 July 1746 in Captain Samuel Perry's company.
McPharan, Matthias, *see* Matthias McFarran.
McPherson, Robert, captain from 10 May 175 of a company in the Third Battalion.
McPherson, Robert, promoted to captain after serving in the Pennsylvania Regiment of Three Battalions in 1758 and 1759.
McPick, James [John], *see* McPeak, James [John].
McQuaid, Patrick, age 22, laborer, born Ireland, enlisted 07 May 1759 in Captain Robert Boyd's company [probably in the Third Battalion]. On a return dated May and June 1759.
McQuoid, Anthony, a private in Captain John Potter's Company, Second Battalion; killed near McDowell's Fort in November 1756.
McSorley, Edward, age 22, born Chester, Pennsylvania, private in Captain John Singleton's company in service between 01 May and 08 May 1758.
McVicker, Peter, age 34, born Scotland, enlisted 18 May 1759, private in Captain Robert Curry's company in Colonel William Clapham's Pennsylvania Regiment. On a return dated June 1759.
McWilliams, Richard, captain in the New Castle Hundred company of Colonel William Armstrong's Upper Regiment of New Castle County in 1756.
Mears, John, ensign.
Mears, John, ensign of Captain William Clapham's Company, Third Battalion (known as the Augusta Regiment) from 20 April 1756.
Meas, Matthias, surgeon of the Second Battalion of the Pennsylvania Regiment from April 1760 and ensign in Captain John Prentice's company of the Second Battalion of the Pennsylvania Regiment from 21 April 1760.

Officers and Soldiers in the Service of the Province of Pennsylvania 1744 to 1764

Meek, Robert, private in Captain Patterson's company from 02 November 1757 stationed eastward of the Susquehanna. On a muster roll dated 08 March 1758.

Meem, Peter, ensign from 10 May 1758 in Captain Robert McPherson's company in the Third Battalion.

Meer, Samuel in Captain Robert Eastburn's company in the Second Battalion.

Mehaffey, John, on a return of Captain David Hunter's Company [probably from York County] in Colonel William Clapham's Regiment of New Levies dated 26 May 1759.

Mehattan, Alexander, age 22, laborer, born Derry, Ireland, enlisted 27 April 1759, corporal in Captain John Haslet's company in the Pennsylvania Regiment. On a list of recruits dated 20 May 1759.

Mehattan, James, age 25, laborer, born Derry, Ireland, enlisted 27 April 1759, sergeant in Captain John Haslet's company in the Pennsylvania Regiment. On a list of recruits dated 20 May 1759.

Mekown, Felix, *see* Felix McGowan.

Mekown, James, *see* James McGown.

Melchior, Leonard, quartermaster in Captain Edward Jones's Independent Company of Horse, Philadelphia in 1756.

Meloney, John, age 26, smith, born Deprair, Ireland, enlisted 06 June 1759, private in Captain John Mathers's company in the Pennsylvania Regiment. On a return dated 15 June 1759.

Mench, Adam, ensign in Captain Edward Biddle's company of the Second Battalion of the Pennsylvania Regiment from 17 April 1760.

Mercer, Dr., captain in the provincial service in 1755 at Fort Shirley.

Mercer, Hugh was promoted to the rank of colonel after having served in the Pennsylvania Regiment of Three Battalions, 1758 and 1759.

Mercer, Hugh, captain of a company of the Second Battalion from 06 March 1756; wounded at Kittanning. Major from 04 December 1757, stationed westward of the Susquehanna. Also identified as a captain of a company in the First Battalion of

Colonel William Denny's Regiment on 04 December 1757. Colonel commandant from 29 May 1758 of the Third Battalion. Colonel from 23 April 1759 of the Third Battalion of the Pennsylvania Regiment.

Mercer, Hugh, colonel of the Second Battalion of the Pennsylvania Regiment from 12 January 1760.

Merchant, Nicholas, age 30, laborer, born England, enlisted 18 July 1746 in Captain William Trent's company.

Merchant, William, age 36, laborer, born Ireland, enlisted 14 July 1746 in Captain John Shannon's company of foot.

Meredith, James, lieutenant in the Associated Regiment of Bucks County in 1748.

Meredith, John, age 25, carpenter, born England, enlisted 01 July 1746 in Captain William Trent's company.

Meredith, Philip, age 28, laborer, born Ireland, enlisted 19 July 1746 in Captain John Shannon's company of foot.

Meyer, Jacob, age 18, laborer, born Germany, enlisted 07 May 1759, private in Captain Joseph Richardson's company of the Third Battalion in the Pennsylvania Regiment. On a return of recruits dated 1759.

Michael, David, private in Captain John Singleton's company in service between 01 May and 08 May 1758.

Michael, Joseph, a private in Captain Charles Batho's Independent Company of Foot, Philadelphia in 1756.

Micheltree, John, private in Captain Patterson's company from 29 December 1757 stationed eastward of the Susquehanna. On a muster roll dated 08 March 1758.

Mifflin, Samuel, captain in the Association Battery Company of Philadelphia in 1756.

Miles, _____, orderly sergeant to the commander-in-chief, then ensign, helped to build the fort at Shamokin, where he remained in garrison until 1758.

Miles, Nathan, captain of a company of the Third Battalion (known as the Augusta Regiment) in 1756.

Miles, Nathaniel, *see* Nathan Miles.

Miles, Samuel, age 16, in a company under the command of Captain Isaac Wayne, of a company that was sent to Northampton in 1755, which rendezvoused at Easton.

Miles, Samuel, captain of a company of the First Battalion of the Pennsylvania Regiment from 21 April 1760.

Miles, Samuel, ensign of Captain Elisha Salter's Company, Third Battalion (known as the Augusta Regiment) from 24 May 1756; promoted to lieutenant from 21 August 1756. Lieutenant in Captain Thomas Lloyd's company in the Second Battalion from 14 December 1757, stationed at Fort Augusta. Wounded by a spent ball at Ligonier before November 1758. Stationed at Fort Ligonier with twenty-five picked men from two battalions in 1759.

Miles, Samuel, promoted to captain after serving in the Pennsylvania Regiment of Three Battalions in 1758 and 1759.

Millekin, Patrick, age 29, laborer, born Down, Ireland, enlisted 06 May 1759, private in Captain John Haslet's company in the Pennsylvania Regiment. On a list of recruits dated 20 May 1759.

Miller, Andrew, lieutenant in the Associated Regiment of Lancaster County over the Susquehanna in 1747–8.

Miller, Anthony, lieutenant in Captain Frederick Smith's company of the First Battalion from 29 December 1755; with sixteen men at Manity [Manada] Fort in June, 1756.

Miller, Anthony, lieutenant on a List of Officers in the Province Pay, 1756 in the First Battalion of the Pennsylvania Regiment with a commission date of 29 December 1755. {PA5, I, 88}

Miller, Francis, age 26, mariner, born Sweedland, enlisted 01 May 1758. On a weekly return of Captain Samuel Jones's company in 1758.

Miller, Gates, on a list of men recruited by Captain Andrew McDowell's company in the Second Battalion, Pennsylvania Regiment dated 04 June 1759.

Miller, George, captain of a company under Commandant James Potter on the Northern Frontier on 02 October 1764.

Miller, George, age 22, smith, born Pennsylvania, enlisted 30 July 1746 in Captain William Trent's company.

Miller, George, age 42, tanner, born England, enlisted 25 June 1746 in Captain John Shannon's company of foot.

Miller, George, lieutenant in Captain John Philip De Hass's company of the First Battalion of the Pennsylvania Regiment from 08 May 1760.

Miller, Henry, age 34, laborer, born Ireland, enlisted 25 July 1746 in Captain John Shannon's company of foot.

Miller, Henry, cooper of the provincial ship *Pennsylvania* on 17 August 1757.

Miller, Hugh, lieutenant in the Associated Regiment of Bucks County in 1748.

Miller, John, age 19, laborer, born Ulster, Ireland, enlisted 01 May 1759, private in Captain James Armstrong's company in Colonel William Clapham's Pennsylvania Regiment. On a return dated 01 June 1759.

Miller, John, captain in the Associated Regiment of Chester County in 1747.

Miller, John, ensign in Captain Francis Johnston's company of the Second Battalion of the Pennsylvania Regiment from 24 April 1760.

Miller, John, ensign in the Associated Regiment of Bucks County in 1748.

Miller, John, lieutenant in one of the Associated Companies of York County in 1756.

Miller, John, major in the Associated Regiment of Chester County in 1747.

Miller, Joseph, age 17, laborer, born Pennsylvania, enlisted 17 May 1758 by Lieutenant William McClay for Captain John Montgomery's company.

Miller, Michael, private who enlisted 20 April 1756 in Captain Nathaniel Miles's company in Colonel William Clapham's Regiment in 1756, the regiment in garrison at Fort Augusta, Shamokin, and listed in Shippen's Account Book. Not the dyer.

Miller, Michael, private who enlisted 28 April 1756 in Captain Joseph Shippen's company in Colonel William Clapham's Regiment in 1756, the regiment in garrison at Fort Augusta, Shamokin, and listed in Shippen's Account Book.

Miller, Nicholas, age 17, born Germany, enlisted 01 September 1757, private in Captain John Nicholas Weatherholt's company which enlisted for a term of three years and stationed in Heydelberg Township, Northampton County, in March and April 1758.

Miller, Peter, age 22, born Germany, enlisted 01 September 1757, private in Captain John Nicholas Weatherholt's company which enlisted for a term of three years and stationed in Heydelberg Township, Northampton County, in March and April 1758.

Miller, Thomas, landsman on the provincial ship *Pennsylvania* on 17 August 1757.

Miller, William, a private in Captain Charles Batho's Independent Company of Foot, Philadelphia in 1756.

Miller, William, landsman on the provincial ship *Pennsylvania* on 17 August 1757.

Miller, William, seaman on the provincial ship *Pennsylvania* on 17 August 1757.

Milliner, Thomas, age 30, surgeon, born England, enlisted 07 July 1746 in Captain John Shannon's company of foot.

Mills, Daniel, age 40, laborer, born England, enlisted 02 May 1749 in Captain Richard Gardiner's company in Colonel William Denney's Pennsylvania Regiment.

Mills, Patrick, age 40, laborer, born Ireland, enlisted 10 May 1759 in Captain Charles Stewart's company [probably one of the Associated Companies of Bucks County]. On a return dated June 1759.

Mindinhurst, John, age 24, tailor, born Germany, enlisted 11 July 1746 in Captain Samuel Perry's company.

Miner, Jeremiah, age 23, farmer, born Pennsylvania, enlisted 24 April 1759 in Captain Charles Stewart's company [probably one of the Associated Companies of Bucks County]. On a return dated June 1759.

Miner, Nathan, age 24, born New England, enlisted 30 April 1759, clerk in Captain Robert Curry's company in Colonel William Clapham's Pennsylvania Regiment. On a return dated June 1759.

Minskey, Emanuel, a private in Captain Hugh Mercer's Company, Second Battalion in 1756; missing at the capture of Kittanning.

Mirerip, John, age 25, laborer, born New Castle, Delaware, enlisted 30 April 1759, private in Captain James Armstrong's company in Colonel William Clapham's Pennsylvania Regiment. On a return dated 01 June 1759.

Mitch, John, hired 29 May 1757 as a battoe man, Master George Allen.

Mitchel, Robert, age 22, born Tyrone, Ireland, private in Captain John Haslett's company enlisted on 13 May 1758 and last paid on 21 May 1758.

Mitchel, William, ensign in the Pencader Hundred company of Colonel Jacob Van Bibber's Lower Regiment of New Castle County in 1756.

Mitchell, James, a member of Captain Joseph Armstrong's Company on 07 August 1755, raised in Cumberland County.

Mitchell, John, a member of Captain Joseph Armstrong's Company on 07 August 1755, raised in Cumberland County.

Mitchell, John, ensign in the Associated Regiment of Lancaster County over the Susquehanna in 1747–8.

Mitchell, John, lieutenant in one of the Associated Companies of Lancaster County in 1756.

Mitchell, John, lieutenant in the Associated Regiment of Lancaster County over the Susquehanna in 1747–8.

Mitchell, Joseph, linquister of the provincial ship *Pennsylvania* on 17 August 1757.

Mitchell, Joseph, private, age 20, cooper, born Down, Ireland, enlisted 12 May 1758 for the campaign in the lower counties. On a return of Captain McClughan's company dated 17 May 1758.

Mitchell, Joshua, a member of Captain Joseph Armstrong's Company on 07 August 1755, raised in Cumberland County.

Mitchell, Nicholas, age 21, mariner, born England, enlisted 01 May 1758. On a weekly return of Captain Samuel Jones's company in 1758.

Mitchell, Thomas, enlisted 23 July 1746 in Captain Samuel Perry's company.

Mitchell, Thomas, ensign in the Associated Regiment of the West End of Lancaster County in 1747–8.

Mitchell, William, a member of Captain Joseph Armstrong's Company on 07 August 1755, raised in Cumberland County.

Mitchell, William, lieutenant in the Associated Regiment of the West End of Lancaster County in 1747–8.

Mitcheltree, James, hired 07 June 1757 as a battoe man, Master George Allen.

Mitcheltree, John, hired 17 June 1757 as a battoe man, Master George Allen.

Mitcheltree, William, hired 27 May 1757 as a battoe man, Master George Allen.

Moffet, Robert, age 22, laborer, born New Castle, Delaware, enlisted 26 April 1759, private in Captain James Armstrong's company in Colonel William Clapham's Pennsylvania Regiment. On a return dated 01 June 1759.

Moffit, Robert, age 27, born Ireland, enlisted 12 June 1759, private in Captain John Mathers's company in the Pennsylvania Regiment. On a return dated 15 June 1759.

Molland, John, Jun., a private in Captain Charles Batho's Independent Company of Foot, Philadelphia in 1756.

Molland, John, a private in Captain Charles Batho's Independent Company of Foot, Philadelphia in 1756.

Molliston, John, lieutenant in the Lower Part of Mispillim Hundred company of Colonel John Vining's Regiment of Kent County Militia, Upon Delaware in 1756.

Money, Robert, age 34, carpenter, born Maryland, enlisted 28 April 1758 by Captain Benjamin Noxon.

Monroe, Rowland, age 48, sail-maker, born Pennsylvania, enlisted 11 May 1749 in Captain Richard Gardiner's company in Colonel William Denney's Pennsylvania Regiment.

Montgomery, Alexander, a private in Captain Charles Batho's Independent Company of Foot, Philadelphia in 1756.

Montgomery, Alexander, ensign in the Miln Creek Hundred company of Colonel William Armstrong's Upper Regiment of New Castle County in 1756.

Montgomery, James, ensign in the Associated Regiment of Chester County in 1747.

Montgomery, James, lieutenant in Captain John Blackwood's company of the Second Battalion of the Pennsylvania Regiment from 26 April 1760.

Montgomery, John, captain from 07 May 1758 of a company in the Third Battalion.

Montgomery, Joseph, captain of a company in the Second Battalion from 05 October 1756.

Montgomery, Samuel, ensign from 17 March 1759 in Captain Jacob Morgan's company in the Second Battalion, vice Harry.

Montgomery, Samuel, ensign from 17 May 1758 in Captain Ludowick Stone's company in the Third Battalion.

Montgomery, Samuel, promoted to lieutenant after serving in the Pennsylvania Regiment of Three Battalions in 1758 and 1759. Reported as "dead".

Montgomery, Thomas, ensign in one of two regiments of New Castle County in 1747–8.

Moody, Alexander, lieutenant in one of two regiments of New Castle County in 1747–8.

Moody, Arthur, hired 25 May 1757 as a battoe man, Master George Allen.

Moody, James, age 27, tailor, born Ireland, enlisted 22 April 1758 by Captain Benjamin Noxon.

Mooney, Michael, age 21, laborer, born Ireland, enlisted 07 July 1746 in Captain William Trent's company.

Moor, John, enlisted 22 May 1758 in Captain French Battell's company of Lower County Provincials.

Moore, Charles, lieutenant in the Associated Regiment of Chester County in 1747.

Moore, George, age 20, mason, born Pennsylvania, enlisted 12 May 1749 in Captain Richard Gardiner's company in Colonel William Denney's Pennsylvania Regiment.

Moore, Guyon, lieutenant in the Associated Regiment of Chester County in 1747.

Moore, James, age 22, born Down, Ireland, fuller, private in Captain John Haslett's company enlisted on 06 May 1758 and last paid on 21 May 1758.

Moore, John, age 24, cordwainer, born Wales, enlisted 15 April 1758 for the campaign in the lower counties and is believed to be in Captain McClughan's company, but not on a return dated 17 May 1758.

Moore, John, age 24, laborer, born Maryland, enlisted 15 April 1758 by Captain Benjamin Noxon.

Moore, John, age 32, mariner, born Ireland, enlisted 15 May 1758. On a return of Captain John Blackwood's company in the Third Battalion dated 22 May 1758.

Moore, Jonathan, a member of Captain Joseph Armstrong's Company on 07 August 1755, raised in Cumberland County.

Moore, Samuel, a private in Captain Charles Batho's Independent Company of Foot, Philadelphia in 1756.

Moore, Samuel, on a list of men recruited by Captain Andrew McDowell's company in the Second Battalion, Pennsylvania Regiment dated 04 June 1759.

Moore, William, private in Captain John Haslett's company enlisted on 10 May 1758 and last paid on 21 May 1758.

Moore, William, age 17, hatter, born Chester, Pennsylvania, enlisted 09 May 1759, private in Captain James Armstrong's company in Colonel William Clapham's Pennsylvania Regiment. On a return dated 01 June 1759.

Moore, William, age 18, laborer, born Ireland, enlisted 27 April 1759. Private in Captain Joseph Richardson's company of the Third Battalion in the Pennsylvania Regiment. On a return of recruits dated 1759.

Moore, William, colonel in the Associated Regiment of Chester County in 1747.

Moore, William, ensign in Captain Samuel Mifflin's Association Battery Company of Philadelphia in 1756.

Moran, John, *see* John Moren.

Moran, John, enlisted 15 May 1759, private in Captain Henry Van Bibber's company of the Lower County. On a return dated 04 June 1759.

Mordecai, Moses, a private in Captain Edward Jones's Independent Company of Horse, Philadelphia in 1756.

Morehead, Matthew, age 28, weaver, born Ireland, enlisted 29 May 1758 by Captain Benjamin Noxon.

Morell, Thomas, seaman on the provincial ship *Pennsylvania* on 17 August 1757.

Moren, John, age 21, laborer, born Delaware, enlisted 26 April 1758 by Captain Benjamin Noxon.

Morgan, George, landsman on the provincial ship *Pennsylvania* on 17 August 1757.

Morgan, Jacob, captain on a List of Officers in the Province Pay, 1756 in the First Battalion of the Pennsylvania Regiment with a commission date of 5 December 1755. {PA5, I, 88}

Morgan, Jacob, provincial officer in 1754 at Fort Lebanon. In the provincial service in 1755 at Forks of Schuylkill. Captain in a company of the First Battalion from 05 December 1755. Captain from 18 December 1757 in a company in the Second Battalion, stationed eastward of the Susquehanna.

Morgan, Jacob, Jr., lieutenant and adjutant of the Second Battalion of the Pennsylvania Regiment from April 1760. Lieutenant in Captain Robert Anderson's company of the Second Battalion of the Pennsylvania Regiment from 21 April 1760.

Morgan, Jacob, Jr., promoted to lieutenant after serving in the Pennsylvania Regiment of Three Battalions in 1758 and 1759.

Morgan, Jacob, Junr., ensign from 12 March 1758 in Captain Levi Trump's company in the Second Battalion, stationed at Fort Augusta.

Morgan, Jacob, Sr., promoted to captain after serving in the Pennsylvania Regiment of Three Battalions in 1758 and 1759.

Morgan, John, ensign of Captain James Burd's Company, Third Battalion (known as the Augusta Regiment) from 24 May 1756. Ensign from 01 December 1757 in Captain John Hambright's company in the Second Battalion, stationed at Fort Augusta.

Morgan, John, promoted to lieutenant after serving in the Pennsylvania Regiment of Three Battalions in 1758 and 1759.

Morgan, John, surgeon from 01 December in the Second Battalion.

Morgan, Thomas, a private in Captain Joseph Inslee's Company of Foot, Newtown, Bucks County, in 1756.

Morgan, Thomas, landsman on the provincial ship *Pennsylvania* on 17 August 1757.

Morgan, William, ensign in Captain John Shannon's company, in winter quarters in Albany, N.Y., 1746–7, discharged 31 October 1747.

Morgen, Peter, a private in Captain Joseph Inslee's Company of Foot, Newtown, Bucks County, in 1756.

Morland, Patrick, age 20, laborer, born Lancaster, Pennsylvania, enlisted 08 May 1759 in Captain Robert Boyd's company [probably in the Third Battalion]. On a return dated May and June 1759.

Morrell, Robert, lieutenant in the Associated Regiment of Chester County in 1747.

Morris, Elijah, lieutenant in the Upper Part of Mispillim Hundred company of Colonel John Vining's Regiment of Kent County Militia, Upon Delaware in 1756.

Morris, Evan, a private in Captain Samuel Mifflin's Association Battery Company of Philadelphia in 1756.

Morris, James, lieutenant in one of two regiments of New Castle County in 1747–8.

Morris, Joshua, on a list of men recruited by Captain Andrew McDowell's company in the Second Battalion, Pennsylvania Regiment dated 04 June 1759.

Morris, Rees, age 28, tailor, born Pennsylvania, enlisted 09 May 1758. On a return of Captain John Bull's company dated 01 July 1758.

Morris, Robert Hunter, governor of the province in 1756.

Morrison, James, age 17, laborer, born Pennsylvania, enlisted 05 May 1759, private in Captain John Haslet's company in the Pennsylvania Regiment. On a list of recruits dated 20 May 1759.

Morrison, James, age 19, laborer, born Ireland, enlisted 11 July 1746 in Captain William Trent's company.

Morrison, James, on a return of Captain David Hunter's Company [probably from York County] in Colonel William Clapham's Regiment of New Levies dated 26 May 1759.

Morrison, John, age 27, born Ireland, enlisted 29 May 1759, private in Captain Robert Curry's company in Colonel William Clapham's Pennsylvania Regiment. On a return dated June 1759.

Morrison, Michael, age 19, tailor, born Pennsylvania, enlisted 05 May 1759, private in Captain John Haslet's company in the Pennsylvania Regiment. On a list of recruits dated 20 May 1759.

Morrison, Samuel, ensign in one of the Associated Companies of Lancaster County in 1756.

Morrow, Charles, captain in the Associated Regiment of Lancaster County over the Susquehanna in 1747–8.

Morrow, John, age 2, laborer, born Scotland, enlisted 08 May 1758 by Lieutenant William McClay for Captain John Montgomery's company.

Morrow, John, hired 30 May 1757 as a battoe man, Master George Allen.

Morrow, Robert, a private in Captain Hugh Mercer's Company, Second Battalion in 1756; missing at the capture of Kittanning.

Mortin, James, landsman on the provincial ship *Pennsylvania* on 17 August 1757.

Moser, Ludwick, age 27, born Germany, enlisted 30 May 1759, private in Captain Robert Curry's company in Colonel William Clapham's Pennsylvania Regiment. On a return dated June 1759.

Moses, Adam, a private in Captain Adam Heylman's Company, of the St. Vincent and Puke's Land Association on 10 May 1756.

Moses, William, age 25, blacksmith, born Pennsylvania, enlisted 07 July 1746 in Captain William Trent's company.

Mosus, William, *see* Moses, William.

Motley, Patt., a private in Captain John Kidd's Independent Company of Foot, Philadelphia in 1756.

Officers and Soldiers in the Service of the Province of Pennsylvania 1744 to 1764

Motley, Paul, ensign in Captain David McAllister's company of the First Battalion of the Pennsylvania Regiment from 20 April 1760.

Mounce, Luke, ensign in one of two regiments of New Castle County in 1747–8.

Mountain, Roger, age 27, barber, born Ireland, enlisted 06 August 1746 in

Moyce, Nicholas, age 20, mariner, born England, enlisted 01 May 1758. On a weekly return of Captain Samuel Jones's company in 1758.

Mulherran, James, age 27, schoolmaster, born Derry, Ireland, enlisted 30 April 1759, private in Captain John Haslet's company in the Pennsylvania Regiment. On a list of recruits dated 20 May 1759.

Mull, Robert, ensign in the Associated Regiment of Lancaster County over the Susquehanna in 1747–8.

Mullan, Daniel, private, age 18, miler, born Dunluce, Ireland, enlisted 29 April 1758 for the campaign in the lower counties. On a return of Captain McClughan's company dated 17 May 1758.

Mullen, John, ensign from 28 April 1759 in Captain Samuel Jones's company of Colonel William Clapham's Regiment of New Levies.

Mullen, John, lieutenant in Captain George Craighead's company of the First Battalion of the Pennsylvania Regiment from 29 April 1760.

Mullen, John, promoted to lieutenant after serving in the Pennsylvania Regiment of Three Battalions in 1758 and 1759. Reported as "dead".

Mullen, Patrick, a private in Captain Hugh Mercer's Company, Second Battalion in 1756; killed at Kittanning.

Muntz, Philip, a private in Captain Adam Heylman's Company, of the St. Vincent and Puke's Land Association on 10 May 1756.

Murphy, Archibald, age 40, sawyer, born Ireland, enlisted 25 July 1746 in Captain William Trent's company.

Murphy, Bryan, age 16, laborer, born Tyrone, Ireland, enlisted 01 May 1759, private in Captain James Armstrong's company in

Colonel William Clapham's Pennsylvania Regiment. On a return dated 01 June 1759.

Murphy, James, age 21, schoolmaster, born Ireland, enlisted 02 May 1758 by Captain Benjamin Noxon.

Murphy, Michael, age 25, laborer, born Ireland, enlisted 20 July 1746 in Captain Samuel Perry's company.

Murphy, Patrick, enlisted 28 July 1746 in Captain Samuel Perry's company.

Murphy, Peter, age 38, laborer, born Ireland, enlisted 08 May 1759 in Captain Charles Stewart's company [probably one of the Associated Companies of Bucks County]. On a return dated June 1759.

Murphy, Thomas, age 40, laborer, born Ireland, enlisted 23 July 1746 in Captain Samuel Perry's company.

Murrain, John, private, age 28, laborer, born Dublin, Ireland, enlisted 07 May 1758 for the campaign in the lower counties. On a return of Captain McClughan's company dated 17 May 1758.

Murray, James, ensign in Captain William Piper's company in Lieutenant Colonel Commandant Asher Clayton's Second Battalion of the Pennsylvania Regiment commanded by the Hon. J. Penn 19 July 1763.

Murray, John, *see* John Morrow.

Murray, John, a private in Captain Charles Batho's Independent Company of Foot, Philadelphia in 1756.

Myer, George, private who enlisted 24 April 1756 in Captain Joseph Shippen's company in Colonel William Clapham's Regiment in 1756, the regiment in garrison at Fort Augusta, Shamokin, and listed in Shippen's Account Book.

Myer, Leonard, private who enlisted 21 April 1756 in Captain Joseph Shippen's company in Colonel William Clapham's Regiment in 1756, the regiment in garrison at Fort Augusta, Shamokin, and listed in Shippen's Account Book.

Myers, Patrick, private in Captain Edward Ward's Company, Second Battalion in 1756; missing at the capture of Kittanning.

Nagle, Casper, age 22, laborer, born Germany, enlisted 14 May 1759, private in Captain Joseph Richardson's company of the

Third Battalion in the Pennsylvania Regiment. On a return of recruits dated 1759.

Nagle, George, an ensign stationed on the frontier in Berks County with twelve men at John Overwinter's, Albany Township, on 01 June 1764 as part of a unit under the command of Major Asher Clayton.

Nagle, George, ensign in Captain Jacob Kern's company in the First Battalion of the Pennsylvania Regiment from 16 July 1764.

Naglee, Jacob, ensign from 04 August 1748, in the Associated Regiment in the County of Philadelphia in 1748. Elected in the room of Jacob Barge. [CR,V,325]

Nagler, John, ensign in one of the companies of Colonel Jacob Duché's Philadelphia Regiment in 1756.

Narrier, Daniel, age 18, laborer, born Tyrone, Ireland, enlisted 03 May 1759, private in Captain James Armstrong's company in Colonel William Clapham's Pennsylvania Regiment. On a return dated 01 June 1759.

Natherland, William, age 32, tailor, born England, enlisted 03 July 1746 in Captain William Trent's company.

Naughan, John, age 42, laborer, born Wales, enlisted 09 July 1746 in Captain John Deimer's company.

Nawood, Daniel, private, age 19, farmer, born Angola Hundred, enlisted 19 April 1758 for the campaign in the lower counties. On a return of Captain McClughan's company dated 17 May 1758.

Nawood, Nathan, private, age 23, planter, born Indian River, Delaware, enlisted 19 April 1758 for the campaign in the lower counties. On a return of Captain McClughan's company dated 17 May 1758.

Neal, Alexander, age 25, laborer, born Ireland, enlisted 04 May 1759 in Captain Robert Boyd's company [probably in the Third Battalion]. On a return dated May and June 1759.

Neal, John, age 20, born New Castle, Delaware, private in Captain John Singleton's company in service between 01 May and 08 May 1758.

Neal, John, age 28, laborer, born Ireland, enlisted 23 July 1746 in Captain John Shannon's company of foot.

Neal, Joseph, age 36, carpenter, born Ireland, enlisted 28 April 1758. On a weekly return of Captain Samuel Jones's company in 1758.

Neal, Lewis, age 30, laborer, born Switzerland, enlisted 25 May 1749 in Captain Richard Gardiner's company in Colonel William Denney's Pennsylvania Regiment.

Nealy, Robert, enlisted 23 July 1746 in Captain Samuel Perry's company.

Nebb, John, captain stationed on the frontier in Northampton County with Ensign Alex Boyd, one sergeant, and twenty-five men at Fort Penn on 01 June 1764 as part of a unit under the command of Major Asher Clayton.

Necle, Martin, age 28, mariner, born Sweedland, enlisted 01 May 1758. On a weekly return of Captain Samuel Jones's company in 1758.

Neidy, Adam, age 50, laborer, born Heidelberg, Germany, enlisted 25 May 1759, private in Captain John Mathers's company in the Pennsylvania Regiment. On a return dated 15 June 1759.

Neifert, Jacob, age 21, born Germany, enlisted 01 September 1757, private in Captain John Nicholas Weatherholt's company, which enlisted for a term of three years and was stationed in Heydelberg Township, Northampton County, in March and April 1758.

Neigle, James, age 21, tailor, born Ireland, enlisted 11 July 1746 in Captain William Trent's company.

Nelson, James, a private in Captain Joseph Inslee's Company of Foot, Newtown, Bucks County, in 1756.

Nelson, John, ensign from 05 May 1758 in Captain Samuel Nelson's company in the Third Battalion. Lieutenant from 26 April 1759 in Captain Samuel Nelson's company of Colonel William Clapham's Regiment of New Levies. Lieutenant in Captain Samuel Nelson's company of the First Battalion of the Pennsylvania Regiment from 13 April 1760.

Nelson, John, promoted to lieutenant after serving in the Pennsylvania Regiment of Three Battalions in 1758 and 1759. Reported as "dead".

Nelson, Samuel, captain from 05 May 1758 of a company in the Third Battalion. Captain from 28 April 1759 of a company of Colonel William Clapham's Regiment of New Levies. Captain of a company of the First Battalion of the Pennsylvania Regiment from 16 April 1760.

Nelson, Samuel, promoted to captain after serving in the Pennsylvania Regiment of Three Battalions in 1758 and 1759. Reported as "dead".

Newbold, John, age 22, carpenter, born Maryland, sergeant in Captain John Wright's company of the Lower County. On a muster dated 11 May 1759.

Newbold, John, captain in the Southern District of Lewes and Rehoboth Hundred company of Colonel Jacob Kollock's Regiment of Sussex County in 1756/8. Described as Rehobeth District Company in 1758.

Newbold, John, private, age 22, farmer, born Somerset, Maryland, enlisted 05 May 1758 for the campaign in the lower counties. On a return of Captain McClughan's company dated 17 May 1758.

Newcomb, Baptist, age 23, born Sussex, Delaware, private in Captain John Wright's company of the Lower County. On a muster dated 11 May 1759.

Newcomb, Thomas, age 19, born Sussex, Delaware, private in Captain John Wright's company of the Lower County. On a muster dated 11 May 1759.

Newman, Edward, age 26, laborer, born Ireland, enlisted 14 July 1746 in Captain William Trent's company.

Newman, Nathaniel, enlisted 28 May 1758 in Captain French Battell's company of Lower County Provincials.

Newton, John, age 18, born Maryland, private in Captain John Wright's company of the Lower County. On a muster dated 11 May 1759.

Nice, John, a lieutenant stationed on the frontier in Northampton County with one sergeant and eighteen men at Thomas

Everitt's, Linn Township, on 01 June 1764 as part of a unit under the command of Major Asher Clayton.

Nice, John, ensign in Captain John Philip De Hass's company of the First Battalion of the Pennsylvania Regiment from 06 May 1760. Lieutenant in Captain Nicholas Housegger's company in the First Battalion of the Pennsylvania Regiment from 14 October 1763.

Nicholas, David, age 21, weaver, born Ireland, enlisted 13 July 1746 in Captain John Shannon's company of foot.

Nichols, John, age 37, laborer, born Ireland, enlisted 30 April 1759 in Captain Charles Stewart's company [probably one of the Associated Companies of Bucks County]. On a return dated June 1759.

Nicholson, James, age 20, laborer, born Yorkshire, England, enlisted 12 May 1758. On a weekly return of Captain Samuel Jones's company in 1758.

Nicholson, John, age 19, laborer, born Ireland, enlisted 27 April 1758. On a weekly return of Captain Samuel Jones's company in 1758.

Nickell, John, private, age 30, laborer, born Bedony, Ireland, enlisted 26 April 1758 for the campaign in the lower counties. On a return of Captain McClughan's company dated 17 May 1758.

Nickelson, Benjamin, private in Captain Patterson's company from 20 January 1758 stationed eastward of the Susquehanna. On a muster roll dated 08 March 1758.

Nieler, George, a private in Captain Adam Heylman's Company, of the St. Vincent and Puke's Land Association on 10 May 1756.

Nilson, William, on a return of Captain David Hunter's Company [probably from York County] in Colonel William Clapham's Regiment of New Levies dated 26 May 1759.

Nisser, Nicholas, age 23, tailor, enlisted 30 June 1746 in Captain John Deimer's company.

Nixon, John, lieutenant in the Dock Ward Company of Colonel Jacob Duché's Philadelphia Regiment in chosen on 20 March

1756 in the stead of Thomas Willing. {PA1, II, 599–600} Return rejected by the assembly as not proper. {CR, VII, 76}

Nixon, Richard, captain in the Associated Regiment of Foot of Philadelphia on 29 Dec 1747.

Noble, William, age 30, plasterer, born England, enlisted 03 June 1758 by Lieutenant William McClay for Captain John Montgomery's company.

Noble, William, age 31, laborer, born England, enlisted 19 April 1758 by Captain Benjamin Noxon.

Noleman, Richard, age 20, carpenter, born Maryland, enlisted 29 April 1758 by Captain Benjamin Noxon.

Noon, George, age 16, laborer, born Arnan, Germany, enlisted 19 May 1759, private in Captain John Mathers's company in the Pennsylvania Regiment. On a return dated 15 June 1759.

Norman, Edward, age 28, laborer, born England, enlisted 13 July 1746 in Captain John Shannon's company of foot.

Norrice, James, a member of Captain Joseph Armstrong's Company on 07 August 1755, raised in Cumberland County.

Norrice, John, a member of Captain Joseph Armstrong's Company on 07 August 1755, raised in Cumberland County.

North, Roger, lieutenant in the Associated Regiment in the County of Philadelphia in 1748.

Norton, Edward, enlisted 15 May 1759, private in Captain Henry Van Bibber's company of the Lower County. On a return dated 04 June 1759.

Norwood, John, age 23, laborer, born Pennsylvania, enlisted 24 May 1759, private in Captain Robert Curry's company in Colonel William Clapham's Pennsylvania Regiment. On a return dated June 1759.

Nouls, Peter, on a return of Captain David Hunter's Company [probably from York County] in Colonel William Clapham's Regiment of New Levies dated 26 May 1759.

Noxon, Benjamin, captain from 15 April 1758, recruiting in April and May 1758, resigned 13 June 1758. On a list of officers of the lower government on Delaware, 1758/9.

Nugent, John, age 35, laborer, born Derry, Ireland, enlisted 04 May 1759, private in Captain John Haslet's company in the

Pennsylvania Regiment. On a list of recruits dated 20 May 1759.

Nutt, John, hired 26 May 1757 as a battoe man, Master George Allen.

Nutter, Henry, landsman on the provincial ship *Pennsylvania* on 17 August 1757.

O'Brien, Daniel, age 40, tailor, born Ireland, enlisted 28 May 1749 in Captain Richard Gardiner's company in Colonel William Denney's Pennsylvania Regiment.

O'Brien, Edward, a private in Captain George Armstrong's Company, Second Battalion in 1756; killed at Kittanning.

O'Brien, Patrick, age 29, laborer, born Ireland, enlisted 18 May 1758 by Lieutenant William McClay for Captain John Montgomery's company.

O'Cain, Richard, *see* O'Kane, Richard.

O'Daniel, James, hired 28 May 1757 as a battoe man, Master George Allen.

O'Donnell, Michael, *see* O'Donnely, Michael.

O'Donnelly, Arthur, age 19, laborer, born Ireland, enlisted 15 July 1746 in Captain Samuel Perry's company.

O'Donnely, Michael, age 22, laborer, born Ireland, enlisted 22 July 1746 in Captain John Shannon's company of foot.

O'Gabing, Owen, age 35, laborer, born Donegal, Ireland, enlisted 30 April 1759, private in Captain Joseph Richardson's company of the Third Battalion in the Pennsylvania Regiment. On a return of recruits dated 1759.

O'Hara, John, seaman on the provincial ship *Pennsylvania* on 17 August 1757.

O'Kane, Richard, captain in the Associated Regiment of Lancaster County over the Susquehanna in 1747–8.

O'Neal, Charles, a private in Captain George Armstrong's Company, Second Battalion in 1756; wounded at Kittanning.

O'Neale, Arthur, enlisted 16 July 1746 in Captain Samuel Perry's company.

Oaley, David in Captain Robert Eastburn's company in the Second Battalion.

Oat, John Martin, enlisted 11 July 1746 in Captain Samuel Perry's company.

Ogle, Thomas, Jun., captain in the Christiana Hundred company of Colonel William Armstrong's Upper Regiment of New Castle County in 1756.

Ogle, Thomas, ensign in one of two regiments of New Castle County in 1747–8.

Oliver, Daniel, age 30, born New England, corporal in Captain John Wright's company of the Lower County. On a muster dated 11 May 1759.

Omuth, John, private who enlisted 21 April 1756 in Captain Joseph Shippen's company in Colonel William Clapham's Regiment in 1756, the regiment in garrison at Fort Augusta, Shamokin, and listed in Shippen's Account Book. Described as being of the Major's Company.

Onslow, Richard, *see* Anslow.

Opdyke, William, a private in Captain Joseph Inslee's Company of Foot, Newtown, Bucks County, in 1756.

Orched, William, age 36, laborer, born England, enlisted 23 April 1758. On a weekly return of Captain Samuel Jones's company in 1758.

Ormsby, Luke, *see* Armsbie, Luke.

Orndt, Jacob, captain on a List of Officers in the Province Pay, 1756 in the First Battalion of the Pennsylvania Regiment with a commission date of 19 April 1756. {PA5, I, 88}

Orndt, Jacob, provincial officer in 1754; at Gnadenhutten in 1755. Captain of a company of the First Battalion from 19 April 1756. Captain from 10 December 1757 in a company in the Second Battalion, stationed eastward of the Susquehanna. Major of the First Battalion (John Armstrong's) of Colonel William Denny's Regiment, 02 June 1758. Major of the First Battalion of the Pennsylvania Regiment in 1759.

Orndt, Jacob, ensign in Captain John Nicholas Wetterholt's company of the First Battalion, 21 March 1759.

Osborn, Charles, a private in Captain John Kidd's Independent Company of Foot, Philadelphia in 1756.

Osman, William, age 22, laborer, born Jersey, enlisted 25 April 1759, private in Captain Joseph Richardson's company of the Third Battalion in the Pennsylvania Regiment. On a return of recruits dated 1759.

Ottaway, George, *see* George Ottway.

Ottway, George, age 24, laborer, born England, enlisted 02 May 1759, private in Captain John Haslet's company in the Pennsylvania Regiment. On a list of recruits dated 20 May 1759.

Overpack, George, ensign in the Associated Regiment of Bucks County in 1748.

Owen, Griffith, captain in the Associated Regiment of Bucks County in 1748.

Owen, Robert, lieutenant in the Associated Regiment of Foot of Philadelphia on 29 Dec 1747.

Packer, Edward, age 22, mason, born Pennsylvania, enlisted 21 May 1758. On a return of Captain John Bull's company dated 01 July 1758.

Painter, Jacob, private in Captain Patterson's company from 22 June 1757 stationed eastward of the Susquehanna. On a muster roll dated 08 March 1758.

Palmer, Jonathan, captain in one of the Associated Companies of Bucks County in 1756.

Parham, George, age 18, laborer, born Wales, enlisted 06 May 1759, private in Captain James Armstrong's company in Colonel William Clapham's Pennsylvania Regiment. On a return dated 01 June 1759.

Parke, Joseph, ensign in the Associated Regiment of Chester County in 1747.

Parke, Thomas, lieutenant in one of the Associated Companies of Kent County in 1747–8.

Parker, Alexander, age 40, weaver, born Ireland, enlisted 21 May 1759, sergeant in Captain Robert Curry's company in Colonel William Clapham's Pennsylvania Regiment. On a return dated June 1759.

Parker, Anthony, age 35, laborer, born Ireland, enlisted 08 July 1746 in Captain John Shannon's company of foot.

Parker, James, age 30, laborer, born Scotland, enlisted 08 May 1759 in Captain Robert Boyd's company [probably in the Third Battalion]. On a return dated May and June 1759.

Parker, Matthew, age 28, smith, born Kent, Delaware, enlisted 20 July 1746 in Captain John Shannon's company of foot.

Parker, Robert, hired 28 May 1757 as a battoe man, Master George Allen.

Parks, James, age 23, born Tyrone, Ireland, private in Captain John Haslett's company enlisted on 15 May 1758 and last paid on 21 May 1758.

Parmela, Charles, age 24, carpenter, born New England, enlisted 27 June 1746 in Captain John Shannon's company of foot.

Parr, James, age 16, laborer, born Chester, Pennsylvania, enlisted 09 May 1759, private in Captain James Armstrong's company in Colonel William Clapham's Pennsylvania Regiment. On a return dated 01 June 1759.

Parr, William, ensign in one of the companies of Colonel Jacob Duché's Philadelphia Regiment in 1756.

Parr, Zephaniah, enlisted 19 May 1759, private in Captain Henry Van Bibber's company of the Lower County. On a return dated 04 June 1759.

Parrager, Charles, age 32, laborer, born Germany, enlisted 02 May 1758. On a return of Captain John Bull's company dated 01 July 1758. Formerly in the Royal Americans.

Parry, David, captain in the Associated Regiment of Chester County in 1747.

Parry, Rowland, ensign in the Associated Regiment of Chester County in 1747.

Parsons, William, major in the provincial service in 1755. Major in the First Battalion from 14 May 1756. Was a captain of a company prior to his promotion.

Parsons, William, major, on a List of Officers in the Province Pay, 1756 in the First Battalion of the Pennsylvania Regiment with a commission date of 14 May 1756. {PA5, I, 88}

Parvour, Peter, age 22, laborer, born Pennsylvania, enlisted 03 May 1749 in Captain Richard Gardiner's company in Colonel William Denney's Pennsylvania Regiment.

Paterson, James, promoted to captain after serving in the Pennsylvania Regiment of Three Battalions in 1758 and 1759.

Patrick, Hugh, captain in one of the Associated Companies of Lancaster County in 1756.

Patrick, Hugh, captain in the Associated Regiment of the West End of Lancaster County in 1747–8.

Patten, Matthew, ensign from 09 May 1758 in Captain Charles McClung's company in the Third Battalion.

Patterson, Henry, seaman on the provincial ship *Pennsylvania* on 17 August 1757.

Patterson, James, a member of Captain Joseph Armstrong's Company on 07 August 1755, raised in Cumberland County.

Patterson, James, captain of a company in the First Battalion from 16 December 1757 to 08 March 1758.

Patterson, James, captain in a company of the First Battalion in 1755/6.

Patterson, James, captain in the Associated Regiment of the West End of Lancaster County in 1747–8.

Patterson, James, captain in the provincial service in 1755. Captain from 16 December 1757 of a company stationed eastward of the Susquehanna.

Patterson, James, captain on a List of Officers in the Province Pay, 1756 in the First Battalion of the Pennsylvania Regiment with a commission date of 10 December 1756. {PA5, I, 88}

Patterson, Joshua, a member of Captain Joseph Armstrong's Company on 07 August 1755, raised in Cumberland County.

Patterson, Nathaniel, lieutenant from 05 May 1758 of Captain Samuel Nelson's company of the Third Battalion.

Patterson, Samuel, captain in the White Clay Creek Hundred company of Colonel William Armstrong's Upper Regiment of New Castle County in 1756.

Patterson, William, captain in one of two regiments of New Castle County in 1747–8.

Patterson, William, ensign of Captain Patrick Work's Company, Third Battalion (known as the Augusta Regiment) from 14 May 1756. Lieutenant from 3/12 December 1757 in Captain

Jacob Orndt's company in the Second Battalion. Stationed at Fort Augusta.

Patterson, William, lieutenant colonel in one of two regiments of New Castle County in 1747–8.

Patterson, William, promoted to captain after serving in the Pennsylvania Regiment of Three Battalions in 1758 and 1759.

Pattin, James, Private who 24 April 1756 in Captain Joseph Shippen's company in Colonel William Clapham's Regiment in 1756, the regiment in garrison at Fort Augusta, Shamokin, and listed in Shippen's Account Book. Killed 19 August 1756.

Pattison, William, age 28, laborer, born Pennsylvania, enlisted 04 May 1758. On a return of Captain John Blackwood's company in the Third Battalion dated 22 May 1758.

Paul, Nicholas, age 21, born Germany, enlisted 01 September 1757, private in Captain John Nicholas Weatherholt's company which enlisted for a term of three years and stationed in Heydelberg Township, Northampton County, in March and April 1758.

Pauling, Henry, captain in the Associated Regiment in the County of Philadelphia in 1748.

Pauling, John, ensign in the Associated Regiment in the County of Philadelphia in 1748.

Paulson, Benjamin, age 30, farmer, born New Castle, Delaware, enlisted 25 April 1759, sergeant in Captain James Armstrong's company in Colonel William Clapham's Pennsylvania Regiment. On a return dated 01 June 1759.

Paulson, Benjamin, age 38, laborer, born Ulster, Ireland, enlisted 25 April 1759, private in Captain James Armstrong's company in Colonel William Clapham's Pennsylvania Regiment. On a return dated 01 June 1759.

Payne, Gilbert, age 33, laborer, born England, enlisted 12 July 1746 in Captain Samuel Perry's company.

Peace, James, *see* James Pease.

Pean, John, on a list of men recruited by Captain Andrew McDowell's company in the Second Battalion, Pennsylvania Regiment dated 04 June 1759.

Pearce, Edward, ensign in the Associated Regiment of Chester County in 1747.

Pearis, Richard, promoted to captain after serving in the Pennsylvania Regiment of Three Battalions in 1758 and 1759. Reported as "discontinued". Captain from 03 May 1759 of a company of Colonel William Clapham's Regiment of New Levies.

Pearson, Arnold, a private in Captain Charles Batho's Independent Company of Foot, Philadelphia in 1756.

Pearson, Benjamin, private in Captain Patterson's company from 14 February 1758 stationed eastward of the Susquehanna. On a muster roll dated 08 March 1758.

Pearson, Joseph, private in Captain Patterson's company from 18 January 1758

Pearson, Samuel, hired 30 May 1757 as a battoe man, Master George Allen.

Pease, James, private, age 32, merchant, born London, England, enlisted 25 April 1758 for the campaign in the lower counties. On a return of Captain McClughan's company dated 17 May 1758.

Peasly, David, ensign from 22 April 1759 in Captain Robert Curry's company in Colonel William Clapham's Regiment of New Levies.

Pedan, Hugh, lieutenant in one of the Associated Companies of Lancaster County in 1756.

Pendergrass, James, age 18, mariner, born England, enlisted 05 May 1758. On a weekly return of Captain Samuel Jones's company in 1758.

Pendergrass, Philip, a private in Captain Hugh Mercer's Company, Second Battalion in 1756; missing at the capture of Kittanning.

Pennington, Highland, enlisted 01 May 1759, private in Captain Henry Van Bibber's company of the Lower County. On a return dated 04 June 1759.

Perkins, Benjamin, private, age 19, farmer, born Cedar Creek, Delaware, enlisted 04 May 1758 for the campaign in the lower counties. On a return of Captain McClughan's company dated 17 May 1758.

Perkins, William, enlisted 17 May 1759, private in Captain Henry Van Bibber's company of the Lower County. On a return dated 04 June 1759.

Permore, Godfrey, age 37, tinker, born Germany, enlisted 25 May 1759 in Captain Charles Stewart's company [probably one of the Associated Companies of Bucks County]. On a return dated June 1759.

Perry, John, age 25, laborer, born Maryland, enlisted 03 May 1758 by Captain Benjamin Noxon.

Perry, Samuel, captain of Pennsylvania troops in Albany, N.Y. on 21 October 1746 and at least through 12 November 1746.

Perry, Samuel, captain in a company in winter quarters in Albany, N.Y., 1746–7, discharged 31 October 1747.

Perse, Alexander, enlisted 19 May 1759, private in Captain Henry Van Bibber's company of the Lower County. On a return dated 04 June 1759.

Peter, Caja, private, age 22, fiddle maker, born Pocomock, Maryland, enlisted May 1758 for the campaign in the lower counties. On a return of Captain McClughan's company dated 17 May 1758.

Peters, John, age 26, laborer, born Pennsylvania, enlisted 17 May 1749 in Captain Richard Gardiner's company in Colonel William Denney's Pennsylvania Regiment.

Peters, Matthew, landsman on the provincial ship *Pennsylvania* on 17 August 1757.

Peters, Moses, on a list of men recruited by Captain Andrew McDowell's company in the Second Battalion, Pennsylvania Regiment dated 04 June 1759.

Peters, William, a private in Captain Charles Batho's Independent Company of Foot, Philadelphia in 1756.

Peterson, Adam, captain in the St. George's Hundred company of Colonel Jacob Van Bibber's Lower Regiment of New Castle County in 1756.

Peterson, Gabril, age 30, born West Jersey, laborer, private in Captain John Shannon's Company, enlisted 16 July 1746. On a roll of deserters dated 22 July 1746. [B3:422:18]

Peterson, Ruloff, lieutenant in one of two regiments of New Castle County in 1747–8.
Petterson, Gabriel, age 30, laborer, born West Jersey, enlisted 16 July 1746 in Captain John Shannon's company of foot.
Petterson, John, age 20, mariner, born England, enlisted 07 May 1758. On a weekly return of Captain Samuel Jones's company in 1758.
Phillips, Edward, seaman on the provincial ship *Pennsylvania* on 17 August 1757.
Phillips, Francis, a private in Captain Hugh Mercer's Company, Second Battalion in 1756; missing at the capture of Kittanning.
Phillips, Jacob, major of Colonel Jacob Kollock's Regiment of Sussex County in 1756/8.
Phillips, Robert, seaman on the provincial ship *Pennsylvania* on 17 August 1757.
Phillips, Thomas, ensign in one of two regiments of New Castle County in 1747–8.
Phillips, Thomas, landsman on the provincial ship *Pennsylvania* on 17 August 1757.
Phillips, Willcox, age 26, bricklayer, born Pennsylvania, enlisted 01 May 1758. On a return of Captain John Bull's company dated 01 July 1758.
Phisler, Jacob, a private in Captain Edward Jones's Independent Company of Horse, Philadelphia in 1756.
Pierce, Cromwell, lieutenant from 08 May 1758 in Captain George Ashton's company in the Third Battalion.
Pierce, James, a member of Captain David Jameson's Company at McCord's Fort on 02 April 1756 when he was killed.
Pierce, Robert, ensign in one of two regiments of New Castle County in 1747–8.
Pike, Isaac, boatswain's mate of the provincial ship *Pennsylvania* on 17 August 1757.
Piper, James, captain of a company in Lieutenant Colonel Commandant Asher Clayton's Second Battalion of the Pennsylvania Regiment commanded by the Hon. J. Penn from 16 July 1763.

Piper, James, ensign from 27 April 1758 in Captain John Byer's Company to what appears to be the headquarters company of Colonel William Denny's Regiment, 18 March 1759. This company was originally Smith's Company stationed east of the Susquehanna.

Piper, James, lieutenant and quartermaster of the Second Battalion of the Pennsylvania Regiment from April 1760. Lieutenant in Captain James Hyndshaw's company of the Second Battalion of the Pennsylvania Regiment from 27 April 1760.

Piper, James, promoted to captain after serving in the Pennsylvania Regiment of Three Battalions in 1758 and 1759.

Piper, John, lieutenant in Captain John Brady's company in Lieutenant Colonel Commandant Asher Clayton's Second Battalion of the Pennsylvania Regiment commanded by the Hon. J. Penn from 19 July 1763.

Piper, Samuel, age 35, tailor, born Derry, Ireland, enlisted 04 May 1759, private in Captain James Armstrong's company in Colonel William Clapham's Pennsylvania Regiment. On a return dated 01 June 1759.

Piper, Samuel, on a list of men recruited by Captain Andrew McDowell's company in the Second Battalion, Pennsylvania Regiment dated 04 June 1759.

Piper, William, captain of a company in Lieutenant Colonel Commandant Asher Clayton's Second Battalion of the Pennsylvania Regiment commanded by the Hon. J. Penn from 20 July 1763.

Pitner, Henry, a private in Captain Joseph Inslee's Company of Foot, Newtown, Bucks County, in 1756.

Pitt, James, age 23, perukemaker, born England, enlisted 29 April 1758. On a return of Captain John Blackwood's company in the Third Battalion dated 22 May 1758.

Platt, Hendrick, age 20, laborer, enlisted 15 July 1746 in Captain John Deimer's company.

Platt, Robert, age 26, millwright, born Ireland, enlisted 28 April 1758. On a return of Captain John Blackwood's company in the Third Battalion dated 22 May 1758.

Platt, Samuel, lieutenant in the White Clay Creek Hundred company of Colonel William Armstrong's Upper Regiment of New Castle County in 1756.

Plumstead, William, a private in Captain Samuel Mifflin's Association Battery Company of Philadelphia in 1756.

Plunkett, William, lieutenant in Captain William Armstrong's company in Lieutenant Colonel Commandant Asher Clayton's Second Battalion of the Pennsylvania Regiment commanded by the Hon. J. Penn from 14 July 1763. Surgeon in Lieutenant Colonel Commandant Asher Clayton's Second Battalion of the Pennsylvania Regiment commanded by the Hon. J. Penn from 07 September 1764.

Plunkett, William, lieutenant of Captain John Hambright's Company, Third Battalion (known as the Augusta Regiment) from 20 August 1756.

Polegreen, James, captain in the Associated Regiment of Foot of Philadelphia on 29 Dec 1747.

Pollock, James, ensign in Captain George Armstrong's company from 04 January 1758, stationed westward of the Susquehanna.

Pollock, James, ensign in Captain Edward Ward's company in the First Battalion, 04 January 1758.

Polstain, Benjamin, ensign from 06 May 1759 in Captain James Armstrong's company of Colonel William Clapham's Regiment of New Levies.

Pool, John George, age 18, laborer, born Germany, enlisted 12 July 1746 in Captain Samuel Perry's company.

Poor, Adam, private in Captain Patterson's company from 28 February 1758 stationed eastward of the Susquehanna. On a muster roll dated 08 March 1758.

Poor, John, seaman on the provincial ship *Pennsylvania* on 17 August 1757.

Poor, Purget, private in Captain Patterson's company from 08 February 1758 stationed eastward of the Susquehanna. On a muster roll dated 08 March 1758.

Poor, William, private in Captain Patterson's company from 26 November 1757 stationed eastward of the Susquehanna. On a muster roll dated 08 March 1758.

Porter, Alexander, captain in one of two regiments of New Castle County in 1747–8.

Porter, Alexander, captain in the New Castle Hundred company of Colonel William Armstrong's Upper Regiment of New Castle County in 1756.

Porter, Alexander, lieutenant in the Pencader Hundred company of Colonel Jacob Van Bibber's Lower Regiment of New Castle County in 1756.

Porter, William, captain in the Associated Regiment of Chester County in 1747.

Porterfield, Joshua, age 20, laborer, born Pennsylvania, enlisted 26 April 1759 in Captain Charles Stewart's company [probably one of the Associated Companies of Bucks County]. On a return dated June 1759.

Postlethwaite, Samuel, captain of a company under Commandant James Potter on the Northern Frontier on 02 October 1764.

Postlewaite, Samuel, lieutenant from 18 May 1758 in Captain John Clark's company of the Third Battalion. Captain from 09 May 1759 of a company of Colonel William Clapham's Regiment of New Levies.

Postlewaite, Samuel, promoted to captain after serving in the Pennsylvania Regiment of Three Battalions in 1758 and 1759.

Potter, James, commandant commanding three companies on the Northern Frontier on 02 October 1764.

Potter, James, ensign in Captain John Armstrong's company of the Second Battalion from 17 February 1756. Stationed westward of Susquehanna. Promoted from lieutenant to captain replacing William Thompson in the First Battalion, 17 February 1759.

Potter, James, ensign in Captain John Potter's Company, Second Battalion from 17 April 1756; wounded at Kittanning.

Potter, James, lieutenant of John Armstrong's company in the First Battalion of Colonel William Denny's Regiment, 04 December 1757. Promoted to captain 17 February 1759. Stationed west of the Susquehanna.

Potter, James, promoted to captain after serving in the Pennsylvania Regiment of Three Battalions in 1758 and 1759.

Potter, John, captain in a company in the Second Battalion from 17 February 1756.

Potter, John, lieutenant in the Associated Regiment of Lancaster County over the Susquehanna in 1747–8.

Potts, John, ensign from 01 May 1759 in Captain Richard Gardiner's company of Colonel William Clapham's Regiment of New Levies.

Pough, Elias, *see* Elias Pugh.

Powell, _____, enlisted 05 June 1749 in Captain Richard Gardiner's company in Colonel William Denney's Pennsylvania Regiment.

Powell, Samuel, landsman on the provincial ship *Pennsylvania* on 17 August 1757.

Powell, Thomas, age 20, private in Captain John Singleton's company in service between 01 May and 08 May 1758.

Power, Robert, boatswain of the provincial ship *Pennsylvania* on 17 August 1757.

Power, Thomas, a private in Captain Lieutenant Robert Callender's Company, Second Battalion in 1756; killed at Kittanning.

Powskner, John Christopher, age 24, laborer, born Germany, enlisted 03 May 1759, private in Captain William Johnston's company in the Pennsylvania Regiment. On a return dated 12 May 1759.

Powvell, *see* Powell.

Preis, John George, age 21, born Germany, enlisted 01 September 1757, private in Captain John Nicholas Weatherholt's company, which enlisted for a term of three years and was stationed in Heydelberg Township, Northampton County, in March and April 1758.

Prentice, John, captain of a company of the Second Battalion of the Pennsylvania Regiment from 13 April 1760.

Prentice, John, ensign in Captain Hance Hamilton's Company, Second Battalion from 22 May 1756. Lieutenant in Captain George Armstrong's company of the First Battalion from 06 December 1757 stationed westward of the Susquehanna.

Promoted to captain vice Garraway in March 1759. Captain from 14 May 1759 of a company in the Old Levies.

Prentice, John, promoted to captain after serving in the Pennsylvania Regiment of Three Battalions in 1758 and 1759.

Prettyman, Thomas, ensign in the Northern District of Indian River Hundred company of Colonel Jacob Kollock's Regiment of Sussex County in 1756. Ensign in Captain Cord Hazzard's company from Angola District, Sussex County, Delaware, in Kollock's Regiment in 1758.

Prettyman, William, ensign in the Southern District of Indian River Hundred in Captain Burton Waples's company of Colonel Jacob Kollock's Regiment of Sussex County in 1756/8.

Price, Charles, a private in Captain Joseph Inslee's Company of Foot, Newtown, Bucks County, in 1756.

Price, Daniel, private, age 25, weaver, born Elizabethtown, New Jersey, enlisted 04 May 1758 for the campaign in the lower counties. On a return of Captain McClughan's company dated 17 May 1758.

Price, George, ensign from 30 April 1758 in Captain Robert Eastburn's company in the Second Battalion. Ensign from 17 March 1759 in Captain James Burd's company in the Second Battalion. Adjutant of the First Battalion in 1760.

Price, George, lieutenant in Captain William Clapham, Jr.'s company of the First Battalion of the Pennsylvania Regiment from 22 April 1760.

Price, Samuel, lieutenant from 12 May 1758 in Captain John Bull's company in the Third Battalion and listed on a company return dated 01 July 1758. Captain from 18 May 1759 of a company of Colonel William Clapham's Regiment of New Levies.

Price, Samuel, promoted to captain after serving in the Pennsylvania Regiment of Three Battalions in 1758 and 1759. Reported as "dead".

Price, Thomas, captain from 12 May 1759 of a company of Colonel William Clapham's Regiment of New Levies.

Price, Thomas, captain of a company of the First Battalion of the Pennsylvania Regiment from 18 April 1760.

Price, Thomas, promoted to captain after serving in the Pennsylvania Regiment of Three Battalions in 1758 and 1759. Reported as moved to "Maryland".

Price, Thompson, ensign in one of the Associated Companies of Bucks County in 1756.

Pride, Southy, private, age 21, planter, born Sussex, Delaware, enlisted 19 April 1758 for the campaign in the lower counties. On a return of Captain McClughan's company dated 17 May 1758.

Pride, Suthy, age 21, born Sussex, Delaware, private in Captain John Wright's company of the Lower County. On a muster dated 11 May 1759.

Priestly, ensign in one of the Associated Companies of Bucks County in 1756.

Priscott, James, age 22, bricklayer, born Ireland, enlisted 11 July 1746 in Captain William Trent's company.

Probater, Michael, age 22, blacksmith, born Sweden, enlisted 13 July 1746 in Captain Samuel Perry's company.

Proctor, John, captain of a company in the First Battalion of the Pennsylvania Regiment during or after 1763.

Proctor, Richard, age 26, weaver, born Lancaster, England, enlisted 29 April 1759, private in Captain James Armstrong's company in Colonel William Clapham's Pennsylvania Regiment. On a return dated 01 June 1759.

Pugh, Elias, age 23, wheelwright, born Philadelphia, Pennsylvania, enlisted 26 April 1759, private in Captain Joseph Richardson's company of the Third Battalion in the Pennsylvania Regiment. On a return of recruits dated 1759.

Pullet, Richard, age 29, born Maryland, private in Captain John Wright's company of the Lower County. On a muster dated 11 May 1759.

Purdey, Alexander, age 27, born Scotland, carpenter, private in Captain John Haslett's company enlisted on 08 May 1758 and last paid on 21 May 1758.

Purgat, George, age 21, laborer, born Germany, enlisted 23 July 1746 in Captain Samuel Perry's company.

Purrins, John, lieutenant in the Associated Regiment of the West End of Lancaster County in 1747–8.

Quay, Alexander, age 25, shoemaker, enlisted 14 July 1746 in Captain John Deimer's company.

Quicksall, Joseph, promoted to lieutenant after serving in the Pennsylvania Regiment of Three Battalions in 1758 and 1759. Reported as "dead".

Quicksell, Joseph, ensign from 09 December 1757 in Captain Jacob Orndt's company in the Second Battalion, stationed eastward of the Susquehanna.

Quigley, John, hired 23 June 1757 as a battoe man, Master George Allen.

Quin, John, age 37, laborer, born Ireland, enlisted 07 May 1758. On a weekly return of Captain Samuel Jones's company in 1758.

Quy, Alexander, *see* Quay, Alexander.

Rabar, John, landsman on the provincial ship *Pennsylvania* on 17 August 1757.

Raddly, John, landsman on the provincial ship *Pennsylvania* on 17 August 1757.

Raerd, Cornelius, age 26, laborer, born Ireland, enlisted 02 August 1746 in Captain John Deimer's company.

Ragg, Robert, a private in Captain Samuel Mifflin's Association Battery Company of Philadelphia in 1756.

Raisley, Hugh, age 27, laborer, born Donegal, Ireland, enlisted 01 May 1759, private in Captain John Haslet's company in the Pennsylvania Regiment. On a list of recruits dated 20 May 1759.

Ralfe, Conrad, age 18, miller, born Hamborough, enlisted 28 April 1758. On a weekly return of Captain Samuel Jones's company in 1758.

Ralston, Hugh, *see* Hugh Rawiston.

Ramsey, David, ensign in Lieutenant Colonel George Armstrong's company of the Second Battalion of the Pennsylvania Regiment from April 1760.

Ramsey, James, age 18, weaver, born Pennsylvania, enlisted 29 May 1759 in Captain Robert Boyd's company [probably in the Third Battalion]. On a return dated May and June 1759.

Ramsey, James, private, age 20, laborer, born Donegal, Ireland, enlisted 20 April 1758 for the campaign in the lower counties. On a return of Captain McClughan's company dated 17 May 1758.

Ramsey, Peter, age 30, laborer, born Scotland, enlisted 09 July 1746 in Captain John Shannon's company of foot.

Ramsey, Samuel, lieutenant in one of the Associated Companies of Lancaster County in 1756.

Ramsey, William, captain in one of the Associated Companies of Bucks County in 1756.

Ramsey, William, captain in the Associated Regiment of Bucks County in 1748.

Randall, Joseph, age 42, born England, enlisted 27 April 1758. On a return of Captain John Blackwood's company in the Third Battalion dated 22 May 1758. Farrier to the Light Horse.

Randals, John, ensign in the Associated Regiment of Lancaster County over the Susquehanna in 1747–8.

Randle, Isaac, a private in Captain Joseph Inslee's Company of Foot, Newtown, Bucks County, in 1756.

Randle, Peter, age 39, laborer, born Inniskillen, Ireland, enlisted 04 May 1759, private in Captain James Armstrong's company in Colonel William Clapham's Pennsylvania Regiment. On a return dated 01 June 1759.

Randle, Warwick, age 38, cordwainer, born England, enlisted 07 July 1746 in Captain William Trent's company.

Randolph, Edward, *see* Fitz Randolph, Edward.

Rankin, George, a private in Captain Samuel Mifflin's Association Battery Company of Philadelphia in 1756.

Rankin, William, a member of Captain Joseph Armstrong's Company on 07 August 1755, raised in Cumberland County.

Raredon, Michael, age 37, weaver, born Ireland, enlisted 11 July 1746 in Captain William Trent's company.

Rawiston, Hugh, private, age 27, laborer, born Argyle, Scotland, enlisted 26 April 1758 for the campaign in the lower counties.

On a return of Captain McClughan's company dated 17 May 1758.

Raye, Christopher, enlisted 23 May 1759, private in Captain Henry Van Bibber's company of the Lower County. On a return dated 04 June 1759.

Rea, Thomas, age 19, laborer, born Ireland, enlisted 19 July 1746 in Captain Samuel Perry's company.

Read, Adam, captain from 04 May 1758 in a company in the Third Battalion.

Read, Adam, captain in the Associated Regiment of the West End of Lancaster County in 1747–8.

Read, James, hired 25 June 1757 as a battoe man, Master George Allen.

Read, John, age 21, laborer, born Ireland, enlisted 09 July 1746 in Captain William Trent's company.

Read, John, lieutenant in one of two regiments of New Castle County in 1747–8.

Read, William, ensign in the White Clay Creek Hundred company of Colonel William Armstrong's Upper Regiment of New Castle County in 1756.

Reag, Peter, age 37, born Germany, baker, enlisted 01 September 1757, private in Captain John Nicholas Weatherholt's company, which enlisted for a term of three years and was stationed in Heydelberg Township, Northampton County, in March and April 1758.

Realy, Terence, age 35, born Chester, Pennsylvania, "pock pitted", private in Captain John Singleton's company in service between 01 May and 08 May 1758.

Redman, Anthony, age 18, tailor, born Pennsylvania, enlisted 12 May 1759, private in Captain Robert Curry's company in Colonel William Clapham's Pennsylvania Regiment. On a return dated June 1759.

Redmond, Joseph, a private in Captain Samuel Mifflin's Association Battery Company of Philadelphia in 1756.

Redmond, Joseph, lieutenant in the Associated Regiment of Foot of Philadelphia on 29 Dec 1747.

Ree, John, on a list of men recruited by Captain Andrew McDowell's company in the Second Battalion, Pennsylvania Regiment dated 04 June 1759.

Reed, Adam, captain in the provincial service in 1755 on the Susquehanna.

Reed, John, age 29, brewer, born Worcester, England, enlisted 11 June 1759, private in Captain John Mathers's company in the Pennsylvania Regiment. On a return dated 15 June 1759.

Reed, John, seaman on the provincial ship *Pennsylvania* on 17 August 1757.

Reed, Thomas, age 43, laborer, enlisted 11 July 1746 in Captain Samuel Perry's company.

Reed, Walter, enlisted 19 May 1758 in Captain French Battell's company of Lower County Provincials.

Reed, William, captain in the Associated Regiment of Chester County in 1747.

Reemer, Michael, age 27, laborer, enlisted 30 July 1746 in Captain John Deimer's company.

Rees, Evan, captain in the Miln Creek Hundred company of Colonel William Armstrong's Upper Regiment of New Castle County in 1756.

Rees, John, lieutenant in one of the Associated Companies of Kent County in 1747–8.

Rees, John, lieutenant in the Associated Regiment of Chester County in 1747. {CR,V, 325}

Rees, William, ensign in one of the Associated Companies of Kent County in 1747–8.

Reese, John, lieutenant in the Upper Part of Duck Creek Hundred company of Colonel John Vining's Regiment of Kent County Militia, Upon Delaware in 1756.

Rehrer, John George, age 21, baker, enlisted 07 July 1746 in Captain John Deimer's company.

Reifel, Jacob, age 23, born Germany, carpenter, enlisted 01 September 1757, private in Captain John Nicholas Weatherholt's company, which enlisted for a term of three years and was stationed in Heydelberg Township, Northampton County, in March and April 1758April 1758.

Reily, Bryan, age 20, laborer, born Ireland, enlisted 17 May 1758 by Lieutenant William McClay for Captain John Montgomery's company.

Reis, Bernard, age 18, laborer, enlisted 11 July 1746 in Captain John Deimer's company.

Rennicks, Henry, ensign in the Associated Regiment of the West End of Lancaster County in 1747–8.

Renox, William, hired 10 June 1757 as a battoe man, Master George Allen.

Renshaw, Richard, lieutenant (a Quaker) in the Associated Regiment of Foot of Philadelphia on 29 Dec 1747. Resigned 17 March 1759, vice Montgomery.

Ress, William, on a list of men recruited by Captain Andrew McDowell's company in the Second Battalion, Pennsylvania Regiment dated 04 June 1759.

Reynolds, Edward, age 23, laborer, born Ireland, enlisted 30 July 1746 in Captain William Trent's company.

Reynolds, George, captain of a company of the First Battalion from 17 May 1756.

Reynolds, George, captain on a List of Officers in the Province Pay, 1756 in the First Battalion of the Pennsylvania Regiment with a commission date of 17 May 1756. {PA5, I, 88}

Reynolds, John, *see* Randals, John.

Reynolds, John, a member of Captain David Jameson's Company at McCord's Fort on 02 April 1756 when he was killed.

Reynolds, John, age 22, born Philadelphia, Pennsylvania, private in Captain John Singleton's company in service between 01 May and 08 May 1758.

Reynolds, Patrick, age 35, laborer, born Ireland, enlisted 07 July 1746 in Captain William Trent's company.

Reynolds, William, promoted to lieutenant after serving in the Pennsylvania Regiment of Three Battalions in 1758 and 1759.

Reynolds, William, wounded while a member of Captain Jamison's company at McCord's Fort on 02 April 1756. Lieutenant from 19 December 1757 in Captain David Jamison's company, stationed at Fort Augusta. Wounded 14

September 1758 at Grant's defeat near Fort Duquesne. Resigned 17 March 1759, vice Hughes.

Rhea, Matthew, lieutenant in the Apoquinimink Hundred company of Colonel Jacob Van Bibber's Lower Regiment of New Castle County in 1756.

Rhoades, William, captain in the Lower Part of Murder Kiln [or Mother-Kill] Hundred company of Colonel John Vining's Regiment of Kent County Militia, Upon Delaware in 1756.

Ribble, Nicholas, a private in Captain John Kidd's Independent Company of Foot, Philadelphia in 1756.

Rice, Evan, captain in one of two regiments of New Castle County in 1747–8.

Rice, John David, age 29, carpenter, born America, enlisted 20 May 1758 by Captain Benjamin Noxon.

Rice, John, age 28, cooper, born Pennsylvania, enlisted 01 May 1758. On a return of Captain John Bull's company dated 01 July 1758.

Rice, Thomas, private, age 21, laborer, born Ware, Virginia, enlisted 12 May 1758 for the campaign in the lower counties. On a return of Captain McClughan's company dated 17 May 1758.

Richard, Anthony, ensign in the Associated Regiment of Chester County in 1747.

Richards, Edward, in Captain Robert Eastburn's company in the Second Battalion.

Richards, Mathias, age 35, laborer, born Wales, enlisted 22 July 1746 in Captain John Deimer's company.

Richardson, Benjamin, age 19, laborer, born Newcastle, Delaware, enlisted 21 July 1746 in Captain John Shannon's company of foot.

Richardson, Joseph, captain from 08 May 1759 of a company of Colonel William Clapham's Regiment of New Levies.

Richardson, Joseph, on a return of Captain David Hunter's Company [probably from York County] in Colonel William Clapham's Regiment of New Levies dated 26 May 1759.

Richardson, Joseph, promoted to captain after serving in the Pennsylvania Regiment of Three Battalions in 1758 and 1759.

Richardson, Richardson, captain in the Associated Regiment of Chester County in 1747.

Richardson, Thomas, age 20, laborer, born Maryland, enlisted 26 July 1746 in Captain Samuel Perry's company.

Richardson, Thomas, age 20, laborer, born Philadelphia, Pennsylvania, enlisted 09 May 1759, private in Captain John Mathers's company in the Pennsylvania Regiment. On a return dated 15 June 1759.

Richardson, Thomas, age 24, laborer, born Pennsylvania, enlisted 03 May 1758 by Captain Benjamin Noxon.

Richardson, William, age 22, laborer, born Ireland, enlisted 02 July 1746 in Captain John Shannon's company of foot.

Richardson, William, age 26, laborer, born Lancaster, Pennsylvania, enlisted 04 May 1759 in Captain Robert Boyd's company [probably in the Third Battalion]. On a return dated May and June 1759.

Richeson, John, age 27, born Chester, Pennsylvania, "cocke nose and smooth faced", private in Captain John Singleton's company in service between 01 May and 08 May 1758.

Riddle, David, corporal in Captain Patterson's company from 11 June 1757 stationed eastward of the Susquehanna. On a muster roll dated 08 March 1758.

Riddle, David, Private who enlisted 15 April 1756 in Captain Joseph Shippen's company in Colonel William Clapham's Regiment in 1756, the regiment in garrison at Fort Augusta, Shamokin, and listed in Shippen's Account Book.

Riddle, Yost, Private who enlisted 19 April 1756 in Captain Joseph Shippen's company in Colonel William Clapham's Regiment in 1756, the regiment in garrison at Fort Augusta, Shamokin, and listed in Shippen's Account Book. Deserted with his arms, regimentals, and blanket on 14 October 1756.

Ridge, Andrew, age 32, barber, born Surry, England, enlisted 13 May 1759, private in Captain John Mathers's company in the Pennsylvania Regiment. On a return dated 15 June 1759.

Riding, Lewis, age 27, laborer, born England, enlisted 02 May 1758. On a return of Captain John Blackwood's company in the Third Battalion dated 22 May 1758.

Rigle, John Conrad, a private in Captain John Kidd's Independent Company of Foot, Philadelphia in 1756.

Riley, Peter, enlisted 15 May 1758 in Captain French Battell's company of Lower County Provincials.

Rinker, J., a lieutenant stationed on the frontier in Northampton County with one sergeant and eleven men at Simon Heller's, Wind Gap, on 01 June 1764 as part of a unit under the command of Major Asher Clayton.

Riple, Jacob, age 19, born Ireland, enlisted 18 May 1759, private in Captain Robert Curry's company in Colonel William Clapham's Pennsylvania Regiment. On a return dated June 1759.

Rippey, Jonathan, a member of Captain Joseph Armstrong's Company on 07 August 1755, raised in Cumberland County.

Rishady, John, age 18, laborer, born Down, Ireland, enlisted 01 May 1759, private in Captain John Haslet's company in the Pennsylvania Regiment. On a list of recruits dated 20 May 1759.

Ritchie, James, ensign in the Associated Regiment in the County of Philadelphia in 1748.

Ritzbaugh, John, lieutenant in Captain Jacob Kern's company in the First Battalion of the Pennsylvania Regiment from 16 July 1764.

Roach, Robert, Private who enlisted 19 April 1756 in Captain Joseph Shippen's company in Colonel William Clapham's Regiment in 1756, the regiment in garrison at Fort Augusta, Shamokin, and listed in Shippen's Account Book. Deserted with arms, regimentals, and blanket on 18 September 1756.

Road, Godfried, age 26, born Germany, blue-dyer, enlisted 01 September 1757, private in Captain John Nicholas Weatherholt's company, which enlisted for a term of three years and was stationed in Heydelberg Township, Northampton County, in March and April 1758.

Road, Jacob, age 23, born Pennsylvania, enlisted 06 September 1757, private in Captain John Nicholas Weatherholt's company, which enlisted for a term of three years and was stationed in Heydelberg Township, Northampton County, in March and April 1758.

Roake, Andrew, age 21, cooper, born Ireland, enlisted 06 May 1749 in Captain Richard Gardiner's company in Colonel William Denney's Pennsylvania Regiment.

Roam, Dietrich, a private in Captain Adam Heylman's Company, of the St. Vincent and Puke's Land Association on 10 May 1756.

Roarty, Edward, landsman on the provincial ship *Pennsylvania* on 17 August 1757.

Roarty, John, landsman on the provincial ship *Pennsylvania* on 17 August 1757.

Robbins, Christopher, captain in the Associated Regiment in the County of Philadelphia in 1748.

Robert Irwin, waggon-master of the Third Battalion (known as the Augusta Regiment) from 12 April 1756.

Roberts, Bignal, enlisted 17 May 1758 in Captain French Battell's company of Lower County Provincials.

Roberts, Jeremiah, age 22, laborer, born Delaware, enlisted 29 April 1758 by Captain Benjamin Noxon.

Roberts, John, ensign in the Associated Regiment in the County of Philadelphia in 1748.

Roberts, John, private, age 27, laborer, born England, enlisted 09 May 1758 for the campaign in the lower counties. On a return of Captain McClughan's company dated 17 May 1758.

Robertson, Barnt., a member of Captain Joseph Armstrong's Company on 07 August 1755, raised in Cumberland County.

Robertson, Charles, age 23, cooper, born England, enlisted 13 July 1746 in Captain John Shannon's company of foot.

Robertson, James (tailor), a member of Captain David Jameson's Company at McCord's Fort on 02 April 1756 when he was killed.

Robertson, James (weaver), a member of Captain David Jameson's Company at McCord's Fort on 02 April 1756 when he was wounded.

Robertson, William, age 27, laborer, born Ireland, enlisted 01 July 1746 in Captain William Trent's company.

Robeson, Matthew, age 20, laborer, born Ireland, enlisted 30 April 1759 in Captain Robert Boyd's company [probably in the Third Battalion]. On a return dated May and June 1759.

Robinson, Daniel, captain in the Murder Kiln [or Mother-Kill] Hundred company of Colonel John Vining's Regiment of Kent County Militia, Upon Delaware in 1756. Resigned before 29 March 1758.

Robinson, Joel, blacksmith, born Philadelphia, Pennsylvania, enlisted 12 May 1759, private in Captain Joseph Richardson's company of the Third Battalion in the Pennsylvania Regiment. On a return of recruits dated 1759.

Robinson, Peter, lieutenant in the Northern District of Indian River Hundred in Captain Cord Hazzard's company of Colonel Jacob Kollock's Regiment of Sussex County in 1756. Also reported as being from Angola District in 1758.

Robinson, Robert, a private in Captain George Armstrong's Company, Second Battalion in 1756; wounded at Kittanning.

Robinson, Robert, ensign in the Christiana Hundred company of Colonel William Armstrong's Upper Regiment of New Castle County in 1756.

Robinson, Septimus, a private in Captain Charles Batho's Independent Company of Foot, Philadelphia in 1756.

Robinson, Septimus, captain in the Associated Regiment of Foot of Philadelphia on 29 Dec 1747.

Robinson, Thomas, steward of the provincial ship *Pennsylvania* on 17 August 1757.

Robinson, William, age 18, carpenter, born New York, enlisted 08 May 1758 by Captain Benjamin Noxon.

Robinson, William, landsman on the provincial ship *Pennsylvania* on 17 August 1757.

Rodgers, James, age 34, laborer, born Ireland, enlisted 05 July 1746 in Captain John Shannon's company of foot.

Rodney, Cæsar, captain in the Dover Hundred company of Colonel John Vining's Regiment of Kent County Militia, Upon Delaware in 1756.

Rody, John Henry, Private who enlisted 24 April 1756 in Captain Patrick Work's company in Colonel William Clapham's

Regiment in 1756, the regiment in garrison at Fort Augusta, Shamokin, and listed in Shippen's Account Book.

Roe, John, age 34, laborer, enlisted 11 July 1746 in Captain John Deimer's company.

Roe, Patrick, age 22, born Chester, Pennsylvania, "bold looking", private in Captain John Singleton's company in service between 01 May and 08 May 1758.

Roe, Thomas Richardson, age 26, laborer, born Maryland, enlisted 24 April 1758 by Captain Benjamin Noxon.

Roen, Thomas Richardson, enlisted 10 May 1759, private in Captain Henry Van Bibber's company of the Lower County. On a return dated 04 June 1759.

Rogers, Hugh, age 20, laborer, enlisted 25 April 1759, private in Captain James Armstrong's company in Colonel William Clapham's Pennsylvania Regiment. On a return dated 01 June 1759.

Rogers, William, age 35, laborer, born Pennsylvania, enlisted 24 April 1758 by Captain Benjamin Noxon.

Roland, John, private, age 23, farmer, born Silver Point, Virginia, enlisted 22 April 1758 for the campaign in the lower counties. On a return of Captain McClughan's company dated 17 May 1758.

Rolten, Josiah, private, age 22, farmer, born Lewistown, Delaware, enlisted 04 May 1758 for the campaign in the lower counties. On a return of Captain McClughan's company dated 17 May 1758.

Romhig, Christian, Private who enlisted 20 April 1756 in Captain Joseph Shippen's company in Colonel William Clapham's Regiment in 1756, the regiment in garrison at Fort Augusta, Shamokin, and listed in Shippen's Account Book.

Rontour, Adam, ensign of Captain Adam Heylman's Company, of the St. Vincent and Puke's Land Association on 10 May 1756.

Rose, John Michael, a private in Captain John Kidd's Independent Company of Foot, Philadelphia in 1756.

Rosenback, John, age 44, weaver, born Lancaster, Pennsylvania, enlisted 06 June 1759, private in Captain John Mathers's company in the Pennsylvania Regiment. On a return dated 15 June 1759.

Ross, James, private, age 17, miller, born Brandywine Hundred, enlisted 02 May 1758 for the campaign in the lower counties. On a return of Captain McClughan's company dated 17 May 1758.

Ross, John, captain in the Associated Regiment of Foot of Philadelphia on 29 Dec 1747.

Ross, Joseph, age 21, born Ireland, private in Captain John Wright's company of the Lower County. On a muster dated 11 May 1759.

Ross, Joseph, lieutenant in one of the Associated Companies of York County in 1756.

Rost, Henry, age 23, born Germany, enlisted 15 February 1758, private in Captain John Nicholas Weatherholt's company, which enlisted for a term of three years and was stationed in Heydelberg Township, Northampton County, in March and April 1758.

Roth, Michael, a private in Captain Adam Heylman's Company, of the St. Vincent and Puke's Land Association on 10 May 1756.

Rothwell, Garrett, ensign in the Apoquinimink Hundred company of Colonel Jacob Van Bibber's Lower Regiment of New Castle County in 1756.

Rothwell, Jerrard, ensign in one of two regiments of New Castle County in 1747–8.

Rourk, Michael, Private who enlisted 16 April 1756 in Major James Bird's company in Colonel William Clapham's Regiment in 1756, the regiment in garrison at Fort Augusta, Shamokin, and listed in Shippen's Account Book.

Row, John, age 30, surgeon, born Dulach, Germany, enlisted 18 May 1759, private in Captain John Mathers's company in the Pennsylvania Regiment. On a return dated 15 June 1759.

Rowell, Constantine, age 25, laborer, born New England, enlisted 15 July 1746 in Captain John Shannon's company of foot.

Rower, John, a private in Captain Edward Jones's Independent Company of Horse, Philadelphia in 1756.

Rowland, David, ensign in one of two regiments of New Castle County in 1747–8.

Rowland, David, ensign in the Pencader Hundred company of Colonel Jacob Van Bibber's Lower Regiment of New Castle County in 1756.

Rowland, John, age 23, born Virginia, private in Captain John Wright's company of the Lower County. On a muster dated 11 May 1759.

Rowland, William, lieutenant in the Associated Regiment of the West End of Lancaster County in 1747–8.

Ruby, John F., on a return of Captain David Hunter's Company [probably from York County] in Colonel William Clapham's Regiment of New Levies dated 26 May 1759.

Ruby, Peter, on a return of Captain David Hunter's Company [probably from York County] in Colonel William Clapham's Regiment of New Levies dated 26 May 1759.

Rudenhaver, John, age 19, laborer, enlisted 14 July 1746 in Captain John Deimer's company.

Rudolph, George, age 19, bricklayer, enlisted 14 July 1746 in Captain John Deimer's company.

Rue, Lewis, lieutenant in the Associated Regiment of Bucks County in 1748.

Runnell, Peter, age 30, laborer, born Ireland, enlisted 04 August 1746 in Captain William Trent's company.

Rush, William, ensign in Captain William Trent's company, in winter quarters in Albany, N.Y., 1746–7, discharged 31 October 1747.

Rush, William, ensign in the Associated Regiment of Foot of Philadelphia on 29 Dec 1747.

Rushton, Job, captain in the Associated Regiment of Chester County in 1747.

Rushton, Job, captain in one of the new levies in May 1758.

Rusk, Joseph, lieutenant in one of the companies of Colonel Jacob Duché's Philadelphia Regiment in 1756.

Russell, Nicholas, age 31, laborer, born Ireland, enlisted 26 July 1746 in Captain John Shannon's company of foot.

Ruston, Job, *see* Rushton, Job.

Rutherford, Alexander, landsman on the provincial ship *Pennsylvania* on 17 August 1757.

Rutherford, Joseph, on a list of men recruited by Captain Andrew McDowell's company in the Second Battalion, Pennsylvania Regiment dated 04 June 1759.

Ryan, James, landsman on the provincial ship *Pennsylvania* on 17 August 1757.

Ryan, John, age 16, tailor, born Maryland, enlisted 02 May 1758 by Captain Benjamin Noxon.

Ryan, John, age 21, laborer, born Psanson, Netherlands, enlisted 28 May 1759, private in Captain John Mathers's company in the Pennsylvania Regiment. On a return dated 15 June 1759.

Ryan, Timothy, age 40, laborer, born Ireland, enlisted 15 June 1759 in Captain Charles Stewart's company [probably one of the Associated Companies of Bucks County]. On a return dated June 1759.

Ryans, James, age 21, laborer, born Kent, Delaware, enlisted 17 July 1746 in Captain John Shannon's company of foot.

Ryder, Christopher, Private who enlisted 20 April 1756 in Captain Nathaniel Miles's company in Colonel William Clapham's Regiment in 1756, the regiment in garrison at Fort Augusta, Shamokin, and listed in Shippen's Account Book.

Ryne, John, age 21, laborer, born Ireland, enlisted 02 May 1758 by Captain Benjamin Noxon.

Sadler, Isaiah, captain in one of the Associated Companies of York County in 1756.

Sailor, Matthias, *see* Sealor, Matthias.

Saltar, Elisha, Commissary General of Musters from 28 March 1756. {B6:1087:349}

Salter, Elisha, captain of a company of the Third Battalion (known as the Augusta Regiment) from 11 May 1756.

Saltwell, John, age 30, gardener, born England, enlisted 24 April 1758 by Captain Benjamin Noxon.

Sammon, Dennis, enlisted 18 July 1746 in Captain William Trent's company, deserted 05 August 1746.

Sample, Henry, age 18, laborer, born Ireland, enlisted 09 May 1758. On a return of Captain John Bull's company dated 01 July 1758.

Sample, James, lieutenant in the Associated Regiment of the West End of Lancaster County in 1747–8.

Sand, Peter, age 25, laborer, born Germany, enlisted 09 May 1758. On a return of Captain John Bull's company dated 01 July 1758.

Sanderson, James, age 27, laborer, born Ireland, enlisted 02 May 1758 by Captain Benjamin Noxon.

Sanding, James, age 46, born England, laborer, private in Captain John Shannon's Company, enlisted 25 July 1746. On a roll of deserters dated 22 July 1746. [B3:422:18]

Sanford, Robert, age 23, laborer, born Chester, Pennsylvania, enlisted 25 May 1759 in Captain Robert Boyd's company [probably in the Third Battalion]. On a return dated May and June 1759.

Sankey, Ezekiel, on a return of Captain David Hunter's Company [probably from York County] in Colonel William Clapham's Regiment of New Levies dated 26 May 1759.

Sankey, Richard, on a return of Captain David Hunter's Company [probably from York County] in Colonel William Clapham's Regiment of New Levies dated 26 May 1759.

Sap, Benjamin, enlisted 20 May 1758 in Captain French Battell's company of Lower County Provincials.

Sarley, George, a private in Captain Edward Jones's Independent Company of Horse, Philadelphia in 1756.

Saunders, William, enlisted 19 May 1759, private in Captain Henry Van Bibber's company of the Lower County. On a return dated 04 June 1759.

Savage, Benjamin, age 18, cordwainer, born Ireland, enlisted May 1759 in Captain Charles Stewart's company [probably one of the Associated Companies of Bucks County]. On a return dated June 1759.

Savage, Patrick, age 25, laborer, born Ireland, enlisted 24 July 1746 in Captain John Shannon's company of foot.

Sax, Martin, age 19, laborer, born German, enlisted 05 May 1749 in Captain Richard Gardiner's company in Colonel William Denney's Pennsylvania Regiment.

Schamby, Behrand, age 23, laborer, enlisted 13 July 1746 in Captain John Deimer's company.

Schauntz, Leonard, age 21, laborer, born Germany, enlisted 19 July 1746 in Captain Samuel Perry's company.

Schiver, John Christian, *see* John Christian Schriver.

Schnyder, George, age 25, laborer, enlisted 07 July 1746 in Captain John Deimer's company.

Schoch, Jacob, age 22, weaver, born Germany, enlisted 13 May 1759, private in Captain Joseph Richardson's company of the Third Battalion in the Pennsylvania Regiment. On a return of recruits dated 1759.

Schriver, John Christian, Private who enlisted 28 April 1756 in Captain Joseph Shippen's company in Colonel William Clapham's Regiment in 1756, the regiment in garrison at Fort Augusta, Shamokin, and listed in Shippen's Account Book.

Schultze, Carl, age 19, joiner, born Germany, enlisted 15 July 1746 in Captain John Deimer's company.

Schwint, John, age 19, barber, born Germany, enlisted 07 July 1746 in Captain Samuel Perry's company.

Scott, Alexander, captain in one of the Associated Companies of Lancaster County in 1756.

Scott, Francis, a member of Captain Joseph Armstrong's Company on 07 August 1755, raised in Cumberland County.

Scott, James, a member of Captain Joseph Armstrong's Company on 07 August 1755, raised in Cumberland County.

Scott, James, ensign in the Associated Regiment of Chester County in 1747.

Scott, John, ensign in Captain Hugh Mercer's Company, Second Battalion from July 1756; wounded at Kittanning.

Scott, John, landsman on the provincial ship *Pennsylvania* on 17 August 1757.

Scott, Joseph, captain of a company of the Second Battalion of the Pennsylvania Regiment from 22 April 1760.

Scott, Joseph, ensign in Captain Joseph Shippen's company in Colonel William Clapham's Regiment in 1756, the regiment in garrison at Fort Augusta, Shamokin, and listed in Shippen's Account Book.

Scott, Joseph, ensign of Captain David Jameson's Company, Third Battalion (known as the Augusta Regiment) from 24 May 1756. Lieutenant in Joseph Shippen's company in the Second Battalion from 15 December 1757 stationed at Fort Augusta.

Scott, Joseph, promoted to captain after serving in the Pennsylvania Regiment of Three Battalions in 1758 and 1759.

Scott, Patrick, a member of Captain Joseph Armstrong's Company on 07 August 1755, raised in Cumberland County.

Scott, Robert, private, age 23, spinner, born Rye, Ireland, enlisted 12 May 1758 for the campaign in the lower counties. On a return of Captain McClughan's company dated 17 May 1758.

Scott, Samuel, lieutenant from 03 May 1759 in Captain John Clark's company of Colonel William Clapham's Regiment of New Levies.

Scott, Samuel, promoted to lieutenant after serving in the Pennsylvania Regiment of Three Battalions in 1758 and 1759.

Scott, Valentine, age 21, laborer, born Ireland, enlisted 15 July 1746 in Captain Samuel Perry's company.

Scott, William, a member of Captain Joseph Armstrong's Company on 07 August 1755, raised in Cumberland County.

Scott, William, age 23, born Lancaster, Pennsylvania, laborer, private in Captain John Haslett's company enlisted on 08 May 1758 and last paid on 21 May 1758.

Scott, William, age 30, laborer, born Monaghan, Ireland, enlisted 02 May 1759, private in Captain John Haslet's company in the Pennsylvania Regiment. On a list of recruits dated 20 May 1759.

Scott, William, age 35, laborer, born Ireland, enlisted 03 May 1759, private in Captain James Armstrong's company in Colonel William Clapham's Pennsylvania Regiment. On a return dated 01 June 1759.

Sealner, John, age 35, born Germany, enlisted 01 September 1757, private in Captain John Nicholas Weatherholt's company, which enlisted for a term of three years and was stationed in Heydelberg Township, Northampton County, in March and April 1758.

Sealor, Matthias, age 21, laborer, born Germany, enlisted 21 July 1746 in Captain Samuel Perry's company.

Searle, John, private in Captain Samuel Mifflin's Association Battery Company of Philadelphia in 1756.

Sears, Andrew, private in Captain Patterson's company from 05 December 1757 stationed eastward of the Susquehanna. On a muster roll dated 08 March 1758.

Seegrist, Jacob, *see* Jacob Segrist.

Seeley, Christopher, lieutenant in Major John Phillip de Haas's Company in the Pennsylvania Regiment commanded by the Hon. J. Penn, Esqr., from 14 July 1764.

Seely, Christopher, a lieutenant stationed on the frontier in Berks County with fourteen men at Rehrer's, Bethel Township, on 01 June 1764 as part of a unit under the command of Major Asher Clayton.

Seely, Jonas, captain in the provincial service in 1755.

Segrist, Jacob, Private who enlisted 23 April 1756 in Captain Nathaniel Miles's company in Colonel William Clapham's Regiment in 1756, the regiment in garrison at Fort Augusta, Shamokin, and listed in Shippen's Account Book.

Seibart, John, age 40, laborer, born Germany, enlisted 13 May 1749 in Captain Richard Gardiner's company in Colonel William Denney's Pennsylvania Regiment.

Seigley, John, Private who enlisted 11 May 1756 in Captain Joseph Shippen's company in Colonel William Clapham's Regiment in 1756, the regiment in garrison at Fort Augusta, Shamokin, and listed in Shippen's Account Book.

Selle, Peter, a private in Captain Adam Heylman's Company, of the St. Vincent and Puke's Land Association on 10 May 1756.

Sellner, Conrad, a private in Captain Adam Heylman's Company, of the St. Vincent and Puke's Land Association on 10 May 1756.

Semple, William, age 28, weaver, born Ireland, enlisted 15 July 1746 in Captain Samuel Perry's company.

Senner, Frans., private in Captain Edward Jones's Independent Company of Horse, Philadelphia in 1756.

Sergon, Thomas, landsman on the provincial ship *Pennsylvania* on 17 August 1757.

Seton, John, age 26, born Scotland, enlisted 23 May 1759, private in Captain Robert Curry's company in Colonel William Clapham's Pennsylvania Regiment. On a return dated June 1759.

Severns, John, ensign in the Associated Regiment of Bucks County in 1748.

Seville, Thomas, age 18, laborer, born Lancaster, Pennsylvania, enlisted 03 May 1759, private in Captain Joseph Richardson's company of the Third Battalion in the Pennsylvania Regiment. On a return of recruits dated 1759.

Shaddock, Charles, age 30, laborer, born Ireland, enlisted 31 May 1759 in Captain Robert Boyd's company [probably in the Third Battalion]. On a return dated May and June 1759.

Shaeffer [also Shafer], _____, corporal in the provincial service in 1754 on scout to Fort Lebanon. {See A Journal in 1754, A(1) 2:159}

Shafer, Henry, age 18, laborer, born Germany, enlisted 12 May 1758. On a return of Captain John Blackwood's company in the Third Battalion dated 22 May 1758.

Shaffner, Jacob, private who enlisted 21 April 1756 in Captain Joseph Shippen's company in Colonel William Clapham's Regiment in 1756, the regiment in garrison at Fort Augusta, Shamokin, and listed in Shippen's Account Book.

Shankmire, Peter, enlisted 07 July 1746 in Captain Samuel Perry's company.

Shannon, captain from 25 June 1746, company in winter quarters in Albany, N.Y., 1746–7, discharged 31 October 1747.

Shannon, James, age 18, born Ireland, enlisted 08 June 1759, private in Captain Robert Curry's company in Colonel William Clapham's Pennsylvania Regiment. On a return dated June 1759.

Shannon, Jno., captain of Pennsylvania troops in Albany, N.Y., on 21 October 1746 and at least through 12 November 1746.

Shannon, John, age 23, born Chester, Pennsylvania, chandler, "Irish man", private in Captain John Singleton's company in service between 01 May and 08 May 1758.

Shans, Leonard, *see* Schauntz, Leonard.

Shantley, Thomas, a private in Captain Joseph Inslee's Company of Foot, Newtown, Bucks County, in 1756.

Sharp, James, Captain from 03 May 1758 in a company in the Third Battalion. Captain from 27 April 1759 of a company of Colonel William Clapham's Regiment of New Levies.

Sharp, James, promoted to captain after serving in the Pennsylvania Regiment of Three Battalions in 1758 and 1759.

Sharp, John, age 25, laborer, born Pennsylvania, enlisted 21 May 1759 in Captain Robert Boyd's company [probably in the Third Battalion]. On a return dated May and June 1759.

Sharp, Joseph, age 25, smith, born Milford, Maryland, enlisted 08 June 1759, private in Captain John Mathers's company in the Pennsylvania Regiment. On a return dated 15 June 1759.

Sharrar, Conrad, age 26, laborer, born Germany, enlisted 09 May 1758. On a return of Captain John Bull's company dated 01 July 1758.

Shaw, John, age 23, laborer, born Ireland, enlisted 26 July 1746 in Captain John Deimer's company.

Shaw, Samuel, captain, then major on 04 August 1748, in the Associated Regiment in the County of Philadelphia in 1748.

Shea, John, age 22, laborer, born Ireland, enlisted 27 April 1759 in Captain Charles Stewart's company [probably one of the Associated Companies of Bucks County]. On a return dated June 1759.

Shea, Timothy, age 23, laborer, born Ireland, enlisted 23 July 1746 in Captain William Trent's company.

Shea, Walter, lieutenant in Captain John Kidd's Independent Company of Foot, Philadelphia in 1756.

Shearer, Conrad, *see* Conrad Sharrar.

Sheerman, James, private, age 20, born Dublin, Ireland, enlisted 20 April 1758 for the campaign in the lower counties. On a return of Captain McClughan's company dated 17 May 1758.

Shelby, Evan, Jr., ensign in the First Battalion of the Pennsylvania Regiment from 12 April 1760.

Shelby, Evan, promoted to Captain after serving in the Pennsylvania Regiment of Three Battalions in 1758 and 1759. Reported as "left the province".

Shelby, John, promoted to lieutenant after serving in the Pennsylvania Regiment of Three Battalions in 1758 and 1759.

Shele, William, *see* William Shell.

Shell, William, age 23, weaver, born Germany, enlisted 12 May 1758. On a return of Captain John Blackwood's company in the Third Battalion dated 22 May 1758.

Shelley, Evan, captain from 04 May 1759 in a company of Colonel William Clapham's Regiment of New Levies.

Shelley, Evan, Jr., ensign from 07 May 1759 in Captain Evan Shelley's company of Colonel William Clapham's Regiment of New Levies.

Shelly, John, lieutenant from 12 May 1759 in Captain Thomas Price's company of Colonel William Clapham's Regiment of New Levies.

Shenk, Jacob, age 20, born Germany, enlisted 06 November 1757, private in Captain John Nicholas Weatherholt's company, which enlisted for a term of three years, and was stationed in Heydelberg Township, Northampton County, in March and April 1758April 1758.

Shepherd, Josiah, seaman on the provincial ship *Pennsylvania* on 17 August 1757.

Sheppard, Edward, age 21, born Chester, Pennsylvania, "red hair and thin visage", private in Captain John Singleton's company in service between 01 May and 08 May 1758.

Sherer, Henry, private who enlisted 10 March 1756 in Captain Joseph Shippen's company in Colonel William Clapham's Regiment in 1756, the regiment in garrison at Fort Augusta, Shamokin, and listed in Shippen's Account Book.

Sherlock, Vander, age 36, tailor, born Germany, enlisted 12 July 1746 in Captain John Deimer's company.

Shickle, Michael, age 24, tailor, born Germany, enlisted 03 May 1758. On a return of Captain John Bull's company dated 01 July 1758.

Shields, David, a member of Captain Joseph Armstrong's Company on 07 August 1755, raised in Cumberland County.

Shields, John, private in Captain Patterson's company from 27 November 1757 stationed eastward of the Susquehanna. On a muster roll dated 08 March 1758.

Shields, Matthew, Jr., a member of Captain Joseph Armstrong's Company on 07 August 1755, raised in Cumberland County.

Shields, Matthew, Sr., a member of Captain Joseph Armstrong's Company on 07 August 1755, raised in Cumberland County.

Shields, Robert, Jun., a member of Captain Joseph Armstrong's Company on 07 August 1755, raised in Cumberland County.

Shields, Robert, Sr., a member of Captain Joseph Armstrong's Company on 07 August 1755, raised in Cumberland County.

Shillberger, John, a private in Captain Edward Jones's Independent Company of Horse, Philadelphia in 1756.

Shineberg, Henry, a private in Captain Edward Jones's Independent Company of Horse, Philadelphia in 1756.

Shiner, Stephen, age 26, laborer, enlisted 07 July 1746 in Captain John Deimer's company.

Shinor, William, age 27, mariner, born Ireland, enlisted 21 May 1758. On a return of Captain John Blackwood's company in the Third Battalion dated 22 May 1758.

Shippen, _____, brigade major. On a list of officers of the lower government on Delaware, 1758/9.

Shippen, Edward, Jun., private in Captain Edward Jones's Independent Company of Horse, Philadelphia in 1756.

Shippen, Joseph, captain of a company in Colonel William Clapham's Regiment in 1756, the regiment in garrison at Fort Augusta, Shamokin.

Shippen, Joseph, captain of a company of the Third Battalion (known as the Augusta Regiment) from 03 April 1756. Captain from 08 December 1757 of a company in the Second Battalion, stationed at Fort Augusta. Commissary of the musters and paymaster of Colonel William Denny's Regiment, 1758. Major from December 1758 of the Second Battalion. Lieutenant colonel of the Second Battalion of the Pennsylvania Regiment in 1759.

Shirtz, John, private who enlisted 03 May 1756 in Captain Joseph Shippen's company in Colonel William Clapham's Regiment in 1756, the regiment in garrison at Fort Augusta, Shamokin, and listed in Shippen's Account Book.

Shmaus, Conrad, age 22, born Germany, enlisted 01 September 1757, private in Captain John Nicholas Weatherholt's company, which enlisted for a term of three years, and was stationed in Heydelberg Township, Northampton County, in March and April 1758.

Shockley, Richard, age 19, laborer, born Kent, Delaware, enlisted 14 July 1746 in Captain John Shannon's company of foot.

Shorr, George, age 20, laborer, born Pennsylvania, enlisted 07 July 1746 in Captain John Deimer's company.

Shortall, John, age 20, laborer, born Ireland, enlisted 17 July 1746 in Captain Samuel Perry's company.

Shortall, Oliver, age 34, laborer, born Ireland, enlisted 16 July 1746 in Captain John Shannon's company of foot.

Shreak, Joseph, age 34, born Ireland, enlisted 23 May 1759, private in Captain Robert Curry's company in Colonel William Clapham's Pennsylvania Regiment. On a return dated June 1759.

Shute, Atwood, lieutenant in the Associated Regiment of Foot of Philadelphia on 29 Dec 1747.

Sibbald, John, private in Captain Samuel Mifflin's Association Battery Company of Philadelphia in 1756.

Sibbald, John, captain of the provincial ship *Pennsylvania* on 17 August 1757.

Siguar, Peter, private in Captain Edward Jones's Independent Company of Horse, Philadelphia in 1756.

Silsby, Nathaniel, lieutenant in the New Castle Hundred company of Colonel William Armstrong's Upper Regiment of New Castle County in 1756.

Silver, James, captain in the Associated Regiment of Lancaster County over the Susquehanna in 1747–8.

Sim, Andrew, age 18, cordwainer, born Pennsylvania, enlisted 29 April 1759 in Captain Charles Stewart's company [probably one of the Associated Companies of Bucks County]. On a return dated June 1759.

Sim, John, age 19, tailor, born Ireland, enlisted 23 July 1746 in Captain John Shannon's company of foot.

Simerel, _____, ensign from 25 April 1759 in Captain Robert Boyd's company of Colonel William Clapham's Regiment of New Levies.

Simmons, James, age 18, laborer, born Pennsylvania, enlisted 09 May 1758. On a return of Captain John Bull's company dated 01 July 1758.

Simmons, John, age 21, laborer, born Maryland, enlisted 23 May 1758 by Captain Benjamin Noxon.

Simon, Anthony, age 30, born Germany, enlisted 01 June 1759, private in Captain Robert Curry's company in Colonel William Clapham's Pennsylvania Regiment. On a return dated June 1759.

Simon, Jacob, age 26, laborer, born Germany, enlisted 23 July 1746 in Captain John Deimer's company.

Simon, John, a private in Captain Edward Jones's Independent Company of Horse, Philadelphia in 1756.

Simpler, Jacob, age 21, laborer, born German, enlisted July 1746 in Captain John Shannon's company of foot.

Simpson, Arthur, age 43, schoolmaster, born Tyrone, Ireland, enlisted 01 May 1759, private in Captain James Armstrong's company in Colonel William Clapham's Pennsylvania Regiment. On a return dated 01 June 1759.

Simpson, James, age 21, weaver, born Ireland, enlisted 21 July 1746 in Captain John Shannon's company of foot.

Simpson, John, lieutenant from 04 May 1758 in Captain Adam Read's company in the Third Battalion.

Simpson, Samuel, captain in one of the Associated Companies of Lancaster County in 1756.

Simpson, Samuel, ensign in the Associated Regiment of the West End of Lancaster County in 1747–8.

Sims, Buckridge, lieutenant in Captain Charles Batho's Independent Company of Foot, Philadelphia. Resigned.

Sims, William, age 27, laborer, born Ireland, enlisted 04 May 1759, private in Captain Joseph Richardson's company of the Third Battalion in the Pennsylvania Regiment. On a return of recruits dated 1759.

Siner, John, a private in Captain Charles Batho's Independent Company of Foot, Philadelphia in 1756.

Singleton, John, captain from 29 April 1758 of a company in the Second Battalion in service between 01 May and 08 May 1758. Captain from 25 April 1759 of a company in Colonel William Clapham's Regiment of New Levies.

Singleton, John, promoted to captain after serving in the Pennsylvania Regiment of Three Battalions in 1758 and 1759. Reported as "resigned".

Sink, Michael, age 22, laborer, born Germany, enlisted 11 July 1746 in Captain John Deimer's company.

Sinkler, James, ensign from 03 May 1759 in Captain David Hunter's company of Colonel William Clapham's Regiment of New Levies.

Sipple, Caleb, lieutenant from 29 March 1758 in Captain Daniel James's company from the Lower District of Mother-Kill Hundred, Kent County, Delaware, vice Hillyard.

Sitzhoupt, John, a lieutenant stationed on the frontier in Berks County with fifteen men at Hagabaugh's, Albany Township, on 01 June 1764 as part of a unit under the command of Major Asher Clayton.

Skeir, Erick, age 34, laborer, born West Jersey, enlisted 07 July 1746 in Captain John Shannon's company of foot.

Skidmore, Edward, age 21, laborer, born Delaware, enlisted 29 April 1758 by Captain Benjamin Noxon.

Skidmore, Edward, enlisted 21 May 1759, private in Captain Henry Van Bibber's company of the Lower County. On a return dated 04 June 1759.

Slack, Henry, a private in Captain Joseph Inslee's Company of Foot, Newtown, Bucks County, in 1756.

Slaughterbergh, George, private who enlisted 24 April 1756 in Captain Joseph Shippen's company in Colonel William Clapham's Regiment in 1756, the regiment in garrison at Fort Augusta, Shamokin, and listed in Shippen's Account Book. Discharged 25 September 1756.

Sleider, Peter, private in Captain Adam Heylman's Company, of the St. Vincent and Puke's Land Association on 10 May 1756.

Sleighter, Galen, private in Captain Charles Batho's Independent Company of Foot, Philadelphia in 1756.

Slevan, John, age 24, weaver, born Ireland, enlisted 19 July 1746 in Captain John Shannon's company of foot.

Sloan, John, private, age 25, weaver, born Tyrone, Ireland, enlisted 04 May 1758 for the campaign in the lower counties. On a return of Captain McClughan's company dated 17 May 1758.

Small, John, age 22, laborer, born Chester, Pennsylvania, enlisted 01 May 1759 in Captain Robert Boyd's company [probably in the Third Battalion]. On a return dated May and June 1759.

Smallman, Thomas, ensign in Captain James Patterson's company of the First Battalion in 1755/6. Ensign of Captain Joseph Montgomery's Company, Second Battalion from 22 May 1756. Lieutenant in Captain Hugh Mercer's Company from 05 December 1757, stationed westward of the Susquehanna. Quartermaster of the First Battalion (John Armstrong's) of Colonel William Denny's Regiment, 05 May 1758. Promoted to captain in March 1759 of a company in the Second Battalion, vice Work. Promoted to major after 1758.

Smallman, Thomas, major of the Second Battalion of the Pennsylvania Regiment from 13 April 1760.

Smidt, Valentine, private in Captain Adam Heylman's Company, of the St. Vincent and Puke's Land Association on 10 May 1756.

Smiley, George, private who enlisted 24 April 1756 in Captain Joseph Shippen's company in Colonel William Clapham's Regiment in 1756, the regiment in garrison at Fort Augusta, Shamokin, and listed in Shippen's Account Book.

Smiley, James, private who enlisted 24 April 1756 in Captain Joseph Shippen's company in Colonel William Clapham's Regiment in 1756, the regiment in garrison at Fort Augusta, Shamokin, and listed in Shippen's Account Book. At Hunter's Fort.

Smiley, John, private who enlisted 24 April 1756 in Captain Joseph Shippen's company in Colonel William Clapham's Regiment in 1756, the regiment in garrison at Fort Augusta, Shamokin, and listed in Shippen's Account Book.

Smiley, Robert, private who enlisted 24 April 1756 in Captain Joseph Shippen's company in Colonel William Clapham's Regiment in 1756, the regiment in garrison at Fort Augusta, Shamokin, and listed in Shippen's Account Book.

Smiley, William, lieutenant in one of the Associated Companies of York County in 1756.

Smith, Alexander, age 23, laborer, born Scotland, enlisted 19 July 1746 in Captain John Shannon's company of foot.

Smith, Benjamin, lieutenant in one of the new levies in May 1758.

Smith, Bernhard, a private in Captain Charles Batho's Independent Company of Foot, Philadelphia in 1756.

Smith, Conrad, age 22, laborer, born Germany, enlisted 22 May 1759 in Captain Robert Boyd's company [probably in the Third Battalion]. On a return dated May and June 1759.

Smith, David, age 18, laborer, born Germany, enlisted 21 July 1746 in Captain Samuel Perry's company.

Smith, Frederick, captain and provincial officer in 1754 at Fort Henry. {See A Journal in 1754, A(1) 2: 159}, in the provincial service in 1755 at Tolehaio and Monody and in a company of the First Battalion from 14 November 1755. On a List of Officers in the Province Pay, 1756 in the First Battalion of the Pennsylvania Regiment with a commission date of 14 Nov 1755. {PA5, I, 88}

Smith, Gilbert, age 28, born Argyle, Scotland, private in Captain John Haslett's company enlisted on 09 May 1758 and last paid on 21 May 1758.

Smith, Hance Caspar, private who enlisted 21 April 1756 in Captain Joseph Shippen's company in Colonel William

Clapham's Regiment in 1756, the regiment in garrison at Fort Augusta, Shamokin, and listed in Shippen's Account Book. Discharged 10 May 1757.

Smith, Isaac, landsman on the provincial ship *Pennsylvania* on 17 August 1757.

Smith, James, age 18, born Pennsylvania, enlisted 19 May 1759, private in Captain Robert Curry's company in Colonel William Clapham's Pennsylvania Regiment. On a return dated June 1759.

Smith, James, age 21, planter, born Sussex, Delaware, enlisted 13 July 1746 in Captain John Shannon's company of foot.

Smith, James, ensign in Captain Samuel Lindsay's company in Lieutenant Colonel Commandant Asher Clayton's Second Battalion of the Pennsylvania Regiment commanded by the Hon. J. Penn from 16 July 1763.

Smith, James, ensign in one of the Associated Companies of York County in 1756.

Smith, James, ensign in the Associated Regiment of the West End of Lancaster County in 1747–8.

Smith, James, lieutenant in the Associated Regiment of the West End of Lancaster County in 1747–8.

Smith, James, on a list of men recruited by Captain Andrew McDowell's company in the Second Battalion, Pennsylvania Regiment dated 04 June 1759.

Smith, John, private in Captain Joseph Inslee's Company of Foot, Newtown, Bucks County, in 1756.

Smith, John, age 23, mariner, born Scotland, enlisted 02 May 1758. On a return of Captain John Blackwood's company in the Third Battalion dated 22 May 1758.

Smith, John, age 35, laborer, born Ireland, enlisted 27 April 1759 in Captain Charles Stewart's company [probably one of the Associated Companies of Bucks County]. On a return dated June 1759.

Smith, John, captain in the Associated Regiment of the West End of Lancaster County in 1747–8.

Smith, John, ensign in the Associated Regiment of Chester County in 1747.

Smith, John, landsman on the provincial ship *Pennsylvania* on 17 August 1757.
Smith, Joseph, private in Captain Charles Batho's Independent Company of Foot, Philadelphia in 1756.
Smith, Joseph, lieutenant in the Associated Regiment of Chester County in 1747.
Smith, Peter, age 40, laborer, enlisted 14 July 1746 in Captain John Deimer's company.
Smith, Peter, sergeant in the provincial service in 1754 on scout to Fort Lebanon.
Smith, Philip, age 23, smith, born Germany, enlisted 15 July 1746 in Captain John Deimer's company.
Smith, Robert, lieutenant in the Associated Regiment of the West End of Lancaster County in 1747–8.
Smith, Robert, seaman on the provincial ship *Pennsylvania* on 17 August 1757.
Smith, Robert, sergeant in Captain Jacob Morgan's company stationed eastward of the Susquehanna in December 1757.
Smith, Samuel, lieutenant in one of the Associated Companies of Lancaster County in 1756.
Smith, Thomas, captain in one of the new levies in May 1758.
Smith, William, lieutenant in the Associated Regiment of Lancaster County over the Susquehanna in 1747–8.
Smith, William, private, age 27, baker, born Belly-shannon, Ireland, enlisted 09 May 1758 for the campaign in the lower counties. On a return of Captain McClughan's company dated 17 May 1758.
Snaidor, Jacob, *see* Jacob Snyder.
Snapes, Paul, age 28, wool comber, born Ireland, enlisted 02 August 1746 in Captain William Trent's company.
Sneider, Jacob, *see* Jacob Snyder.
Sner, Casper, age 24, laborer, born Germany, enlisted 03 May 1758. On a return of Captain John Bull's company dated 01 July 1758.
Snider, John, private who enlisted 24 April 1756 in Captain Joseph Shippen's company in Colonel William Clapham's Regiment

in 1756, the regiment in garrison at Fort Augusta, Shamokin, and listed in Shippen's Account Book.

Snodgrass, James, captain in the Associated Regiment of the West End of Lancaster County in 1747–8.

Snodgrass, John, ensign in the Associated Regiment of the West End of Lancaster County in 1747–8.

Snodgrass, John, lieutenant in one of the Associated Companies of Lancaster County in 1756.

Snuble, Johan, a private in Captain Charles Batho's Independent Company of Foot, Philadelphia in 1756.

Snyder [Snaidor] [Sneider], Jacob, ensign in Captain John Van Etten's company of the First Battalion in 1756. Lieutenant in Hance Hamilton's company from 13 December 1757, stationed westward of the Susquehanna. Resigned at Fort Bedford 12 April 1759.

Snyder, Christain, a private in Captain Charles Batho's Independent Company of Foot, Philadelphia in 1756.

Snyder, Christain, private in Captain Edward Jones's Independent Company of Horse, Philadelphia in 1756.

Soden, Thomas, age 23, laborer, born Jersey, enlisted 21 July 1746 in Captain Samuel Perry's company.

Soile, John, hired 28 May 1757 as a battoe man, Master George Allen.

Sollar, Andrew, age 40, laborer, enlisted 14 July 1746 in Captain John Deimer's company.

Souber, Michael, private in Captain John Kidd's Independent Company of Foot, Philadelphia in 1756.

Soverhill, Abraham, hired 30 May 1757 as a battoe man, Master George Allen.

Sowersmith, John, private in 1756 in Captain Joseph Shippen's company in Colonel William Clapham's Regiment in 1756, the regiment in garrison at Fort Augusta, Shamokin, and listed in Shippen's Account Book.

Sparks, William, private in Captain John Singleton's company in service between 01 May and 08 May 1758.

Spear, Charles, private, age 24, born Faughboyne, Ireland, enlisted 1758 for the campaign in the lower counties. On a return of Captain McClughan's company dated 17 May 1758.

Spearing, William, lieutenant in the provincial service in 1755.

Spice, Matthias, a private in Captain John Kidd's Independent Company of Foot, Philadelphia in 1756.

Spillander, John, age 26, mariner, born Sweden, enlisted 09 May 1749 in Captain Richard Gardiner's company in Colonel William Denney's Pennsylvania Regiment.

Spire, Matthias, *see* Spice, Matthias.

Sportz, Lorentz, a private in Captain Edward Jones's Independent Company of Horse, Philadelphia in 1756.

Springham, Thomas, hired 27 May 1757 as a battoe man, Master George Allen.

Springham, Thomas, private who enlisted 20 April 1756 in Captain Joseph Shippen's company in Colonel William Clapham's Regiment in 1756, the regiment in garrison at Fort Augusta, Shamokin, and listed in Shippen's Account Book.

Sprogell, Samuel, landsman on the provincial ship *Pennsylvania* on 17 August 1757.

Sprout, John, age 24, laborer, born Down, Ireland, enlisted 30 April 1759, private in Captain John Haslet's company in the Pennsylvania Regiment. On a list of recruits dated 20 May 1759.

Squires, Richard, age 25, born Bristol, Pennsylvania, drummer in Captain John Wright's company of the Lower County. On a muster dated 11 May 1759.

St. Clair, John, on a return of Captain David Hunter's Company [probably from York County] in Colonel William Clapham's Regiment of New Levies dated 26 May 1759.

St. Clair, William, on a return of Captain David Hunter's Company [probably from York County] in Colonel William Clapham's Regiment of New Levies dated 26 May 1759.

Stack, Richard, enlisted 17 July 1746 in Captain Samuel Perry's company.

Staddly, Jacob, age 44, carpenter, born Germany, enlisted 08 May 1758. On a return of Captain John Bull's company dated 01 July 1758.

Stadley, Jacob, age 29, born Ireland, enlisted 20 May 1759, private in Captain Robert Curry's company in Colonel William Clapham's Pennsylvania Regiment. On a return dated June 1759.

Stadtler, Casper, ensign in Captain Edward Ward's company in the First Battalion, 20 March 1759.

Stahl, George, age 23, born Germany, enlisted 01 September 1757, private in Captain John Nicholas Weatherholt's company, which enlisted for a term of three years, and was stationed in Heydelberg Township, Northampton County, in March and April 1758.

Stammers, John, age 28, laborer, born Pennsylvania, enlisted 30 April 1759 in Captain Charles Stewart's company [probably one of the Associated Companies of Bucks County]. On a return dated June 1759.

Stanley, Thomas, *see* Shantley, Thomas.

Stanly, Joseph, enlisted 05 July 1746 in Captain William Trent's company, died 25 July 1746.

Stant, Joseph, enlisted 10 May 1758 in Captain French Battell's company of Lower County Provincials.

Starland, William, age 17, mariner, born South Carolina, enlisted 26 June 1746 in Captain John Shannon's company of foot.

Starr, Moses, ensign in the Associated Regiment of Lancaster County over the Susquehanna in 1747–8.

Starry, Peters, on a list of men recruited by Captain Andrew McDowell's company in the Second Battalion, Pennsylvania Regiment dated 04 June 1759.

stationed eastward of the Susquehanna. On a muster roll dated 08 March 1758.

Steap, Peter, age 22, born Germany, enlisted 01 September 1757, private in Captain John Nicholas Weatherholt's company, which enlisted for a term of three years, and was stationed in Heydelberg Township, Northampton County, in March and April 1758.

Stedman, Alexander, private in Captain Edward Jones's Independent Company of Horse, Philadelphia in 1756.

Stedman, Charles, private in Captain Samuel Mifflin's Association Battery Company of Philadelphia in 1756.

Steel, Andrew, enlisted 20 May 1759, private in Captain Henry Van Bibber's company of the Lower County. On a return dated 04 June 1759.

Steel, Arthur, age 23, born Kent, Delaware, private in Captain John Wright's company of the Lower County. On a muster dated 11 May 1759.

Steel, Hugh, age 27, laborer, born Ireland, enlisted 01 May 1758 by Captain Benjamin Noxon.

Steel, James, enlisted 24 May 1758 in Captain French Battell's company of Lower County Provincials.

Steel, Joseph, private in Captain Joseph Inslee's Company of Foot, Newtown, Bucks County, in 1756.

Steel, Rev. John, captain in the provincial service in 1755 at McDowell's Mill.

Steel, Rev. John, captain of a company of the Second Battalion from 25 March 1756. Chaplain from 01 December 1757 of the Second Battalion.

Steel, William, captain in one of the Associated Companies of Lancaster County in 1756.

Steiger, Peter, a private in Captain Adam Heylman's Company, of the St. Vincent and Puke's Land Association on 10 May 1756.

Stein, A., ensign in Captain Caleb Grayden's company in the First Battalion of the Pennsylvania Regiment in or after 1763.

Stein, John, private in Captain Adam Heylman's Company, of the St. Vincent and Puke's Land Association on 10 May 1756.

Stephens, Alexander, private who enlisted 26 April 1756 in Captain Joseph Shippen's company in Colonel William Clapham's Regiment in 1756, the regiment in garrison at Fort Augusta, Shamokin, and listed in Shippen's Account Book. Discharged 26 April 1757.

Stephenson, George, private in Captain Samuel Mifflin's Association Battery Company of Philadelphia in 1756.

Stephenson, Samuel, enlisted 12 August 1746 in Captain William Trent's company, deserted 27 August 1746.

Stevens, Andrew, hired 27 May 1757 as a battoe man, Master George Allen.

Stevens, Levi, chaplain in the Pennsylvania Regiment commanded by the Hon. J. Penn, Esqr., in 1764.

Stevenson, James, age 21, laborer, born Ireland, enlisted 13 July 1746 in Captain John Shannon's company of foot.

Stevenson, James, ensign in Captain Samuel Perry's company, in winter quarters in Albany, N.Y., 1746–7, discharged 31 October 1747.

Steward, David, captain in one of two regiments of New Castle County in 1747–8.

Stewart, Archibald, private in Captain Samuel Mifflin's Association Battery Company of Philadelphia in 1756.

Stewart, Charles, lieutenant stationed on the frontier in Lancaster County with one sergeant and fifteen men at John McFarling's, Hanover Township, on 01 June 1764 as part of a unit under the command of Major Asher Clayton.

Stewart, Charles, captain in one of the Associated Companies of Bucks County in 1756. On a return dated June 1759.

Stewart, Charles, captain in the Associated Regiment of Bucks County in 1748.

Stewart, Charles, lieutenant in Captain Timothy Green's company in Lieutenant Colonel Commandant Asher Clayton's Second Battalion of the Pennsylvania Regiment commanded by the Hon. J. Penn from 18 July 1763.

Stewart, Robert, ensign in one of two regiments of New Castle County in August 1748.

Stewart, William, enlisted 23 May 1758 in Captain French Battell's company of Lower County Provincials.

Stillwagen, John, lieutenant in one of the companies of Colonel Jacob Duché's Philadelphia Regiment in 1756.

Stiltzer, _____, ensign stationed westward of Susquehanna.

Stoakley, Solomon, age 23, born Sussex, Delaware, private in Captain John Wright's company of the Lower County. On a muster dated 11 May 1759.

Stoddard, Thomas, promoted to lieutenant after serving in the Pennsylvania Regiment of Three Battalions in 1758 and 1759. Reported as "left the Province".

Stoler, Adam, seaman on the provincial ship *Pennsylvania* on 17 August 1757.

Stone, Adam, private in Captain Adam Heylman's Company, of the St. Vincent and Puke's Land Association on 10 May 1756.

Stone, John, age 22, mariner, born England, enlisted 14 May 1749 in Captain Richard Gardiner's company in Colonel William Denney's Pennsylvania Regiment.

Stone, Ludowick, captain from 17 May 1758 of a company in the Third Battalion.

Stone, Ludwick, promoted to captain after serving in the Pennsylvania Regiment of Three Battalions in 1758 and 1759.

Storman, Richard, on a return of Captain David Hunter's Company [probably from York County] in Colonel William Clapham's Regiment of New Levies dated 26 May 1759.

Storrie, Peters, *see* Peters Starry.

Stouder, Henry, private who enlisted 27 April 1756 in Captain David Jameson's company in Colonel William Clapham's Regiment in 1756, the regiment in garrison at Fort Augusta, Shamokin, and listed in Shippen's Account Book.

Stout, Jacob, lieutenant in the Lower Part of Duck Creek Hundred company of Colonel John Vining's Regiment of Kent County Militia, Upon Delaware in 1756.

Stouter, Casper, age 25, born Germany, fiddler, enlisted 01 September 1757, private in Captain John Nicholas Weatherholt's company, which enlisted for a term of three years, and was stationed in Heydelberg Township, Northampton County, in March and April 1758.

Stow, Jacob, age 20, tailor, born Germany, enlisted 07 May 1758. On a return of Captain John Blackwood's company in the Third Battalion dated 22 May 1758.

Straghan, John, private, age 24, laborer, born Derry, Ireland, enlisted 18 April 1758 for the campaign in the lower counties. On a return of Captain McClughan's company dated 17 May 1758.

Streader, Jacob, age 33, born Germany, commissioned 01 September 1757, surgeon in Captain John Nicholas Weatherholt's company, which enlisted for a term of three years, and was stationed in Heydelberg Township, Northampton County, in March and April 1758April 1758.

Streaker, George, age 23, weaver, born Germany, enlisted 15 May 1758. On a weekly return of Captain Samuel Jones's company in 1758.

Street, David, age 23, born Sussex, Delaware, private in Captain John Wright's company of the Lower County. On a muster dated 11 May 1759.

Street, Ezekiel, private, age 22, planter, born Black Swamp, Delaware, enlisted 10 April 1758 for the campaign in the lower counties. On a return of Captain McClughan's company dated 17 May 1758.

Strettle, Amos, private in Captain Charles Batho's Independent Company of Foot, Philadelphia in 1756.

Strickland, James, a private in Captain Lieutenant Robert Callender's Company, Second Battalion in 1756; wounded at Kittanning.

Strickler, Christopher, age 28, laborer, enlisted 07 July 1746 in Captain John Deimer's company.

Stringer, Holdcraft, a private in Captain George Armstrong's Company, Second Battalion in 1756; killed at Kittanning.

Stringer, William, age 22, laborer, born England, enlisted 29 May 1758 by Captain Benjamin Noxon.

Stringer, William, enlisted 01 May 1759, private in Captain Henry Van Bibber's company of the Lower County. On a return dated 04 June 1759.

Stroud, Jacob, age 21, laborer, born Newcastle, Delaware, enlisted 20 July 1746 in Captain John Shannon's company of foot.

Strunck, Henry, age 34, born Ireland, enlisted 25 May 1759, private in Captain Robert Curry's company in Colonel William Clapham's Pennsylvania Regiment. On a return dated June 1759.

Stuart, Charles, a member of Captain Joseph Armstrong's Company on 07 August 1755, raised in Cumberland County.

Stuart, Charles, lieutenant from 13 May 1759 in Captain Samuel Price's company of Colonel William Clapham's Regiment of New Levies.

Stuart, Daniel, a member of Captain Joseph Armstrong's Company on 07 August 1755, raised in Cumberland County.

Stuart, David, age 21, born Sussex, Delaware, private in Captain John Wright's company of the Lower County. On a muster dated 11 May 1759.

Stuart, John, a member of Captain Joseph Armstrong's Company on 07 August 1755, raised in Cumberland County.

Stuart, John, age 20, laborer, born Ireland, enlisted 30 April 1759 in Captain Charles Stewart's company [probably one of the Associated Companies of Bucks County]. On a return dated June 1759.

Stuart, John, private in Captain John Singleton's company in service between 01 May and 08 May 1758.

Stubbs, Joseph, age 21, laborer, born England, enlisted 03 May 1759, private in Captain John Haslet's company in the Pennsylvania Regiment. On a list of recruits dated 20 May 1759.

Stuckey, George, age 32, bricklayer, enlisted 21 July 1746 in Captain John Deimer's company.

Studham, John, seaman on the provincial ship *Pennsylvania* on 17 August 1757.

Sturges, John, drummer in Captain Patterson's company from 28 July 1757 stationed eastward of the Susquehanna. On a muster roll dated 08 March 1758.

Sturgis, Stokely, ensign in the Lower Part of Little Creek Hundred company of Colonel John Vining's Regiment of Kent County Militia, Upon Delaware in 1756.

Sturk, Edward, age 20, miller, born Pennsylvania, enlisted 01 May 1758. On a return of Captain John Bull's company dated 01 July 1758.

Suff, Peter, private in Captain Samuel Mifflin's Association Battery Company of Philadelphia in 1756.

Sullivan, Andrew, age 27, laborer, enlisted 23 July 1746 in Captain John Deimer's company.

Sullivan, Daniel, age 30, laborer, born Ireland, enlisted 14 July 1746 in Captain William Trent's company.

Sullivan, Samuel, ensign in Captain Thomas Price's company of the First Battalion of the Pennsylvania Regiment from April 1760.

Sullivan, Samul, ensign in Captain John Blackwood's company of the Second Battalion of the Pennsylvania Regiment from 08 May 1760.

Supplee, Jacob, age 39, cordwainer, born Pennsylvania, enlisted 08 May 1759, private in Captain Robert Curry's company in Colonel William Clapham's Pennsylvania Regiment. On a return dated June 1759.

Supplee, Josiah, age 23, born Pennsylvania, enlisted 12 May 1759, private in Captain Robert Curry's company in Colonel William Clapham's Pennsylvania Regiment. On a return dated June 1759.

Sutliff, Michael, age 23, laborer, born Ireland, enlisted 29 July 1746 in Captain John Shannon's company of foot.

Sutton, Bartholomew, seaman on the provincial ship *Pennsylvania* on 17 August 1757.

Sutton, John, private, age 28, weaver, born Wiltshire, England, enlisted 30 April 1758 for the campaign in the lower counties. On a return of Captain McClughan's company dated 17 May 1758.

Swab, Frederick, private in Captain Adam Heylman's Company, of the St. Vincent and Puke's Land Association on 10 May 1756.

Swack, Jacob, age 26, shoemaker, born Germany, enlisted 06 May 1758. On a return of Captain John Bull's company dated 01 July 1758.

Swan, Jonathan, a member of Captain Joseph Armstrong's Company on 07 August 1755, raised in Cumberland County.

Swan, Joshua, a member of Captain Joseph Armstrong's Company on 07 August 1755, raised in Cumberland County.

Swan, Richard, lieutenant in the Associated Regiment of Foot of Philadelphia on 29 Dec 1747.

Swan, Thomas, a private in Captain George Armstrong's Company, Second Battalion in 1756; missing at the capture of Kittanning.

Swan, Thomas, age 23, schoolmaster, born Ireland, enlisted 25 May 1759 in Captain Robert Boyd's company [probably in the Third Battalion]. On a return dated May and June 1759.

Swan, William, a member of Captain Joseph Armstrong's Company on 07 August 1755, raised in Cumberland County.

Swaney, Thomas, age 23, laborer, born Ireland, enlisted 07 July 1746 in Captain William Trent's company.

Swanson, Samuel, enlisted 26 June 1746 in Captain William Trent's company, deserted 04 August 1746.

Swartz, Henry, on a return of Captain David Hunter's Company [probably from York County] in Colonel William Clapham's Regiment of New Levies dated 26 May 1759.

Swenck, John, ensign in Captain Jacob Kern's company of the Second Battalion of the Pennsylvania Regiment from 16 April 1760.

Swerner, Adam, private in Captain Adam Heylman's Company, of the St. Vincent and Puke's Land Association on 10 May 1756.

Swetsky, Joseph, age 55, baker, born Bremen, Germany, enlisted 21 May 1759, private in Captain John Mathers's company in the Pennsylvania Regiment. On a return dated 15 June 1759.

Swift, Joseph, private in Captain Edward Jones's Independent Company of Horse, Philadelphia in 1756.

Swift, Samuel, ensign in one of the companies of Colonel Jacob Duché's Philadelphia Regiment in 1756.

Swinglius, Henry, lieutenant in Captain Jacob Kern's company of the Second Battalion of the Pennsylvania Regiment from 05 May 1760.

Swins, Conrad, age 40, stocking weaver, born Germany, enlisted 01 May 1759, private in Captain William Johnston's company in the Pennsylvania Regiment. On a return dated 12 May 1759.

Sword, William, private in Captain John Kidd's Independent Company of Foot, Philadelphia in 1756.

Sykes, James, lieutenant in the Dover Hundred company of Colonel John Vining's Regiment of Kent County Militia, Upon Delaware in 1756.

Tabar, John, a private in Captain John Kidd's Independent Company of Foot, Philadelphia in 1756.

Tabin, Thomas, lieutenant in the Red Lyon Hundred company of Colonel Jacob Van Bibber's Lower Regiment of New Castle County in 1756.

Taggart, Archibald, private in Captain John Singleton's company in service between 01 May and 08 May 1758.

Talbert, Joseph, ensign in the Associated Regiment of Chester County in 1747.

Talkington, Stephen, age 20, cooper, born Pennsylvania, enlisted 29 April 1758 by Captain Benjamin Noxon.

Talkington, Stephen, enlisted 19 May 1759, private in Captain Henry Van Bibber's company of the Lower County. On a return dated 04 June 1759.

Tanning, Dennis, age 29, tailor, born Ireland, enlisted 30 April 1758. On a return of Captain John Blackwood's company in the Third Battalion dated 22 May 1758.

Taries, William, *see* William Ferris.

Tartum, William, age 23, cooper, born Pennsylvania, enlisted 26 June 1746 in Captain William Trent's company.

Tate, Anthony, captain in one of the Associated Companies of Bucks County in 1756.

Tay, Daniel, age 19, laborer, born Ireland, enlisted 19 July 1746 in Captain Samuel Perry's company.

Taylor, Abraham, a private in Captain John Kidd's Independent Company of Foot, Philadelphia in 1756.

Taylor, Edward, age 21, laborer, enlisted 27 July 1746 in Captain John Deimer's company.

Taylor, George, captain in the Associated Regiment of Chester County in 1747.

Taylor, James, ensign in one of the companies of Colonel Jacob Duché's Philadelphia Regiment in 1756.

Taylor, John, private in Captain Hugh Mercer's Company, Second Battalion in 1756; missing at the capture of Kittanning.

Taylor, John, Cornet, in Captain Edward Jones's Independent Company of Horse, Philadelphia in 1756.

Taylor, John, enlisted 10 May 1758 in Captain French Battell's company of Lower County Provincials.

Taylor, Thomas, age 36, cooper, born England, enlisted 23 July 1746 in Captain John Shannon's company of foot.

Teat, John, age 31, laborer, born Derry, Ireland, enlisted 08 May 1759, private in Captain John Mathers's company in the Pennsylvania Regiment. On a return dated 15 June 1759.

Teat, Joseph, enlisted 10 May 1758 in Captain French Battell's company of Lower County Provincials.

Teate, Anthony, lieutenant in the Associated Regiment of Bucks County in 1748.

Tennent, William, age 22, cabinetmaker, born Scotland, enlisted 29 April 1758. On a return of Captain John Blackwood's company in the Third Battalion dated 22 May 1758.

Tharp, Michael, landsman on the provincial ship *Pennsylvania* on 17 August 1757.

Thomas, Aaron, age 28, born New England, enlisted 30 April 1759, corporal in Captain Robert Curry's company in Colonel William Clapham's Pennsylvania Regiment. On a return dated June 1759.

Thomas, Cornelius, age 25, laborer, born "on the high seas", enlisted 10 May 1759, private in Captain Joseph Richardson's company of the Third Battalion in the Pennsylvania Regiment. On a return of recruits dated 1759.

Thomas, Elias, ensign in Captain Joseph Scott's company of the Second Battalion of the Pennsylvania Regiment from 05 April 1760.

Thomas, Jacob, private in Captain Adam Heylman's Company, of the St. Vincent and Puke's Land Association on 10 May 1756.

Thomas, James, age 22, born Chester, Pennsylvania, laborer, private in Captain John Haslett's company enlisted on 08 May 1758 and last paid on 21 May 1758.

Thomas, John, age 23, smith, born England, enlisted 04 May 1759 in Captain Robert Boyd's company [probably in the Third Battalion]. On a return dated May and June 1759.

Thomas, Joshua, lieutenant in the Associated Regiment in the County of Philadelphia in 1748.

Thomas, Lewis, captain in the Pencader Hundred company of Colonel Jacob Van Bibber's Lower Regiment of New Castle County in 1756.

Thomas, Micha, age 31, carpenter, born Pennsylvania, enlisted 13 May 1758 by Captain Benjamin Noxon.

Thomas, Morris, lieutenant in the Associated Regiment of Chester County in 1747.

Thomas, Phineas, age 21, mason, born Pennsylvania, enlisted 09 May 1749 in Captain Richard Gardiner's company in Colonel William Denney's Pennsylvania Regiment.

Thomas, Rees, age 34, laborer, born Wales, enlisted 11 July 1746 in Captain John Shannon's company of foot.

Thomas, Simon, lieutenant in one of the companies of Colonel Jacob Duché's Philadelphia Regiment in 1756.

Thomas, William, age 23, laborer, born Wales, enlisted 29 May 1759, private in Captain Robert Curry's company in Colonel William Clapham's Pennsylvania Regiment. On a return dated June 1759.

Thompson, David, private in Captain Samuel Mifflin's Association Battery Company of Philadelphia in 1756.

Thompson, James, landsman on the provincial ship *Pennsylvania* on 17 August 1757.

Thompson, John, age 33, laborer, born Germany, enlisted 01 May 1749 in Captain Richard Gardiner's company in Colonel William Denney's Pennsylvania Regiment.

Thompson, John, age 35, sailor, born Pennsylvania, enlisted 24 April 1759 in Captain Charles Stewart's company [probably one of the Associated Companies of Bucks County]. On a return dated June 1759.

Thompson, John, ensign in the Associated Regiment of Lancaster County over the Susquehanna in 1747–8.

Thompson, John, on a list of men recruited by Captain Andrew McDowell's company in the Second Battalion, Pennsylvania Regiment dated 04 June 1759.

Thompson, John, promoted to lieutenant after serving in the Pennsylvania Regiment of Three Battalions in 1758 and 1759.

Thompson, Mordecai, deputy wagonmaster of Colonel William Denny's Regiment, 1758, from Chester County.

Thompson, Richard, enlisted 12 May 1758 in Captain French Battell's company of Lower County Provincials.

Thompson, Robert, enlisted 15 May 1758 in Captain French Battell's company of Lower County Provincials.

Thompson, Theophilus, private in Captain Hugh Mercer's Company, Second Battalion in 1756; killed at Kittanning.

Thompson, William, age 23, laborer, born Down, Ireland, enlisted 05 May 1759, private in Captain John Haslet's company in the Pennsylvania Regiment. On a list of recruits dated 20 May 1759.

Thompson, William, captain from 01 May 1758 in a troop of Light Horse in the First Battalion.

Thompson, William, enlisted 01 May 1759, private in Captain Henry Van Bibber's company of the Lower County. On a return dated 04 June 1759.

Thompson, William, lieutenant in Captain Hance Hamilton's County, Second Battalion from 16 January 1756. Captain of a company in the First Battalion from 21 December 1757 stationed westward of the Susquehanna. Resigned 17 February 1759.

Thompson, William, lieutenant in one of the Associated Companies of York County in 1756.

Thompson, William, promoted to captain after serving in the Pennsylvania Regiment of Three Battalions in 1758 and 1759.

Thompspon, James, age 18, linen-printer, born Ireland, enlisted 28 April 1758 by Captain Benjamin Noxon.

Thomson, Robert, age 30, sail maker, born Germany, enlisted 14 May 1758. On a weekly return of Captain Samuel Jones's company in 1758.

Thornton, Joseph, age 30, carpenter, born Ireland, enlisted 28 April 1759 in Captain Charles Stewart's company [probably one of the Associated Companies of Bucks County]. On a return dated June 1759.

Thornton, Joseph, private in Captain John Singleton's company in service between 01 May and 08 May 1758.

Thorp, Henry, age 17, laborer, born Delaware, enlisted 15 May 1758. On a return of Captain John Blackwood's company in the Third Battalion dated 22 May 1758.

Thorp, Michael, *see* Tharp, Michael.

Throp, Samuel, enlisted 16 May 1758 in Captain French Battell's company of Lower County Provincials.

Till, Thomas, captain in the Southern District of Cedar Creek Hundred company of Colonel Jacob Kollock's Regiment of Sussex County in 1756. Described as Slaughter Neck District company in 1758.

Tillinger, George, age 19, saddler, born Germany, enlisted 06 May 1759, private in Captain James Armstrong's company in Colonel William Clapham's Pennsylvania Regiment. On a return dated 01 June 1759.

Tilt, John, age 21, mariner, born England, enlisted 18 July 1746 in Captain William Trent's company.

Tilton, Thomas, ensign in the Lower Part of Duck Creek Hundred company of Colonel John Vining's Regiment of Kent County Militia, Upon Delaware in 1756.

Todman, John, gunner's yeoman of the provincial ship *Pennsylvania* on 17 August 1757.

Toll, Nicholas, age 20, shoemaker, born England, enlisted 11 July 1746 in Captain John Deimer's company.

Tomey, John, age 32, laborer, born Ireland, enlisted 21 July 1746 in Captain William Trent's company.

Tomlinson, Benjamin, private in Captain Joseph Inslee's Company of Foot, Newtown, Bucks County, in 1756.

Tomlinson, Thomas, private in Captain Joseph Inslee's Company of Foot, Newtown, Bucks County, in 1756.

Tong, Peter, age 40, laborer, born Germany, enlisted 30 May 1759 in Captain Robert Boyd's company [probably in the Third Battalion]. On a return dated May and June 1759.

Tonson, John, private in Captain Joseph Inslee's Company of Foot, Newtown, Bucks County, in 1756.

Tornage, Richard, age 25, laborer, born England, enlisted 08 May 1759 in Captain Robert Boyd's company [probably in the Third Battalion]. On a return dated May and June 1759.

Tort, Nathan, master's mate of the provincial ship *Pennsylvania* on 17 August 1757.

Towers, Isaac, landsman on the provincial ship *Pennsylvania* on 17 August 1757.

Towland, William, age 22, laborer, born Delaware, enlisted 25 April 1758 by Captain Benjamin Noxon.

Towland, William, age 22, laborer, born New Castle County, Delaware, enlisted 25 April 1758 for the campaign in the lower counties and is believed to be in Captain McClughan's company, but not on a return dated 17 May 1758.

Towney, Archibald, lieutenant from 22 May 1759 of a company from the Lower County.

Travers, Francis, age 22, smith, born Ireland, enlisted 17 May 1759 in Captain Robert Boyd's company [probably in the Third Battalion]. On a return dated May and June 1759.

Travers, John, age 20, tailor, born Chester, Pennsylvania, enlisted 11 May 1759 in Captain Robert Boyd's company [probably in the Third Battalion]. On a return dated May and June 1759.

Trent, George, captain of Pennsylvania troops in Albany, N.Y., on 21 October 1746 and at least through 12 November 1746.

Trent, William, captain of a company in winter quarters in Albany, N.Y., 1746–7, discharged 31 October 1747.

Trent, William, captain in the provincial service in 1755.

Trexler, _____, captain in the provincial service in 1755 in Lyn & Heidelberg Townships, Northampton County.

Trindle, William, lieutenant in the Associated Regiment of Lancaster County over the Susquehanna in 1747–8.

Trump, Levi, lieutenant of Captain William Clapham's Company, Third Battalion (known as the Augusta Regiment) from 03 April 1756. Captain from 17 December 1757 of a company in the Second Battalion, stationed at Fort Augusta.

Trump, Levi, lieutenant in Captain William Clapham's Company, Third Battalion (known as the Augusta Regiment);captain of that company after Clapham was promoted to lieutenant colonel on 29 March 1756; in charge of the building of the fort at Shamokin.

Trump, Levi, promoted to captain after serving in the Pennsylvania Regiment of Three Battalions in 1758 and 1759. Reported as "Settled in Barbadoes".

Tucker, William, age 23, enlisted 08 June 1759, private in Captain Robert Curry's company in Colonel William Clapham's Pennsylvania Regiment. On a return dated June 1759.

Tuffrey, Simon, enlisted 21 May 1759, private in Captain Henry Van Bibber's company of the Lower County. On a return dated 04 June 1759.

Tulton, William, age 21, laborer, born Ireland, enlisted 07 August 1746 in Captain William Trent's company.

Turbutt, Francis, lieutenant colonel in the Pennsylvania Regiment commanded by the Hon. J. Penn, Esqr., from 06 June 1764.

Turner, Edward, enlisted 26 May 1758 in Captain French Battell's company of Lower County Provincials.

Turner, Ephraim, age 18, born Sussex, Delaware, private in Captain John Wright's company of the Lower County. On a muster dated 11 May 1759.

Turner, John, age 25, laborer, born Donegal, Ireland, enlisted 29 May 1759, private in Captain John Mathers's company in the Pennsylvania Regiment. On a return dated 15 June 1759.

Turner, Joseph, private in Captain Charles Batho's Independent Company of Foot, Philadelphia in 1756.

Turner, Peter, Jun., private in Captain Charles Batho's Independent Company of Foot, Philadelphia on 12 March 1756.

Turner, Peter, private in Captain Edward Jones's Independent Company of Horse, Philadelphia in 1756.

Turner, Samuel Bevens, ensign in the Middle Part of Mispillim Hundred company of Colonel John Vining's Regiment of Kent County Militia, Upon Delaware in 1756.

Turner, Samuel, age 22, stocking-weaver, born Ireland, enlisted 14 July 1746 in Captain John Shannon's company of foot.

Turner, Thomas, private in Captain Edward Jones's Independent Company of Horse, Philadelphia in 1756.

Tusey, Stephen, private, age 26, laborer, born Brandywine Hundred, Delaware, enlisted 24 April 1758 for the campaign in the lower counties. On a return of Captain McClughan's company dated 17 May 1758.

Twining, Benjamin, private in Captain Joseph Inslee's Company of Foot, Newtown, Bucks County, in 1756.

Tybout, James, lieutenant in the Upper Part of Little Creek Hundred company of Colonel John Vining's Regiment of Kent County Militia, Upon Delaware in 1756.

Unger, Baltus, age 24, laborer, born Germany, enlisted 09 May 1758. On a return of Captain John Bull's company dated 01 July 1758.

Van Bibber, Henry, second lieutenant from 21 April 1758 in Captain Benjamin Noxon's company; promoted to adjutant from 04 June 1758, and promoted to first lieutenant 13 June 1758. On a list of officers of the lower government on Delaware, 1758/9. Captain from 23 May 1759 of a company from the Lower County. On a return dated 04 June 1759.

Van Bibber, Jacob, colonel of the Lower Regiment of New Castle County in 1756.

Van Bibber, Jacob, lieutenant in one of two regiments of New Castle County in 1747–8.

Van Bibber, Jacob, major in one of two regiments of New Castle County in 1747–8.

Van Bokirk, Andrew, ensign in one of the Associated Companies of Bucks County in 1756.

Van Dyke, John, lieutenant in one of two regiments of New Castle County in 1747–8.

Van Etten, John, Jun., color-sergeant in Captain John Van Etten's company of the First Battalion in 1756.

Van Etten, John, captain in the provincial service in 1755 in Upper Smithfield, Northampton County.

Van Etten, John, captain of a company of the First Battalion from May 1756.

Van Hombach, Frederick, promoted to lieutenant after serving in the Pennsylvania Regiment of Three Battalions in 1758 and 1759.

Van Hombackh, Frederick, ensign of John Armstrong's company in the First Battalion of Colonel William Denny's Regiment, 02 April 1758. Stationed west of the Susquehanna.

Van Horn, John, lieutenant in one of the companies of Colonel Jacob Duché's Philadelphia Regiment in 1756.

Van Lunanigh, Zachariah, ensign in the New Castle Hundred company of Colonel William Armstrong's Upper Regiment of New Castle County in 1756.

Van Warnsdorff, Charles, ensign from 12 May 1758 in Captain John Bull's company in the Third Battalion. Stationed at Fort Allen in June 1758. On a return for that company dated 01 July 1758. Later reported as an ensign in Captain Ludowick Stone's company in the Third Battalion.

Van Winkle, James, age 18, born Pennsylvania, enlisted 19 May 1759, private in Captain Robert Curry's company in Colonel William Clapham's Pennsylvania Regiment. On a return dated June 1759.

Van Winkle, John, ensign in one of the Associated Companies of Kent County in 1747–8.

Vanberg, John Michael, on a list of men recruited by Captain Andrew McDowell's company in the Second Battalion, Pennsylvania Regiment dated 04 June 1759.

Vance, John, captain in one of two regiments of New Castle County in 1747–8.

Vance, John, captain in the St. George's Hundred company of Colonel Jacob Van Bibber's Lower Regiment of New Castle County in 1756.

Vanderford, Vincent, enlisted 15 May 1758 in Captain French Battell's company of Lower County Provincials.

Vanderspeigle, William, captain of the Philadelphia Company in 1760.

Vanderwit, Conrad, age 26, laborer, born Germany, enlisted 14 May 1759 in Captain Charles Stewart's company [probably one of the Associated Companies of Bucks County]. On a return dated June 1759.

Vandike, Andrew, age 20, laborer, born Delaware, enlisted 02 May 1758 by Captain Benjamin Noxon.

Vandiver, Jacob, age 18, laborer, born Wilmington, Delaware, enlisted 02 May 1759, private in Captain James Armstrong's company in Colonel William Clapham's Pennsylvania Regiment. On a return dated 01 June 1759.

Vanduren, Godfrey, private in Captain Joseph Inslee's Company of Foot, Newtown, Bucks County, in 1756.

Vandyke, John, lieutenant in the St. George's Hundred company of Colonel Jacob Van Bibber's Lower Regiment of New Castle County in 1756.

Vanetton, John, captain on a List of Officers in the Province Pay, 1756 in the First Battalion of the Pennsylvania Regiment. {PA5, I, 88}

Vanhorn, Barnett, ensign in the Associated Regiment of Bucks County in 1748.

Vanhorn, Benjamin, private in Captain Joseph Inslee's Company of Foot, Newtown, Bucks County, in 1756.

Vanhorn, Bernard, Jr., captain in the Associated Regiment of Bucks County in 1748.

Vanhorn, Henry, private in Captain Joseph Inslee's Company of Foot, Newtown, Bucks County, in 1756.

Vanhorn, John, private in Captain Joseph Inslee's Company of Foot, Newtown, Bucks County, in 1756.

Vanhorn, Richard, ensign in the Associated Regiment of Bucks County in 1748.

Vansant, Garrett, lieutenant in the Associated Regiment of Bucks County in 1748.

Vansant, Isaiah, lieutenant in the Associated Regiment of Bucks County in 1748.

Vansant, John, lieutenant in one of the Associated Companies of Bucks County in 1756.

Vashan, Michael, age 30, laborer, born Armagh, Ireland, enlisted 07 May 1759, private in Captain James Armstrong's company in Colonel William Clapham's Pennsylvania Regiment. On a return dated 01 June 1759.

Vaughe, Groves, enlisted 09 July 1746 in Captain William Trent's company, deserted 23 July 1746.

Vaughn, John, lieutenant in the Associated Regiment of Chester County in 1747.

Vine, Jacob, private in Captain Adam Heylman's Company, of the St. Vincent and Puke's Land Association on 10 May 1756.

Vining, John, captain in one of the Associated Companies of Kent County in 1747–8.

Vining, John, colonel in the Regiment of Militia for Kent Co, upon the Delaware in 1756.

Vinney, Peter, private, age 24, shoemaker, born Newport, Delaware, enlisted 24 April 1758 for the campaign in the lower counties. On a return of Captain McClughan's company dated 17 May 1758.

Vittler, Valentine, private in Captain Adam Heylman's Company, of the St. Vincent and Puke's Land Association on 10 May 1756.

Von Humboch, Frederick, lieutenant in Captain (Brigade Major) David Jamison's Company of the First Battalion of the Pennsylvania Regiment from 19 April 1760.

Wackenberg [Wackerberg], Andrew, ensign in Captain Hugh Mercer's Company of the First Battalion (John Armstrong's) of William Denny's Regiment, replacing Robert Anderson, 19 March 1759. Lieutenant in Captain Thomas Price's Company of the First Battalion of the Pennsylvania Regiment from 28 April 1760.

Waddell, John, age 27, stonecutter, born Pennsylvania, enlisted 10 May 1758. On a return of Captain John Bull's company dated 01 July 1758.

Wade, Henry, private who enlisted 20 April 1756 in Captain Joseph Shippen's company in Colonel William Clapham's Regiment in 1756, the regiment in garrison at Fort Augusta, Shamokin, and listed in Shippen's Account Book. Discharged 10 May 1757.

Waldraven, Tobias, age 20, tanner, born New Castle, Delaware, enlisted 26 April 1759, private in Captain James Armstrong's company in Colonel William Clapham's Pennsylvania Regiment. On a return dated 01 June 1759.

Walker, Hugh, age 26, born Derry, Ireland, private in Captain John Haslett's company enlisted on 10 May 1758 and last paid on 21 May 1758.

Walker, James, lieutenant in one of two regiments of New Castle County in 1747–8.

Walker, James, lieutenant in the Miln Creek Hundred company of Colonel William Armstrong's Upper Regiment of New Castle County in 1756.

Walker, John, age 36, laborer, born Ireland, enlisted 02 May 1759, private in Captain Robert Curry's company in Colonel William Clapham's Pennsylvania Regiment. On a return dated June 1759.

Walker, Richard, captain from 24 April 1758 in a company in the First Battalion.

Walker, Richard, captain in the Associated Regiment of Bucks County in 1748.

Walker, Richard, promoted to captain after serving in the Pennsylvania Regiment of Three Battalions in 1758 and 1759.

Walker, Robert, lieutenant in the Associated Regiment of Bucks County in 1748.

Walker, Samuel, age 21, laborer, born Pennsylvania, enlisted 08 May 1759 in Captain Charles Stewart's company [probably one of the Associated Companies of Bucks County]. On a return dated June 1759.

Walker, William, ensign in the Associated Regiment of Bucks County in 1748.

Wall, John, private who enlisted 19 April 1756 in Captain Joseph Shippen's company in Colonel William Clapham's Regiment in 1756, the regiment in garrison at Fort Augusta, Shamokin, and listed in Shippen's Account Book.

Wallace, Arthur, ensign not assigned in the First Battalion of the Pennsylvania Regiment from 30 April 1760.

Wallace, Hugh, age 17, shoemaker, born Chester, Pennsylvania, enlisted 12 June 1759, private in Captain John Mathers's company in the Pennsylvania Regiment. On a return dated 15 June 1759.

Wallace, William, private in Captain Samuel Mifflin's Association Battery Company of Philadelphia in 1756.

Wallace, William, age 25, mariner, born Ireland, enlisted 23 May 1758. On a return of Captain John Blackwood's company in the Third Battalion dated 22 May 1758.

Walter, Jacob, private in Captain John Kidd's Independent Company of Foot, Philadelphia in 1756.

Walter, Jacob, landsman on the provincial ship *Pennsylvania* on 17 August 1757.

Walton, Joseph, seaman on the provincial ship *Pennsylvania* on 17 August 1757.

Walton, Joshua, *see* Walton, Joseph.

Waples, Burton, captain in the Southern District of Indian River Hundred company of Colonel Jacob Kollock's Regiment of Sussex County in 1756/8.

Ward, _____, ensign in Captain Trent's Company, who was in command at Fort DeQuesne [Duquesne] with thirty men when it was captured by seven hundred French in March 1754.

Ward, Edward, captain of a company in the Second Battalion from 22 May 1756. Captain in a company in the First Battalion from 13 December 1757 stationed westward of the Susquehanna. Major from 26 April 1759 of the Third Battalion of the Pennsylvania Regiment.

Ward, John, age 20, miller, born Donegal, Ireland, enlisted 06 May 1759, private in Captain James Armstrong's company in Colonel William Clapham's Pennsylvania Regiment. On a return dated 01 June 1759.

Ward, John, age 40, born Jersey, private in Captain John Wright's company of the Lower County. On a muster dated 11 May 1759.

Ward, John, on a list of men recruited by Captain Andrew McDowell's company in the Second Battalion, Pennsylvania Regiment dated 04 June 1759.

Ward, Richard, age 24, farmer, born New Jersey, enlisted 26 April 1759, private in Captain William Johnston's company in the Pennsylvania Regiment. On a return dated 12 May 1759.

Warfield, William, enlisted 30 July 1746 in Captain William Trent's company, deserted 14 August 1746.

Warren, Benjamin, Jun., ensign in the Murder Kiln [or Mother-Kill] Hundred company of Colonel John Vining's Regiment of Kent County Militia, Upon Delaware in 1756. Ensign in Captain Daniel Robinson's company from the Lower District of Mother-Kill Hundred, Kent County, Delaware. Resigned before 29 March 1758.

Warren, John, age 24, weaver, born Berks, Pennsylvania, enlisted 27 May 1759, private in Captain John Mathers's company in the Pennsylvania Regiment. On a return dated 15 June 1759.

Warrington, Zachariah, private, age 19, planter, born Angola Hundred, Delaware, enlisted 20 April 1758 for the campaign in the lower counties. On a return of Captain McClughan's company dated 17 May 1758.

Wasson, Robert, age 20, tailor, born Ireland, enlisted 30 July 1746 in Captain William Trent's company.

Wassum, Conrad, age 39, born Germany, enlisted 01 September 1757, sergeant in Captain John Nicholas Weatherholt's company, which enlisted for a term of three years, and was stationed in Heydelberg Township, Northampton County, in March and April 1758.

Waters, William, age 19, laborer, born Pennsylvania, enlisted 26 April 1759 in Captain Charles Stewart's company [probably one of the Associated Companies of Bucks County]. On a return dated June 1759.

Wathell, John, *see* John Waddell.

Watkins, James, age 26, laborer, born England, enlisted 03 May 1758 by Captain Benjamin Noxon.

Watkins, Solomon, age 22, laborer, born Maryland, enlisted 11 July 1746 in Captain John Deimer's company.

Watson, Alexander, age 40, laborer, born Scotland, enlisted 07 May 1758. On a return of Captain John Blackwood's company in the Third Battalion dated 22 May 1758.

Watson, Bethuel, lieutenant in the Northern District of Cedar Creek Hundred in Captain Benjamin Wynkoop's company of Colonel Jacob Kollock's Regiment of Sussex County in 1756.

Watson, Henry, adjutant in the Pennsylvania Regiment commanded by the Hon. J. Penn, Esqr., from 06 September 1764.

Watson, Isaac, lieutenant in the Southern District of Cedar Creek Hundred Captain Thomas Till's company of Colonel Jacob Kollock's Regiment of Sussex County in 1756. Described as Slaughter Neck District company in 1758.

Watson, Nathaniel, age 30, shoemaker, born Ireland, enlisted 19 May 1758. On a return of Captain John Blackwood's company in the Third Battalion dated 22 May 1758.

Watson, Thomas, age 35, laborer, born England, enlisted 12 July 1746 in Captain John Deimer's company.

Watson, Thomas, on a return of Captain David Hunter's Company [probably from York County] in Colonel William Clapham's Regiment of New Levies dated 26 May 1759.

Watson, William, private in Captain Patterson's company from 27 December 1757 stationed eastward of the Susquehanna. On a muster roll dated 08 March 1758.

Watt, Robert, age 19, laborer, enlisted 27 July 1746 in Captain John Deimer's company.

Way, David, age 24, born Chester, Pennsylvania, tanner, private in Captain John Singleton's company in service between 01 May and 08 May 1758.

Wayne, Isaac, captain of a company that was sent to Northampton in 1755, rendezvoused at Easton, under the command of General Dr. Benjamin Franklin. Order to Canoteu Hatten (Gnadenhutten) where they erected a stockade, Fort Allen. Father of General Wayne. At Nazareth.

Weasle, Francis, private in Captain Joseph Inslee's Company of Foot, Newtown, Bucks County, in 1756.

Weatherby, Benjamin, ensign in the Associated Regiment of Chester County in 1747.

Weatherholt, John Nicholas, age 34, born Germany, commissioned 16 December 1755, Captain of a company, which enlisted for a term of three years, and was stationed in Heydelberg Township, Northampton County, in March and April 1758.

Weaver, Peter, age 35, born Germany, enlisted 12 May 1759, private in Captain Robert Curry's company in Colonel William Clapham's Pennsylvania Regiment. On a return dated June 1759.

Webb, John, captain of a company in the First Battalion of the Pennsylvania Regiment from 09 November 1763.

Weber, Henry, age 28, miller, born Germany, enlisted 06 August 1746 in Captain John Deimer's company.

Weeks, Thomas, private in Captain John Singleton's company in service between 01 May and 08 May 1758.

Weels, Thomas, on a return of Captain David Hunter's Company [probably from York County] in Colonel William Clapham's Regiment of New Levies dated 26 May 1759.

Weer, Hugh, *see* Hugh Weir.

Weherholt, Nicholas, captain in the provincial service in 1755.

Weidle, John, on a list of men recruited by Captain Andrew McDowell's company in the Second Battalion, Pennsylvania Regiment dated 04 June 1759.

Weir [Weer], Hugh, age 28, born Enniskillen, Ireland, private in Captain John Haslett's company enlisted on 10 May 1758 and last paid on 21 May 1758.

Weir, John, age 18, weaver, born Antrim, Ireland, enlisted 05 May 1759, private in Captain John Haslet's company in the Pennsylvania Regiment. On a list of recruits dated 20 May 1759.

Weir, Owen, age 22, laborer, born Ireland, enlisted 27 August 1746 in Captain Samuel Perry's company.

Weirick, Christian, sergeant in Captain Charles Foulk's company of the First Battalion in 1755/6.

Weiser, Capt., lieutenant colonel on a List of Officers in the Province Pay, 1756 in the First Battalion of the Pennsylvania Regiment with a commission date of 5 May 1756. {PA5, I, 88}

Weiser, Conrad, a provincial officer in 1754 and 1755, Lt. Col., in the provincial service in 1755. Lt. col., First Battalion, from 05 May 1756. Was a captain of a company in the First Battalion prior to his promotion. Stationed eastward of Susquehanna.

Weiser, Conrad, Indian interpreter for the province and counties in 1749.

Weiser, Philip, lieutenant on a List of Officers in the Province Pay, 1756 in the First Battalion of the Pennsylvania Regiment with a commission date of 3 July 1756. {PA5, I, 88}

Weiser, Philip, lieutenant, a provincial officer in 1754, in Captain George Reynolds company of the First Battalion from 03 July 1756.

Weiser, Samuel, captain lieutenant on a List of Officers in the Province Pay, 1756 in the First Battalion of the Pennsylvania Regiment with a commission date of 3 July 1756. {PA5, I, 88}

Weiser, Samuel, lieutenant in Captain Conrad Weiser's Company in the First Battalion; captain lieutenant from 03 July 1756. Stationed eastward of Susquehanna. Captain from 20 December 1757 of a company in the Second Battalion, stationed eastward of the Susquehanna.

Welch, Daniel, private in Captain Joseph Inslee's Company of Foot, Newtown, Bucks County, in 1756.

Welch, James, private in Captain Joseph Inslee's Company of Foot, Newtown, Bucks County, in 1756.

Welch, John, age 30, laborer, born Ireland, enlisted 18 May 1758 by Lieutenant William McClay for Captain John Montgomery's company.

Welch, William, private in Captain Edward Ward's Company, Second Battalion in 1756; killed at Kittanning.

Weldon, Daniel, ensign in the Apoquinimink Hundred company of Colonel Jacob Van Bibber's Lower Regiment of New Castle County in 1756.

Wells, George, ensign from 16 June 1758.

Wells, James, age 19, born Kent on Delaware, laborer, private in Captain John Shannon's Company, enlisted 18 July 1746. On a roll of deserters dated 22 July 1746. [B3:422:18]

Wells, James, age 19, laborer, born Kent, Delaware, enlisted 18 July 1746 in Captain John Shannon's company of foot.

Wells, James, ensign in the Town of Dover company of Colonel John Vining's Regiment of Kent County Militia, Upon Delaware in 1756.

Wells, Joseph, age 18, laborer, born Maryland, enlisted 14 July 1746 in Captain John Shannon's company of foot.

Wells, Richard, ensign in one of the Associated Companies of Kent County in 1747–8. Captain from 17 April 1758 of company raised for the campaign in the lower counties. Major from June 1758. On a list of officers of the lower government on Delaware, 1758/9.

Wells, Robert, age 22, laborer, born Ireland, enlisted 15 May 1759 in Captain Robert Boyd's company [probably in the Third Battalion]. On a return dated May and June 1759.

Wells, Thomas, lieutenant in one of the companies of Colonel Jacob Duché's Philadelphia Regiment in 1756.

Welsh, George, hired 10 June 1757 as a battoe man, Master George Allen.

Welsh, Nicholas, landsman on the provincial ship *Pennsylvania* on 17 August 1757.

Welsh, Robert, enlisted 12 May 1758 in Captain French Battell's company of Lower County Provincials.

Werny, George, a private in Captain Adam Heylman's Company, of the St. Vincent and Puke's Land Association on 10 May 1756.

West, Samuel, captain of a company of the First Battalion of the Pennsylvania Regiment from 30 April 1760.

West, Samuel, lieutenant from 07 May 1759 in Captain Joseph Richardson's company of Colonel William Clapham's Regiment of New Levies.

West, Samuel, promoted to captain after serving in the Pennsylvania Regiment of Three Battalions in 1758 and 1759. Reported to have "left the province".

West, Samuel, promoted to lieutenant after serving in the Pennsylvania Regiment of Three Battalions in 1758 and 1759.

Westcott, Thomas, private, age 23, farmer, born Indian River, Maryland, enlisted 04 May 1758 for the campaign in the lower counties. On a return of Captain McClughan's company dated 17 May 1758.

Wetherholt, John Nicholas, captain in a company from 19 December 1757 stationed eastward of the Susquehanna.

Wetterholt, Jacob, lieutenant in Captain William Parson's Company in the First Battalion from 20 December 1755. Left out in the reorganization of December 1757.

Wetterholt, Jacob, lieutenant on a List of Officers in the Province Pay, 1756 in the First Battalion of the Pennsylvania Regiment with a commission date of 20 December 1755. {PA5, I, 88}

Wetterholt, John Nicholas, captain in a company of the First Battalion from 21 December 1755. Captain in a company of the First Battalion from 19 December 1757.

Wetterholt, John Nicholas, promoted to captain after serving in the Pennsylvania Regiment of Three Battalions in 1758 and 1759. Reported as "discontinued."

Weyerbacher, John, age 30, born Germany, tailor, enlisted 01 September 1757, private in Captain John Nicholas Weatherholt's company, which enlisted for a term of three years, and was stationed in Heydelberg Township, Northampton County, in March and April 1758.

Wharey, Samuel, age 22, born Antrim, Ireland, laborer, private in Captain John Haslett's company enlisted on 10 May 1758 and last paid on 21 May 1758.

Wheeler, Joseph, ensign in Captain George Craighead's company of the First Battalion of the Pennsylvania Regiment from 23 April 1760.

Wheeler, Joshua, age 20, born Kent County, laborer, private in Captain John Shannon's Company, enlisted 16 July 1746. On a roll of deserters dated 22 July 1746. [B3:422:18]

Whellan, Luke, private, age 35, miller, born Waterford, Ireland, enlisted 22 April 1758 for the campaign in the lower counties. On a return of Captain McClughan's company dated 17 May 1758.

Whiler, John, a private in Captain Edward Jones's Independent Company of Horse, Philadelphia in 1756.

White, Brooks, age 22, born Donegal, Ireland, private in Captain John Haslet's company in the Pennsylvania Regiment. On a list of recruits dated 20 May 1759.

White, James, age 24, born Antrim, Ireland, weaver, private in Captain John Haslett's company enlisted on 08 May 1758 and last paid on 21 May 1758.

White, John, lieutenant from 11 May 1758 in Captain Paul Jackson's company of the Third Battalion.

White, John, sergeant in Captain Charles Foulk's company of the First Battalion in 1755/6.

White, Samuel, age 26, born Chester, Pennsylvania, private in Captain John Haslett's company enlisted on 10 May 1758 and last paid on 21 May 1758.

White, Samuel, private in Captain John Singleton's company in service between 01 May and 08 May 1758.

White, Thomas, age 40, carpenter, born England, enlisted 02 May 1759, private in Captain Robert Curry's company in Colonel William Clapham's Pennsylvania Regiment. On a return dated June 1759.

White, William, private, age 24, farmer, born Cedar Creek, Delaware, enlisted 04 May 1758 for the campaign in the lower counties. On a return of Captain McClughan's company dated 17 May 1758.

Whiteford, Hugh, lieutenant in the Associated Regiment of the West End of Lancaster County in 1747–8.

Whitehall, James, in the Regiment of the West End of Lancaster County in 1747–8.

Whitehead, John, age 21, carpenter, born Pennsylvania, enlisted 01 May 1749 in Captain Richard Gardiner's company in Colonel William Denney's Pennsylvania Regiment.

Whitford, John, enlisted 13 May 1758 in Captain French Battell's company of Lower County Provincials.

Whitman, Jacob, captain in one of the companies of Colonel Jacob Duché's Philadelphia Regiment in 1756.

Whittel, William, lieutenant in the St. George's Hundred company of Colonel Jacob Van Bibber's Lower Regiment of New Castle County in 1756.

Wickley, Andrew, landsman on the provincial ship *Pennsylvania* on 17 August 1757.

Wiggans, John, surgeon in the Pennsylvania Regiment commanded by the Hon. J. Penn, Esqr., from 20 December 1763.

Wilcox, John, private in Captain Charles Batho's Independent Company of Foot, Philadelphia in 1756.

Wild [Wiles], William, an ensign stationed on the frontier in Berks County with one sergeant and thirteen men at Christopher Young's, Tulpehocking Township, on 01 June 1764 as part of a unit under the command of Major Asher Clayton.

Wild, William, *see* William Wiles.

Wildman, John, private in Captain Joseph Inslee's Company of Foot, Newtown, Bucks County, in 1756.

Wildman, Martin, private in Captain Joseph Inslee's Company of Foot, Newtown, Bucks County, in 1756.

Wildt, John, lieutenant in Captain John Diemer's company, in winter quarters in Albany, N.Y., 1746–7, discharged 31 October 1747.

Wiles [Wild], William, ensign in Major John Phillip de Haas's Company in the Pennsylvania Regiment commanded by the Hon. J. Penn, Esqr., from 30 December 1763.

Wiles, William, *see* William Wild

Wilkey, Andrew, ensign in Captain George Ashton's company in the Third Battalion. Transferred to Captain Ward's company 17 March 1759.

Wilkey, James, ensign in the Associated Regiment of Lancaster County over the Susquehanna in 1747–8.

Wilkins, Hance George, age 26, mariner, born Sweedland, enlisted 01 May 1758. On a weekly return of Captain Samuel Jones's company in 1758.

Wilkins, James, ensign from 12 February 1745–6, company raised in Rathmullin Township, Lancaster County.

Wilkins, Richard, age 25, laborer, born England, enlisted 28 July 1746 in Captain John Shannon's company of foot.

Willey, James, age 20, laborer, born Ireland, enlisted 17 May 1758 by Lieutenant William McClay for Captain John Montgomery's company.

Williams, Derrick, lieutenant in the Apoquinimink Hundred company of Colonel Jacob Van Bibber's Lower Regiment of New Castle County in 1756.

Williams, Devard, a member of Captain Joseph Armstrong's Company on 07 August 1755, raised in Cumberland County.

Williams, George, private in Captain Patterson's company from 26 December 1757 stationed eastward of the Susquehanna. On a muster roll dated 08 March 1758.

Williams, Henry, age 22, born Chester, Pennsylvania, drummer in Captain John Singleton's company in service between 01 May and 08 May 1758.

Williams, James, age 19, born Tyrone, Ireland, weaver, private in Captain John Haslett's company enlisted on 08 May 1758 and last paid on 21 May 1758.

Williams, John, age 20, laborer, born Wales, enlisted 05 May 1759, private in Captain James Armstrong's company in Colonel William Clapham's Pennsylvania Regiment. On a return dated 01 June 1759.

Williams, John, age 44, miner, born Wales, enlisted 08 May 1759 in Captain Charles Stewart's company [probably one of the Associated Companies of Bucks County]. On a return dated June 1759.

Williams, Peregrin, age 40, born Pembroke, Wales, "has some old wounds", private in Captain John Haslett's company enlisted on 16 May 1758 and last paid on 21 May 1758.

Williams, William, captain in the Apoquinimink Hundred company of Colonel Jacob Van Bibber's Lower Regiment of New Castle County in 1756.

Williams, William, ensign in the Associated Regiment of Bucks County in 1748.

Williamson, _____, ensign in the White Clay Creek Hundred company of Colonel William Armstrong's Upper Regiment of New Castle County in 1756.

Williamson, Abraham, lieutenant from 14 May 1758 in Captain William Biles's company in the Third Battalion.

Williamson, John, captain in the Associated Regiment of Chester County in 1747.

Williamson, Joseph, private who enlisted 23 April 1756 in Captain Joseph Shippen's company in Colonel William Clapham's Regiment in 1756, the regiment in garrison at Fort Augusta, Shamokin, and listed in Shippen's Account Book.

Williamson, Thomas, landsman on the provincial ship *Pennsylvania* on 17 August 1757.

Willing, Charles, captain in the Associated Regiment of Foot of Philadelphia on 29 Dec 1747.

Willing, Thomas, lieutenant who resigned his commission in the Dock Ward Company in 1756. {PA1, II, 599–600}

Willis, Thomas, age 17, born Sussex, Delaware, private in Captain John Wright's company of the Lower County. On a muster dated 11 May 1759.

Willong, Andrew, hired 10 June 1757 as a battoe man, Master George Allen.

Wills, Caleb, age 21, born Sussex, Delaware, private in Captain John Wright's company of the Lower County. On a muster dated 11 May 1759.

Wills, Lawrence, age 21, born Sussex, Delaware, private in Captain John Wright's company of the Lower County. On a muster dated 11 May 1759.

Willson, James, corporal, present at battle of Sideling Hill. {PA1, III, 315} {B8:1691:625}

Willson, John, age 20, laborer, born Chester, Pennsylvania, enlisted 07 May 1759 in Captain Robert Boyd's company [probably in the Third Battalion]. On a return dated May and June 1759.

Willson, Robert, age 24, laborer, born Ireland, enlisted 11 June 1759 in Captain Robert Boyd's company [probably in the Third Battalion]. On a return dated May and June 1759.

Willy, Waitman, age 25, born Maryland, private in Captain John Wright's company of the Lower County. On a muster dated 11 May 1759.

Wilson, David, age 40, laborer, born England, enlisted 08 May 1749 in Captain Richard Gardiner's company in Colonel William Denney's Pennsylvania Regiment.

Wilson, Edward, enlisted 04 June 1759, private in Captain John Mathers's company in the Pennsylvania Regiment. On a return dated 15 June 1759.

Wilson, Hezekiah, age 21, laborer, born Pennsylvania, enlisted 06 August 1746 in Captain John Deimer's company.

Wilson, John, captain in the Associated Regiment of Bucks County in 1748.

Wilson, John, ensign in the Associated Regiment of the West End of Lancaster County in 1747–8.

Wilson, Jonathan, a member of Captain Joseph Armstrong's Company on 07 August 1755, raised in Cumberland County.

Wilson, Joseph, captain in the Associated Regiment of Chester County in 1747.

Wilson, Joseph, on a list of men recruited by Captain Andrew McDowell's company in the Second Battalion, Pennsylvania Regiment dated 04 June 1759.

Wilson, Samuel, private, age 15, laborer, born Kennett, Pennsylvania, enlisted 12 May 1758 for the campaign in the lower counties. On a return of Captain McClughan's company dated 17 May 1758.

Wilson, Solomon, private, age 18, laborer, born Chester River, Maryland, enlisted 01 May 1758 for the campaign in the lower counties. On a return of Captain McClughan's company dated 17 May 1758.

Wilson, Thomas, age 21, miller, born Ireland, enlisted 26 July 1746 in Captain Samuel Perry's company.

Wilson, William, age 23, cooper, born Pennsylvania, enlisted 08 May 1758. On a return of Captain John Bull's company dated 01 July 1758.

Wilson, William, age 25, cooper, born Pennsylvania, enlisted 09 May 1758. On a weekly return of Captain Samuel Jones's company in 1758.

Windsor, Thomas, age 43, laborer, born England, enlisted 01 July 1746 in Captain William Trent's company.

Winer, James, private in Captain Joseph Inslee's Company of Foot, Newtown, Bucks County, in 1756.

Winford, John, age 19, shoemaker, born Ireland, enlisted 07 May 1758. On a return of Captain John Blackwood's company in the Third Battalion dated 22 May 1758.

Winford, John, age 27, shoemaker, born Cork, Ireland, enlisted 23 April 1759, private in Captain William Johnston's company in the Pennsylvania Regiment. On a return dated 12 May 1759.

Winslow, John, private in Captain Patterson's company from 01 January 1758 stationed eastward of the Susquehanna. On a muster roll dated 08 March 1758.

Winton, John, lieutenant in the Associated Regiment of Lancaster County over the Susquehanna in 1747–8.

Wirth, Jacob, age 34, tailor, enlisted 28 June 1746 in Captain John Deimer's company.

Witherow, Samuel, ensign in one of the Associated Companies of York County in 1756.

Witherspoon, David, captain in one of two regiments of New Castle County in 1747–8. Lt. Col, of Colonel Jacob Van Bibber's Lower Regiment of New Castle County in 1756.

Witherspoon, Robert, age 22, weaver, born Down, Ireland, enlisted 01 May 1759, private in Captain James Armstrong's company in Colonel William Clapham's Pennsylvania Regiment. On a return dated 01 June 1759.

Witterhold, John, captain on a List of Officers in the Province Pay, 1756 in the First Battalion of the Pennsylvania Regiment with a commission date of 21 December 1755. {PA5, I, 88}

Wolf, Nicholas, age 17, laborer, born Germany, enlisted 19 July 1746 in Captain Samuel Perry's company.

Wolf, Peter, age 17, nailsmith, born York, Pennsylvania, enlisted 24 May 1759, private in Captain John Mathers's company in the Pennsylvania Regiment. On a return dated 15 June 1759.

Wolf, Rice, lieutenant in the Southern District of Lewes and Rehoboth Hundred Captain John Newbold's company of Colonel Jacob Kollock's Regiment of Sussex County in 1756/8. Described as Rehobeth District Company in 1758.

Wolpp, John, private in Captain Edward Jones's Independent Company of Horse, Philadelphia in 1756.

Wood, Joseph, second lieutenant in Captain William Vanderspeigle's Philadelphia Company in 1760.

Wood, Joseph, ensign in the Associated Regiment of Foot of Philadelphia on 29 Dec 1747.

Wood, Richard, age 22, tanner, born Long Island, enlisted 26 June 1746 in Captain John Shannon's company of foot.

Woodnought, Robert, age 30, cordwainer, born England, enlisted 29 July 1746 in Captain William Trent's company.

Woods, James, captain in the Associated Regiment of Lancaster County over the Susquehanna in 1747–8.

Woodside, John, lieutenant in the Associated Regiment of the West End of Lancaster County in 1747–8.

Woolf, Rees, Sr., *see* Wolf, Rice.

Work, Andrew, captain in one of the Associated Companies of Lancaster County in 1756.

Work, Patrick, captain of a company of the Third Battalion (known as the Augusta Regiment) from 22 April 1756. Captain from 11 December 1757 of a company in the Second Battalion stationed at Fort Augusta. Lieutenant colonel of the First Battalion (John Armstrong's) of Colonel William Denny's Regiment, March 1759. Lieutenant colonel from 01 June 1758 in the Third Battalion. Lieutenant colonel from 24 April 1759 of the Third Battalion of the Pennsylvania Regiment. Lieutenant colonel of the First Battalion of the Pennsylvania Regiment from 12 April 1760.

Work, William, ensign in one of the Associated Companies of Lancaster County in 1756. Lieutenant from 04 May 1759 in Captain Richard Pearis's company of Colonel William Clapham's Regiment of New Levies.

Workman, Andrew, age 17, laborer, born Pennsylvania, enlisted 10 May 1759 in Captain Charles Stewart's company [probably one of the Associated Companies of Bucks County]. On a return dated June 1759.

Workman, Joseph, age 24, laborer, born Pennsylvania, enlisted 22 April 1759 in Captain Charles Stewart's company [probably one of the Associated Companies of Bucks County]. On a return dated June 1759.

Workman, Stephen, age 16, laborer, born Pennsylvania, enlisted 05 May 1759 in Captain Charles Stewart's company [probably one of the Associated Companies of Bucks County]. On a return dated June 1759.

Wornell, Jacob, private in Captain Patterson's company from 03 March 1758 stationed eastward of the Susquehanna. On a muster roll dated 08 March 1758.

Wright, Anthony, captain in the Associated Regiment of Bucks County in 1748.

Wright, Ezekeil, enlisted 10 May 1759, private in Captain Henry Van Bibber's company of the Lower County. On a return dated 04 June 1759.

Wright, Henry, age 18, laborer, born Pennsylvania, enlisted 10 May 1758. On a weekly return of Captain Samuel Jones's company in 1758.

Wright, Isaac, age 27, laborer, born West Jersey, enlisted 21 July 1746 in Captain Samuel Perry's company.

Wright, James, captain in the provincial service in 1755.

Wright, John, age 22, laborer, born Maryland, enlisted 02 May 1758 by Captain Benjamin Noxon.

Wright, John, first lieutenant from 19 April 1758 in Captain John McClughan's company raised for the campaign in the lower counties. Captain from 24 May 1759 of a company from the Lower County, but on a muster rolled dated 11 May 1759 as a captain.

Wurtenberg, Michael, age 22, born Germany, enlisted 01 December 1757, private in Captain John Nicholas Weatherholt's company, which enlisted for a term of three years, and was stationed in Heydelberg Township, Northampton County, in March and April 1758.

Wyer, Samuel, private in Captain Patterson's company from 28 December 1757 stationed eastward of the Susquehanna. On a muster roll dated 08 March 1758.

Wyle, John, private who enlisted 16 April 1756 in Captain Joseph Shippen's company in Colonel William Clapham's Regiment in 1756, the regiment in garrison at Fort Augusta, Shamokin, and listed in Shippen's Account Book. Transferred to Captain Thomas Lloyd's company 30 June 1756.

Wynkoop, Benjamin, captain in the Northern District of Cedar Creek Hundred company of Colonel Jacob Kollock's Regiment of Sussex County in 1756.

Wynkoop, Garrett, lieutenant in the Associated Regiment of Bucks County in 1748. Lieutenant in one of the Associated Companies of Bucks County in 1756.

Wynkoop, Philip, ensign in the Associated Regiment in the County of Philadelphia in 1748.

Yeates, John, landsman on the provincial ship *Pennsylvania* on 17 August 1757.

Yenle, Hendry, age 19, laborer, born Pennsylvania, enlisted 01 May 1749 in Captain Richard Gardiner's company in Colonel William Denney's Pennsylvania Regiment.

Yoder, Jacob, age 22, born Pennsylvania, saddler, enlisted 06 November 1757, private in Captain John Nicholas Weatherholt's company, which enlisted for a term of three years, and was stationed in Heydelberg Township, Northampton County, in March and April 1758.

Yorgen, Dennis, age 20, laborer, born Ireland, enlisted 22 July 1746 in Captain William Trent's company.

York, Thomas, captain and then lt. colonel on 04 August 1748, in the Associated Regiment in the County of Philadelphia in 1748.

Yorkson, John, age 20, carpenter, born Maryland, enlisted 02 May 1758 by Captain Benjamin Noxon.

Young, Archibald, ensign in the Associated Regiment of Chester County in 1747.

Young, Frederick Christian, age 27, laborer, enlisted 17 July 1746 in Captain John Deimer's company.

Young, Goodman, age 22, weaver, born Ireland, enlisted 03 May 1758 by Captain Benjamin Noxon.

Young, Isaac, age 20, laborer, born Down, Ireland, enlisted 07 May 1759, private in Captain James Armstrong's company in Colonel William Clapham's Pennsylvania Regiment. On a return dated 01 June 1759.

Young, Jacob, age 25, born Germany, enlisted 29 May 1749 in Captain Richard Gardiner's company in Colonel William Denney's Pennsylvania Regiment.

Young, James, private in Captain John Kidd's Independent Company of Foot, Philadelphia in 1756.

Young, James, age 20, weaver, born New England, enlisted 15 May 1758 by Captain Benjamin Noxon.

Young, James, enlisted May 1759, private in Captain Henry Van Bibber's company of the Lower County. On a return dated 04 June 1759.

Young, John Carsum, age 30, mariner, born Denmark, enlisted 26 June 1746 in Captain William Trent's company.

Young, John, age 20, weaver, born Maryland, private in Captain John Wright's company of the Lower County. On a muster dated 11 May 1759.

Young, John, enlisted 15 May 1758 in Captain French Battell's company of Lower County Provincials.

Young, John, ensign in the Associated Regiment of the West End of Lancaster County in 1747–8.

Young, Peter, age 20, carpenter, born Germany, enlisted July 1746 in Captain Samuel Perry's company.

Yunge, Jacob, *see* Young, Jacob.

Zahn, Casper, age 30, laborer, born Germany, enlisted 07 July 1746 in Captain John Deimer's company.

Zips, Joseph, age 20, born Germany, tailor, enlisted 01 September 1757, private in Captain John Nicholas Weatherholt's company, which enlisted for a term of three years, and was stationed in Heydelberg Township, Northampton County, in March and April 1758April 1758.

Ziseger, John Godfrey, private who enlisted 23 April 1756 in Captain Joseph Shippen's company in Colonel William Clapham's Regiment in 1756, the regiment in garrison at Fort Augusta, Shamokin, and listed in Shippen's Account Book.

Zubers, Benjamin, private in Captain Joseph Inslee's Company of Foot, Newtown, Bucks County, in 1756.

Zubers, John, lieutenant in Captain Joseph Inslee's Company of Foot, Newtown, Bucks County, in 1756.

Zuimell, Daniel, age 27, laborer, enlisted 14 July 1746 in Captain John Deimer's company.

Craig R. Scott

Appendix A

An Incomplete Table of Organization of Pennsylvania Units
In the French and Indian War

Lower County Provincials
   Capt French Battell, 1758
   Capt Henry Van Bibber, 1759
Capt John Wright, 1759

    Kent
       Associated Company, 1748
       Associated Company, 1748

    New Castle
       Lower Regiment of New Castle County
          Col. Jacob Van Bibber
          St. George's Hundred Company, 1756

Upper Regiment of New Castle County
       Col. William Armstrong
          New Castle Hundred Company, 1756
            Lt. Samuel Aldricks
   Christiana Hundred Company, 1756
Regiment, 1747, 1748
      Regiment, 1747, 1748
      Capt John Almond, 1747

   Capt Robert Anderson, 1758,1759 [served in Regt. of 3 Batln.]
Capt John Bull, 1758
   Capt John Deimer, 1746
   Capt Samuel Jones, 1758
   Capt McClughan
Capt Benjamin Noxon, 1758
Capt Samuel Perry
Capt John Shannon

Capt John Singleton, 1758
Capt William Trent, 1746

Pennsylvania Regiment
   Capt John Haslett's, 1758, 1759

Bucks
   Associated Regiment, 1748
   Associated Companies, 1756

Chester
   Associate Regiment, 1747

Lancaster
   Associated Regiment, 1747, 1748

West End
      Associated Regiment, 1747, 1748
          Capt Samuel Anderson, 1747

   Associated Companies, 1756
      Capt James Anderson, 1756
      Capt Samuel Anderson, 1756 same as 1747

Philadelphia
   Philadelphia Regiment, 1756
      Col. Jacob Duche, 1756
          Capt William Allen
   Capt Edward Jones Independent Company of Horse, 1756
   Capt Edward Kidd Independent Company of Foot, 1756
   Capt Samuel Mifflin Association Battery Company, 1756

York
   Associated Companies, 1756

   Capt Thomas Armour, new levies)

St. Vincent and Puke's Land Association
    Capt Adam Heylmans, 1756

Pennsylvania Regiments
Col. William Denney Regiment
    Capt Richard Gardiner, 1749

Col. William Clapham Regiment
    (aka Regt. Of New Levies)
    Capt James Armstrong, 1759
Capt Joseph Shippen, 1756
Capt Robert Curry, 1759

Col. William Denny's Regiment, 1757
    (aka Pennsylvania Regiment of the Three Battalions
1st Battalion, 1756
    Col. John Armstrong's Battalion, 1757, 1758
    Capt Hugh Mercer, 1757)
Capt John Van Etten
    Capt Smith then was Van Etten
    Capt John Nicholas Weatherholts, 1758 [Northampton County]
    Capt William Thompson Troop of Light Horse, 1758
    Capt George Armstrong, 1757 from 2nd Batln.

2nd Battalion, 1760
    Capt George Armstrong, 1756
    Capt Robert Anderson, 1760
    Capt Edward Ward, 1756

3rd Battalion, 1758
    (aka Augusta Regiment)
    Capt John Blackwood, 1758
    Capt James Burd, 1756
    Capt Archibald McGrew

Navy

Pennsylvania, 1757
Battoe, 1757, 1758

Appendix B

Snippets of information or questions found in the material that might be of help

Murder Kiln [or Mother-Kill] Hundred which is it?
Kill or Kiln in all cases.
In July 1756 the station of Provincial Forces was:
Reading – Lt. Col. Weiser's Company
Fort at North Kill (above Alleminga) – Lt. Eagle, sergeant, and sixteen men of Captain Jacob Morgan's Company
Fort Lebanon – Captain Morgan's militia detachment
Fort Henry – Captain Christian Bussé
Fort Allen (at Gnadenhutton) – Lt. Jacob Meas with twenty-five men of Captain Charles Foulk's Company
Fort Norris – Captain Jacob Orndt and twenty-one men
Fort Hyndshaw – Lt. James Hyndshaw of Captain Wetterholt's company
Wind Gap – Ensign Daniel Harry of Captain Wetterholt's company
Nazareth Mill – Captain Enslee, Ensign Enslee, and twenty-four men
Lehigh Gap (north side) – Sergeant and eight men
Fort Hamilton – Lt. and fifteen men
Dupui's – Captain Wetterholt's company
Harris's Fort – Sergeant and twelve men
Hunter's Fort – Ensign Mears and twenty-four men
Fort Halifax – Captain Nathaniel Miles and thirty men
"In the Hole," at Moravian House – eight men from Captain Frederick Smith's Company.
"Fort under the Hill" – twenty-four men from Captain Frederick Smith's Company.
Manity [Manada] Fort – Lt. Miller and sixteen men from Captain Frederick Smith's Company.
"At Bernhard Friedli's" (next to the Moravians) – ten men from Captain Christian Bussé's Company.

"At Casper Snebelie's – eight men from Captain Christian Bussé's Company.

"At Daniel Shue's or Peter Klop's" – six men from Captain Christian Bussé's Company.

"At Bernhard Friedli's" (next to the Moravians) – ten men from Captain Christian Bussé's Company.

Second Battalion – In the year 1758, the expedition against Fort Du Quesne [Duquesne], now Pittsburgh, was undertaken, and the Second Battalion joined the British Army at Carlisle. At this time, Captain Lloyd had been promoted to Lt. Col., but retained his company, and was left for some time as the garrison commander at Shippensburg. On marching from Shippensburg with a brigade of wagons under the command of Miles, at Chambers about eleven miles from Shippensburg the men mutinied. Most were convinced to resume the march to Fort Loudoun, where Lieutenant Scott was with eight or ten month's pay. While the army was at Ligonier, they were attacked by a body of French and Indians. On 25 November 1758 the army took possession of Fort Duquesne, under the command of General Forbes.

At Hunter's Fort. May have been in Captain Elisha Saltar's company instead of Captain Shippen's.

Colonel Burd's Journal covers period of 1754 to 1758. Second Series, Volume II, p745 to 820

Boquet, Col. served in 1764.

_____ stationed on the frontier in Berks County with ten men in Bern Township on 01 June 1764 as part of a unit under the command of Major Asher Clayton.

Appendix C

French and Indian War and Post-War Pennsylvania Sources

The Indian Wars of Pennsylvania, C. Hale Sipe

A (1) I
A (4) I–III,

Pennsylvania Archives, First Series, Volume 3
Pennsylvania Archives, Second Series, Volume 2
Pennsylvania Archives, Fifth Series, Volume I
C.R. V; Colonial Records, Volume 5

Shannon, John, Capt.: Muster Roll of Company, 1746: printed (in part) PA2, II, 496–498, 1876 ed., 425–427, 1890 ed. {B3:419;3}

Trent, William, Capt.: Muster Roll of Company, 1746: printed (in part) PA2, II, 492–495, 1876 ed., 422–425, 1890 ed. {B3:420:9}

Perry, Samuel, Capt.: Muster Roll of Company, 1746: printed (in part) PA2, II, 498–501, 1876 ed., 427–429, 1890 ed. {B3:421:13}

Shannon, John, Capt.: List of Deserters from Company, 1746 {B3:422:18}

Diemer, John, Capt.: Muster Roll of Company, 1746: printed (in part) PA2, II, 490–492, 1876 ed., 420–422, 1890 ed. {B3:423:21}

Perry, Samuel, Capt.: Expenses of Company, July 7 – Aug. 4, 1746 {B3:424:24} [Not transcribed into book]

Associators, List of Officers, 1748 Aug 4; printed CR, V, 325 {B3:517:383}

Lower Counties (Del.): Return of Militia 1756; printed PA1, III, 87 {B6:1000:11}

Pennsylvania Troops, List of Officers, 1756; printed PA5, I, 70–71 [not finished]

Inslee, Joseph, Capt., Return of Election of Officers for the Company of; 7 March 1756 {B6:1067:283} Not transcribed

Knowles, John, Certification of Election as Militia Ensign, 12 March 1756 {B6:1074:304}

Kidd, John, Capt., Return of Election of Officer for the Company of, 13 March 1756 {B6:1076:310} [Not transcribed]

Mifflin, Samuel, Capt., Return of Election of Officers for Company of, 13 March 1756 {B6:1077:313} [Not transcribed]

Jones, Edward, Capt., Return of Election of Officers for Company of, 13 March 1756 {B6:1078:316} [Not transcribed]

Batho, Charles, Capt., Return of Election of Officers for Company of, 13 March 1756 {B6:1078:319} [Not transcribed]

Chester County, St. Vincent Township, "Picke Land," Return of Associated Militia company, 10 May 1756 printed PA1, II, 656–657, {B6:1155:602}.

Pennsylvania Regiment, List of Officers, Oct. 1756 {B7:1279:204} [Not transcribed]

York and Lancaster Counties, Officers of Associated Militia, 4 Nov 1756, printed PA1, III, 20–21 {B7:1320:375, B7:1321:379}

Kent and Sussex Counties (Del.), Officers of Associated Militia, 4 Nov 1756, printed PA1, III, 23–24 {B7:1322:383}

Philadelphia City and Bucks County, Officers of Associated Militia, 4 Nov 1756, printed PA1, III, 19–20 {B7:1323:387, B7:1324:391}

New Castle County (Del.), Officers of Associated Militia, 4 Nov 1756, printed PA1, III, 21–22 {B7:1325:396}

Pennsylvania Regiment, 1st Battalion, 20 Nov 1756; printed PA5, I, 73–74 {B7:1378:626}

Provincial Troops, List of Officers, 19 August 1757; printed PA5, I, 62–63 {B8:1617:257}

Pennsylvania Frigate, List of Officers and Men, 26 August 1757; printed PA1, III, 260–261 {B8:1620:269}

Isaac (Indian), Certificate Regarding Sgt. Falconer and Corpl. James Willson, 31 Oct 1757, printed PA1, III, 315 {B8:1691:625

Fort Augusta, Return of, 1 Feb 1758, printed PA5, I, 110–112 {B8:1750:912} [Not transcribed]

New Levies, Officers Recommended, April 1758 {B8:1828:1221} [Not transcribed]

Lower Counties (Del.), Military Officers Commissions for, April 1758{B8:1829:1224} [Not transcribed]

Lower Counties (Del.) recommendation of Military Officers, 12 April 1758, {B8:1850:1306} [Not transcribed]

Lower Counties (Del.) Recommendation of Military Officers, 14 April 1758, {B8:1852:1311} [Not transcribed]

Pennsylvania Regiment, First Battalion, List of Officers, 26 August 1758 {B8:1865:1365}

Pennsylvania Regiment, List of Officers, May 1758, {B9: 1875: 37 and B9:1876:41} [Not transcribed]

New Levies, Applicants for Commissions, May 1758, {B9:1879:50} [Not transcribed]

Fort Augusta, Returns of, 1 May 1758, printed PA5, I, 123–125 {B9:1880:53}

New Levies, List of Officers, May 1758, printed PA5, I, 174–175 {B9:1881:58}

Pennsylvania Regiment, List of Officers, 12 May 1758 printed PA1, III, 336–337 {B9:1901:156}

Singleton, John, Capt., Return of Company, 17 May 1758, printed: PA2, II, 553–554, 1876 ed., 474–475, 1890 ed., PA5, I, 145–147 {B9:1903:165}

McClughan, John, Capt.: Return of Recruits, 17 May 1758, printed: PA2, II, 570–573, 1876 ed., 489–491, 1890 ed., PA5, I, 142–144 {B9:1904:168}

Singleton, John, Return of Company, 17 May 1758 {B9:1905:173} [Not transcribed]

Haslet, John, Capt., Return of Company, 21 May 1758, printed PA2, II, 551–552, 1876 ed., 472– 474, 1890 ed., PA5, I, 148–149 {B9:1910:185}

Blackwood, John, Capt., Return of Company, 22 May 1758, printed PA2, II, 569–570, 1876 ed., 487– 488, 1890 ed., PA5, I, 151–152 {B9:1911:190}

New Levies, Memoranda Regarding, 24 May 1758 {B9:1913:197} [Not transcribed]

Noxon, Benjamin, Capt., Return of Recruits, 27 May 1758 {B9:1915:204} [Not transcribed]

Pennsylvania Regiment, List of Officers, June 1758, printed PA5, I, 128–132 {B9:1919:219}

Fort Augusta, Returns of, 2 June 1758, printed PA1, 111, 408 {B9:1925:239}

Provincial Arms, Return of, 8 June 1758 {B9:1931:261} [Not transcribed]

Fort Augusta, Returns of, 1 August 1758, printed PA1, 111, 503 {B9:1996:553}

Fort Augusta, Returns of, 1 September 1758, printed PA1, 111, 513 {B9:2007:593}

Pennsylvania Regiment, 2nd Battalion, Return of at Raystown, 2 September 1758 {B9:2008:598}

Craig R. Scott

www.ingramcontent.com/pod-product-compliance
Lightning Source LLC
Chambersburg PA
CBHW062003220426
43662CB00010B/1215